FOREVER BOYS

THE DAYS OF CITIZENS AND HEROES

JAMES LAWTON

John Wisden & Co Ltd
An imprint of Bloomsbury Publishing Plc

50 Bedford Square
London
WC1B 3DP
UK

1385 Broadway
New York
NY 10018
USA

www.bloomsbury.com

WISDEN and the wood-engraving device are trademarks of
John Wisden & Company Ltd, a subsidiary of Bloomsbury Publishing Plc

First published 2015
This paperback edition published 2016

www.wisden.com
www.wisdenrecords.com
Follow Wisden on Twitter @WisdenAlmanack
and on Facebook at Wisden Sports

British Library Cataloguing-in-Publication Data
A catalogue record for this book is available from the British Library.

Library of Congress Cataloguing-in-Publication data has been applied for.

ISBN: PB: 978-1-4729-1242-8
ePub: 978-1-4729-1241-1

2 4 6 8 10 9 7 5 3 1

Typeset in 11.75pt Minion by Deanta Global Publishing Services, Chennai, India
Printed and bound in Great Britain by CPI Group (UK) Ltd, Croydon CR0 4YY

To find out more about our authors and books visit www.wisden.com.
Here you will find extracts, author interviews, details of forthcoming
events and the option to sign up for our newsletters.

*For Stuart and the fallen heroes of the team he loved
with a quiet but steadfast passion . . .*

Neil Young (1944–2011)
Mike Doyle (1946–2011)
George Heslop (1940–2006)
Harry Dowd (1938–2015)

A NOTE ON THE AUTHOR

James Lawton first started covering top-flight football as a 19-year-old for the *Daily Telegraph* in 1963 and, after a seven-year stint in North America, went on to become chief sports writer of the *Daily Express* and the *Independent*. He was three times voted sportswriter of the year and was also awarded the sports columnist and sports feature writer of the year titles. He has written 12 books, including an award-winning collaboration with Sir Bobby Charlton on his two volumes of autobiography.

Prologue

One of the lesser distinctions of the Manchester City side which filled the late sixties with football of sometimes heartbreaking ambition was that, as it turned out, they were the team of my youth. They were the bearers of light, the recreators of long-dormant hope, the boys who said to anyone who was listening that if you wanted something badly enough, well, there might just be ways and means of getting it.

The best part of 50 years may strike you as a long time to gain a proper understanding of the meaning of a single football team but then, don't we know the older we get, there are a few distractions along the way.

Maybe you will also find it strange that the impetus to return to a side that was filled with the most thrilling optimism and spirit, and some gloriously swift accomplishment, should be born in, of all places, a cemetery.

Odd, perhaps, because so often we go to a funeral not so much to recognise the passing of another's life, however dear or engaging or influential it was to brush against, or even inhabit to some degree, but the loss of a certain purpose and optimism in our own. We sit in a church stall and we think of how it once was – and how it can never be so again. We consider the erosion of the years and the seepage of hope, in our own existence and that of the one we are there to acknowledge.

Yet it isn't always so, and certainly it wasn't when we came out of the bright autumn sunshine and into the crematorium chapel to pay our last respects to Malcolm Allison.

Maybe we had gone there to regret the pain and the sad detachment and confusions of his last years, but we felt another force, sudden and contagious, and afterwards when we stood in the churchyard we spoke of it freely, even exultantly. We were no longer mourners but celebrants. And what was it we celebrated? It was a time in our lives when anything seemed possible, when everything was before us, and when a group of young footballers, ageing now but extremely proud, so brilliantly embraced the idea that if they worked hard enough, if they explored all of their resources, there might not be anything they'd fail to achieve.

There was, of course – there always is a degree of failure – and the reality of this weighed most heavily on the man to whom we said farewell that October afternoon in 2010. But there was solace for those who cared most about him, so often in spite of the worst of his destructive nature, and it was expressed in this surge of the spirit, this quickening of the stride.

It was as though he was, as the imprisonment of dementia slid away, restored to all of his old outrageous glory.

We could look around and see how many people he had touched, for good and bad, for great and no doubt frequently reckless pleasure and also pain. Francis Lee, the superbly pugnacious player so important to the achievements of Manchester City between 1967 and 1970 that would always represent the peak of Allison's work, put it most succinctly. He cocked his ear at the sound of a police car siren blaring along the nearby Princess Parkway and as he thought of all the scrapes and dramas of the man he had once described, not without a degree of affection and admiration, as an 'arrogant bastard', he said with his most puckish grin, 'They're too late. Malcolm's got away one last time.'

From their first meeting, Lee had been a particular delight of Allison's as he shaped his startling team in those brief, good years when he still listened to his mentor, Joe Mercer. Allison loved Lee's hauteur, his edge, his ability to inflict himself on any situation and, maybe most of all, the sense that he would never renege on the commitments he had made to himself. One of Allison's warmest memories was of Lee's protest at slow service in a San Francisco restaurant. In mock exasperation, Lee had plucked flowers from a bowl on the table and began to chew them.

Allison, with some reason, believed that he had created extraordinary potential – and appetites – in his team, and having done so was entitled to speak of his players in superlatives.

So Lee was filled with the authority of a gunfighter. Colin Bell was 'Nijinsky', named for the great thoroughbred not the mad dancer. Mike Summerbee was a man of fierce talent and unbreakable pride. Tony Book was the quick and knowing veteran, rescued, almost entirely by him, from a mediocrity which would have been the most unjust of fates.

They mingled now, the old elite of Manchester City in the last of the sunlight, and they formed an animated consensus with former colleagues like Joe Corrigan, the young, towering goalkeeper who had, with Allison's help, defied all doubts about his native talent, and the Cheshire cousins Glyn Pardoe and Alan Oakes, who were so quickly persuaded by their new coach that they were great players. Everything they said was a vindication of a man they believed had been too easily discounted, too readily scorned.

Allison had his faults, and not too few to mention, but still they had to be measured against quite what he had first given, and when you thought of that, when you considered the extent of the gift, so many of his misadventures, and the ensuing red ink which had so smeared the details of his later life, were surely reduced sharply in this last accountancy, if not washed away.

Allison's striking eldest daughter, Dawn, had stood up in the chapel and put aside all of the disruptions and discomfort and hurts that had accompanied her fierce love for a father who was so often absent. She said that if she had learned anything from him it was that you should never waste a second of your life. That was his dogma when his career was most exciting and productive, and here were so many witnesses to say that his ability to transmit the value of that belief had never left them, even in the most unpromising of circumstances.

But then this, if you were wondering, is not the story of Malcolm Allison, the details of which have been recounted and, perhaps, retouched often enough, but it is one which would never have begun to unfold had he not parked his beaten-up Borgward – which had a Shell sticker on the windscreen in place of a current road tax label – in front of City's old Maine Road stadium on an early summer morning of 1965. It is an account of a brief passage of time seen through the eyes of a football team which made itself permanent in the hearts of all those who played in it and so many who saw it. Certainly for a young reporter of those thrilling years it seemed that the strength of what happened, the extraordinary force of it, might now be assessed afresh, not just for its impact on those half-forgotten days but for the durability of a legacy that was still so alive and evocative in all the lives that it had touched.

At least that was my instinct as I drove away from Southern Cemetery, Manchester, with such an overwhelming sense that something from deep in the past had been awakened. I may have gone there to consign, with sadness and maybe a tinge of old guilt, those players and their creator to some obscure page of sporting history, some recess of an unformed, abandoned memory, but now there was the feeling that maybe this just wouldn't do. Perhaps there was something more to be said about what happened all those years ago – and its unshakeable consequences for all those who took part? Maybe there were questions to ask again, a time, a mood, a state of mind to reassess along those iron chains of recollection that ultimately hold against all neglect?

It should not, I guessed, be a book about the ephemeral nature of any kind of success. Nor the casual sentiment that came at the end of the funeral service when, having noted the blue colours of City and a bottle of champagne beside Malcolm Allison's coffin, those of sufficient age sang along with Frank Sinatra's old anthem, 'Fly Me To The Moon'.

No, the account would be about a desire to retrace the experiences and shifting emotions of young men who had been invaded by a great inspiration – one that, to a man, they swore would always be with them, because it could be conjured so easily it might all have happened yesterday.

It was with them again in this concentration of the mind demanded by the most solemn and conclusive of occasions. They felt all of it again. They felt the soaring exhilaration of once knowing that they could beat anyone, that they had been given the means to conquer their world. They were back at those landmarks of their best achievements. They were revisiting all of the old terrain of their glory, on the training fields, the running tracks, the science labs and, supremely, famous old stadiums like the Prater in the Viennese woods, the now refurbished Wembley and St James' Park on Tyneside. They were playing again a game which surged with life and self-belief, football filled with speed and skill and competitive nerve. They were drinking champagne in London, of course, and beer with their fans back in Manchester. They were doing what old Joe Mercer impressed so strongly on Allison and his players after a particularly notable triumph. 'Lads, always remember to celebrate your victories,' he said, 'because in this old game, and this old life, you never know if you will have another one.'

It was something else to remember as they were returned to the best of their days. It touched them all in the churchyard and, yes, you could feel among them these eddies of that old spirit, that certainty about who they were and what they had achieved. Indeed, in the end they hadn't come to mourn Malcolm Allison. They were there to thank him. And for what precisely? He had given an enduring meaning to their lives.

I had my own reasons for gratitude, and my hope is that they are implicit enough in all that follows. A character in the Sebastian Faulks novel *Human Traces*, which deals with the roots of modern psychology, says that the past does not vanish, it can be recreated – but this is not the overriding objective here.

There is, after all, a library of grainy film that speaks more eloquently than any words of the spirit and the panache of the football team that erupted so dramatically all those years ago. There is more than a half-shelf of autobiography and at least as many studies of the rise and fall of the young men who ran so hard before the sun.

This, if you like, is an attempt not to augment the memory of achievement that passed long ago but, maybe, to illuminate the resonance of it that still lives so strongly today.

Maybe it is true that to some degree we are all prisoners of our past, but then perhaps we should sometimes go back to it a little more carefully. Then, who knows, some if not all of the chains may just fall away.

Chapter 1

Three years had passed since the last rites of the hell-raising coach, and it was only then that I began revisiting the team he made and saw develop with such skill and adventure – and which down the years lingered like some passing but not quite forgotten romance. This, however, was not meant to be a mere dalliance with the past, and if there was a reason for delay it no longer seemed so disabling as I stood outside the house of Tony Book in the tree-lined street in the Manchester suburb of Sale on a dark, damp November morning.

It was quite the opposite, when I thought about it, because if you wanted to deal soundly with the realities of where you were rather than where you would have liked to be, was there a better place to start than with a man who had his own best hopes restored long after he had consigned them, and with only a tinge of bitterness, to his past? Book was 30 when they were returned to him – in his words as an 'amazing gift' – and now, on the approach to his eightieth birthday, it was as though he had read my mind.

He led me to a glass cabinet in the corner of his lounge. It housed the medals of a winner – something which came so late to him, so tumultuously – and it was, he revealed, the place which he visited with some intensity on those bad days when the house so beautifully kept by his wife Sylvia seemed like a prison. Those were days suddenly invaded by depression, and when they came without warning Book went to the cabinet and ran his old bricklayer hands along the glass and was calmed by the memories and the reinforcement they brought at those times when he had to tell himself who he still was and what it was he had achieved.

For my part, I might offer you various explanations for the delay in arriving at this place. Most of them, though, would concern the disconnections that so often come between good intentions and a little action and, in all honesty, they would not represent the truth, at least not all of it. The fact was that I too had come to understand a little better what can happen to you when quite suddenly a large part of your identity is removed, when, say, an ageing footballer is told that whatever else he does in what is left of his time it cannot be that which made him feel most complete, most at ease with everything around him. Or when a young one is cut down cruelly by random injury – and is handed the rest of his lifetime to tend to his regrets.

And also to grasp, like the victim of a sneak punch, that there is no preparing for the moment when somebody, maybe a doctor in his antiseptic surgery or a football manager, his sensitivities calloused by time, from the other end of a telephone tells you that you are no longer who you thought you were, that something at the core of your existence has been taken away.

This, as it happened, came to me so late, so absurdly so when measured against the experiences of so many of the heroes of this story, the idea of self-pity could not be entertained, not even when putting down the phone on a man I had never met who told me that my days as the chief sports writer of a national newspaper were over. Still, it was a longer, more reflective journey than I had imagined from Southern Cemetery to the doorstep of Tony Book.

It probably needs to be said right away that at no time in that process of adjustment did I confuse the new terrain that had to be negotiated with that of the men whose time of their greatest, most heightened experience comes so quickly and then can disappear with scarcely a warning – and at a stage of their lives when others are still far from sure where their futures lie. Old sportswriters tend to subside down the years. For the men they write about fate is rarely so gentle. One day they can be demigods, the next they are required to ask, 'Who am I now, and what do I do with myself from this point on?'

There are not so many professional sportsmen who have engaged this question without a degree of anguish. Once I asked the great fighter Sugar Ray Leonard why it was he risked a terrible beating at the end of a glorious career. We were in a gym on New York's Eighth Avenue, a traditionally muggy place impregnated by the smell of so many years of sweat, but when he fixed his eyes on me the chill went as deep as the one out on the street where the snow fell copiously.

'You are a writer and you write and you will always want to write,' he said, 'and I'm a fighter and I will always want to fight. Fighting is what I do best and this will always be what I most want to do. Maybe you will understand this one day.' I didn't a few days later when he suffered over 12 brutal rounds at the hands of Terry Norris, a younger, stronger man, but I did when I went to talk to Tony Book.

I knew now how it was to awake from nightmares of phantom challenges, in my case deadlines which had gone, irrecoverably. I knew now at least a little of how my father felt when he walked across the airfield adjacent to the factory training school where he worked to say hello to some young members of his old Bomber Command squadron who shuffled in embarrassment over this visit from an ageing man who suddenly felt clumsy and out of place.

Certainly I understood better the agonies of Gareth Edwards when over a lunch in Cardiff he spoke of one of the last dilemmas of his superb career. He worried whether he was still strong enough, young enough, to submit again to the trials of a New Zealand tour. 'But if I worry about this,' he said, 'I'm also aware that this might be the last call to do something I still love passionately.'

Most haunting for me was the drive away from covering my last major sporting occasion – the 2013 Open at Muirfield, where Phil Mickelson, maybe ransacking the last of his burning but sometimes fragile brilliance, added another prize to buttress the last days of his prime. Maybe distracted by the weight of memory, I missed the motorway turn to the south and found myself wending slowly through the border country. At one point I stopped to smoke a cigarette above a small, richly hued valley where a farmer was bringing in his herd, and wondered how he might, as he went his seamless way, look upon the writhing angst and vanities of a time-expired sportswriter. Probably with not much more sympathy, I had to suspect, than that of the old man at the bar who a little earlier was surprised to hear that the stranger was lost and offered the sketchiest re-directions. 'Go left for the south not right,' he said, 'for that is the road to hell – and Glasgow.'

There was much to remember on that last drive away from the excitement of a life which for so long had been enjoyed not as a privilege but a randomly bestowed birthright.

But if I could be sure where it ended as night fell on the borders, where, precisely, did it start?

It was on a 19-year-old's train ride across the Pennines to cover a wild-talking Scotsman's emerging Liverpool play at the old three-sided ground of Sheffield United, and as the miles rolled by it wasn't so hard to reconstruct some of that long-ago action. Most vividly, I could recall two short, perfectly balanced men who were so dynamic in their different styles – Ian St John, who Bill Shankly likened to the most aggressive of natural-born middleweights; and Joe Shaw, a short, neat man, an oddity in those days of hulking central defenders, but of a skill and a poise which made nonsense of such classifications.

On the following Monday morning I marched to the newsagent's to see my name in a national newspaper for the first time. It was over a modestly displayed piece in the sports pages of the *Daily Telegraph*. I had to tear at the string tightly binding the bundle lying on the street before the shop door was opened. Only later did I notice a newspaper stigmata, the dried blood on my hands.

Now, half a century later on that retreat to the south, there was a great skein of sensation to untangle. If I had the heart and the stamina, I could at least begin the task.

I could remember George Best's first game for Manchester United, against West Bromwich, and most of all the moment he made space for himself in his own penalty area and released a 50-yard pass to Denis Law, and the crowd, gathering in what they had seen, gave a great belated roar. And then I could run so far ahead of the spool of time and recall the cold, rainy night 40 years later when I returned to Old Trafford to stand among all those who brought flowers and notes to grieve the end of his troubled life in a London clinic earlier that day.

I could think of my first visit to Madison Square Garden, when Muhammad Ali rummaged among the last of his gifts to withstand and then triumph over the power of the hard-hitting Earnie Shavers, and how my heart had beaten so alarmingly fast; and then, when his time as the greatest sportsman of the twentieth century was truly running to a close, how he invited me to breakfast in his training camp amid the Amish-painted barns in the Poconos hill country of Pennsylvania, and his long-time friend and retainer Gene Kilroy confided, 'He gets very restive now when he looks around and doesn't see a writer with his notebook open.'

A little later, there was the sight of his former sparring partner Larry Holmes pounding him to defeat in the open-air stadium at Caesars Palace in Las Vegas – and the difficulty of normally tough men who had seen the best of him in Kinshasa and Manila and the Garden fighting to keep the tears from their eyes.

There was the rise and fall of Mike Tyson, and I saw much of that – from his tenement birthplace in Brownsville, where rats scurried down the dank corridors, the prison in Indianapolis and the night he bit into the ear of Evander Holyfield and said that he had come from hell and so what if he was going back there. Even that horror, though, was barely preparation for his final, exhausted efforts in the ring when he was beaten in Louisville and Washington DC by such heavyweight obscurities as Danny Williams from England and Ireland's Kevin McBride, which were his final public humiliations after Lennox Lewis had come close to tearing him apart on a humid night in the big dome on the banks of the Mississippi in Memphis.

I saw the rise and fall of Ben Johnson, too; I saw the bewildered look on Carl Lewis's face when he flashed a glance at the stadium clock in Seoul and saw Johnson's startling time, and then afterwards I saw the rough skin and yellow-tinged eyes of this explosive man who, a little earlier in the year, had been fêted at the Ferrari factory when he went to collect a shining new model; and I heard the dire talk of his drugging, and then in the small hours, I got the call that he had fallen from his pedestal and an old, white Canadian columnist cruelly joked as we hurried to the story, 'What odds on Johnson's next quote, "Would you like fries with that, sir?"'

The great Viv Richards, who I admired so much, came into the little wooden press box in Antigua to threaten me for something I had written when he should have been leading the West Indian team out at the start of a day of Test cricket. And that was another day's work, as was the arraignment of O. J. Simpson for the murder of his former wife and her young friend just a few streets away from the Santa Monica hotel where I was staying for the 1994 World Cup.

Earlier that year, after covering a fight in Las Vegas, I was told to fly to Indianapolis to get Nigel Mansell's reaction to the death of Ayrton Senna and I was surprised, when we collided in a steakhouse, that he invited me to the track the following morning, where he said he had spent most of the night trying to compose a letter to the great, driven Brazilian's father.

It was a remarkable document, laying bare the psychology of the men who still lived so dangerously in pursuit of their passion to drive faster than any other man on earth, but I suppose I should not have been surprised when a phone call from London asked if I could massage Mansell's emotionally complex reaction into a statement that Senna's demise might persuade him to walk away from the track. It would, didn't I see, make such an arresting headline.

On the road back from Muirfield I was bound to think of the fierce compression of the brilliance of Tiger Woods, how lost and bewildered he had looked when his nemesis Mickelson made his killing move at Muirfield and once again he had failed to respond.

I thought of his astonishing mastery in the 1997 Masters and how so many experts were saying he had reinvented the game in a place which for so long had tolerated black men only in the caddies' shack and the uniform of the club cocktail bar and the terrace with its thinly muffled resentment of such a spectacular, unstoppable intrusion into the old order.

I could hardly put a check on the cast of characters teeming in the memory. For one example, Diego Maradona strutting into a restaurant in Mexico City in 1986 with the bearing of a fighting cock, and everyone getting to their feet and shouting, '*Olé.*' A virtuoso bullfighter would surely have been pleased by such a salute.

And there was that night in Barcelona when I went to see Johan Cruyff a few days before he beat England at Wembley while scarcely crossing the halfway line. It was a beautiful, sweet-scented night at the Nou Camp before they set alight the television vans and sent up the acrid smoke after the Golden Dutchman was sent off in the league match against Malaga, and in the rioting and the chaos there was one ineradicable cameo. It was of the big man leading the pursuit of the referee. He swept along at an astonishing pace, especially when you noted he was on crutches, but when he caught the official and swung his right hand he lost his footing and slowly fell on his back. A great roar of laughter rocked the stadium and later on Las Ramblas the gaiety was only enhanced by the news that there had been no loss of life only dignity, which, of course, in Spain is sometimes almost if not quite the same thing.

Spain has its own storehouse of memories, including Manchester United's astounding Champions League win and the need for a thousand-word rewrite in half an hour, and the complicated emotions accompanying Linford Christie's gold medal at the Barcelona Olympics. But then the one that in the circumstances probably had most resonance on the road back from Scotland was the time I had dinner in the old part of Madrid with the Formula One champion Jody Scheckter and the late English matador Henry Higgins.

Roy Rutter, the *Daily Express* stringer and an old Madrid hand, arranged the affair, and I was invited along with David Benson, the paper's motoring correspondent. Much Rioja was consumed over the wild boar in a restaurant which retained the décor of its former life as one of the King of Spain's favourite brothels, and then in order to continue a conversation which raced along the pit lanes and over the sand of the great plazas we adjourned to the Cervecería Alemana, whose patrons once included Ernest Hemingway.

Madrid is a late town but even by its elastic standards we went deep into the night. Eventually our table was an island in a sea of upturned chairs, but there was no sign of impatience from our elderly waiter. He stood, smiling contentedly in the presence of a great foreign driver and torero, and at one point he went down the street to replenish the Marlboros.

Later, as we walked into the breaking dawn, Rutter asked me if I had ever read the Hemingway short story 'A Clean Well-Lighted Place', and he was pleased when I said not only did I know it, it was one of my favourites. 'Well,' he said, 'you know the theme of the old and the young waiter and how the young one grew so angry when a newly widowed patron ordered another cognac and lingered long on the terrace and prevented him seeing a new girlfriend – and the old waiter lectured the boy, said that the function of the cafe was to attend fastidiously to the needs of every decent patron, whatever the hour? I thought you might like to know that the young waiter grew to be the old one who went for your cigarettes tonight.'

Privileges had indeed heaped down the years, too many to record the more you thought about it, but that didn't make their disappearance any easier to handle.

When I attended the Allison funeral I still had a few miles to run, however arthritically, and certainly there was no sense of impending ambush. No doubt it is true that the victim of such an event is, by its very nature, the last to know, but there had been some camouflage. It included a recent night at the Savoy to receive a Sportswriter of the Year award for a third time, and a request by my employers to write a column for the London *Evening Standard* on top of the five I produced for the *Independent* each week.

Such underpinning is, of course, arbitrary and thus unreliable, but still it was not, I had re-assured myself from time to time against the background of increasing frugality in the newspaper business, an invitation to insecurity.

And so when the call came on a summer's evening, a few days after covering Andy Murray's triumph at Wimbledon, a certain hollowness was felt in the bones.

It is not an uncommon fate, heaven knows, and if it has any beneficial effect, I know now, it is a reminder to everyone of their duty to see the world, sooner or later, not only as it impacts on you – and also to recognise the folly you may have entertained that somehow you were removed from its ultimately dispassionate cycles. Or put another way, the requirement it makes that you understand, finally, that there will always be a time to fold your cards with a degree of grace.

I certainly made a stab at that kind of exit from the only life I'd known since a kindly schoolmaster, fearful about my preparation for the grown-up world, liked an essay I wrote and recommended me to a friend who happened to be the editor of the local newspaper. I vowed to serve out faithfully the terms of a contract depleted by the forward planning of the oligarchs when they bought the *Independent*.

I went to the first Ashes Test at Trent Bridge, and felt the kindness of old colleagues, including Simon Barnes and Matthew Engel and Jim Holden, and the former captain of England, Mike Atherton, and I said, cheerfully, that I could serve out my time with a philosophical shrug or two. It didn't really work, not in the last of the hotel rooms in the small hours and not on the countdown of morning drives to Muirfield from Edinburgh, when each new sunlit day took me closer to what, for a little time at least, seemed to resemble nothing so much as an abyss.

I passed on what would have been the last Test match, the third Ashes Test at Old Trafford, though I did drive into Manchester for a warm but inevitably wrenching last dinner with some of the men with whom I shared the road, Paul Hayward, Ollie Holt, Steven Howard, Martin Samuel and my successor at the *Express*, John Dillon. There was a last column to be written from my home in North Wales in the little study cluttered with what was now the memorabilia of a way of life that had come to pass, and, finally, with one last reproach to the self-indulgences of the modern professional footballer as represented by another sullen manifestation of Wayne Rooney.

The last credential was hung on the wall, to go along with all those for fights in Toyko (Tyson–Douglas), New Orleans (Leonard–Durán), Las Vegas (Leonard–Hearns 1, maybe the greatest I ever saw) and so many others that had come to merge in a kaleidoscope embracing just about every sports event I had ever wanted to cover.

They ranged from the Olympics and World Cups and Super Bowls and Test matches to Jonny Wilkinson's dropped goal in Sydney and the Tours de France in the mountains and in Paris for the grand climax – with the bands playing and the city *en fête* and disregarding the certainty that a drug culture had taken hold so strongly that each summer the communist newspaper *L'Humanité* proclaimed the race a capitalist farce. Included was the Masters in Augusta in April, down to that last Ryder Cup in Medinah near Chicago where the beauty of the course, over which each day you could see the great southward passage of the Canadian geese high in a vast blue sky, at certain times threatened to break your heart.

There were oddities, too: amid all those laminated press passes hanging on a wall there is a boxing glove signed and presented to me by Tommy Hearns on the night we met in the Vegas dressing room of his friend Tom Jones, who went out on the stage to tell the farmers' wives from Nebraska and Montana that he had been performing for them for more than 30 years and now there were times when it didn't seem a second less than that. The ladies laughed, uproariously at what they plainly considered an improbable joke.

There is a picture of me taken before my descent of the Cresta Run back in the seventies, and the anxiety on my face is something that really should be turned to the wall. There is a credential issued in the basement of the sandbagged hotel around the corner from the palace of the Croatian president in Zagreb, which a day or two earlier had been bombed by the Serbs. That was an assignment I was given by the editor of the *Daily Express*, Sir Nick Lloyd, who explained in an early morning phone call to Warsaw, where I was in transit after seeing Gary Lineker score the goal on a cold night in Poznań which carried England to the 1992 European Championships in Sweden, that the paper's chief news writer Daniel McGrory had been delayed en route to the Balkans.

Still immersed in the relatively harmless dramas of the games we play, I wondered what was happening in Croatia and the editor told me, quite laconically, 'They bombed Dubrovnik last night.'

Maybe it should take a little time to absorb the loss of such a stimulating life – and measure the extent of the good fortune that, sooner or later, was always going to be withdrawn. Perhaps you need a little time in a decompression chamber, and when that is served you can get back on what is left in your legs, with some of that purpose which carried you through the ravages of fatigue and hangover and, at the lowest point, a self-inflicted medical crisis that I survived only with the help of my eldest daughter, Jacinta, who administered mouth-to-mouth resuscitation in the house in Marbella lent to us by the great Irish midfield general, John Giles.

I had joined my family weary and dislocated from covering the Barcelona Olympics and, then, immediately, South Africa's return from international exile in rugby union Test matches against the All Blacks and Australia in Johannesburg and Cape Town. The first match was an extraordinary occasion, remarkable not only for the vigour of the Springbok return to the big stage but also for the evidence that the Boer tribe remained utterly unrepentant in the matter of apartheid. The great Voortrekker hymn, 'Die Stem van Suid-Afrika', thundered around the old Ellis Park stadium, and it was necessary to note that the only black presence was that of a few African National Congress officials and men and women carrying pails and cleaning mops.

After the second game in Cape Town I felt a knife stab in my stomach, which was diagnosed among other problems as the bursting of a peptic ulcer, and the debilitating effects became most apparent a few days later in the old town of Ronda, when a blue, cloudless sky turned dark before my eyes. Later, in the house, I lost consciousness and would, I was told later, have been gone without my daughter's intervention.

There were two sobering conversations before I was discharged from the Málaga clinic where in the days after being moved from the high dependency unit I watched unbroken, Spanish-dubbed reruns of the old TV western series *Bonanza* and a large lady hanging out vast arrays of washing on a balcony across the street. First, a German nurse told me that on the night of my admission I was in the company of a Finnish man of the same age and almost precisely the same condition and that he was lost before the morning. Then I was told by the tall, imposing head doctor that I really should try to enjoy Fanta Orange as much as I had a shot of Scotch. I said that on balance I thought I would rather die and he replied, with a small frown, 'Señor, it is entirely your choice.'

Chastened, of course, I vowed to spare my family further alarms and that never again would the good luck of enjoying such an absorbing way of life be put so carelessly at risk. When I was his young ghostwriter, Malcolm Allison had always told me that life should always be lived to the full, but then he never defined the risks that such a resolve could so easily incite. Perhaps if he had known he might have mentioned it, perhaps even to himself, but if he ever did it was probably too casually – and too late.

My good fortune was that I had survived for so long a frequently joyful but, looking back, in some respects punishing existence and that, with the worst pangs of the separation from it over, I still had something to do. And now, as I pressed Tony Book's doorbell there was indeed a feeling of renewal, a sense that if I had come full circle it did not have to be in the mood of some long drawn-out defeat.

The possibility of this dissipated in the few minutes before I reported to the Book house, just as the idea that I was going back to around where it all started was almost eerily enforced. He said for me to arrive 9.30 a.m., and Book is a military man, the son of a professional soldier, one who square-bashed himself in the years of National Service – so for a notoriously erratic time-keeper like me the obligation was to be neither late nor early. So I parked just around the corner from Queens Road, in the wet, leaf-strewn forecourt of a block of flats and there it was, suddenly, the confirmation that indeed the full circle had been completed.

Windsor Court was to where we moved when the birth of our first daughter, the heroine of Marbella, made our 'studio' flat a few miles away in Withington impractical not only for its categorisation as a 'rabbit hutch' by my aghast mother (when my wife Linda proudly invited her to admire the 'Swedish design', the balcony bedroom and the vast skylight) but also because our neighbour, the manager of a disco, insisted on entertaining much of his female clientele until at least the first streaks of dawn.

In Windsor Court there was a little more room but hardly less excitement. It was the thrill of starting off, of believing that all was before us in the most invigorating of times which, however gauche and naïve they may now be labelled by social historians picking away at the myths of the Swinging Sixties, seemed to have a vibrancy which had been reserved for us.

So the Beatles were compared with Mozart as they composed 'Lucy In The Sky With Diamonds', their hymn to the effects of hallucinogenic drugs, and in the clubs you rubbed shoulders with visiting, putative rock giants like Mick Jagger and Brian Jones, and for a little while were persuaded that Manchester, the old home of the Industrial Revolution, might just have become one of the key centres of a new universe. It certainly didn't damage civic pride when it was widely reported that a delegation of leading London gangsters, agog for a share in the profits of a booming nightlife, had been stopped and turned back at Piccadilly Station by the local constabulary.

By now George Best was the pick of the city's most exotic fauna. He had come back from Lisbon christened 'the Fifth Beatle' after a sublime performance against Benfica, a giant of European football, and for a little while the incongruity of his living in a Chorlton-cum-Hardy council house, without any kind of protection from the worst effects of the new celebrity culture, was lost on the majority of us, and most critically his employers Manchester United. He was astonishingly gifted – and beautiful – and no one, to be fair, could have reasonably guessed the traumas that were lying in wait, no more than they could those which would soon enough engulf his admirer Malcolm Allison who, at the most critical and forlornly decisive point of his career, risked everything, and lost so much of it, by hazardously attempting to import some of the Irishman's glamour in the signing of Rodney Marsh.

Marsh, too, was extravagantly gifted but it was a talent that for a crucial time was misplaced, and when he arrived at Manchester airport, less than fully fit and with his leather coat tugging at his hips, it was also true that we had seen the best, the unforgettable best, of the man whose glory he was expected to, if not completely match, in some ways reproduce.

Some years later, when Best was stretching out thinly some of the last of his ability at Fulham in the company of Marsh, and I had moved to the London office of the *Express*, a beautifully written note landed on my desk. I had disputed the theory of a newspaper rival that it would be wrong to take a son to see a once great player who had largely destroyed his own career. Provoked by the fact that Best had just wrapped his white Rolls Royce around a lamp post in Knightsbridge, the columnist said he would never take a boy to see someone who had so spectacularly ruined the best of his gifts. He said it would be a salute to the folly of waste.

My argument, such as it was, said that Best was still capable of moments of great beauty and that maybe a father could tell his son that life was full of perils and that maybe we should understand that there are many degrees of failure and that some of them are quite complicated. Best's note was poignantly brief. It said, 'Thank you for remembering I did a few things on the field.'

It was hardly a hardship, I said, a few years later when he came to Vancouver, where I was a writing a column for the afternoon paper, and he asked me to take him to the local racetrack one evening. He wasn't drinking (it was soon after he'd had capsules inserted into his stomach that created nausea at the first drop of alcohol) but it was clear soon enough that he had undergone a medical procedure that guarded against only one type of obsessive behaviour.

I told him that form was unreliable at the track, but this did not prevent him betting heavily – and losing on every race. His entire coaching fee disappeared that night, but his only reaction was to smile a little wanly.

Such pain, though, for Best and Allison and even the resolute, disciplined Book had seemed to belong on another universe when 'Lucy In The Sky With Diamonds' played in Windsor Court.

Some of the lyrics were still in my ears as Tony Book came to his door, and they included, 'Newspaper taxis appear on the shore/ Waiting to take you away/ Climb in the back with your head in the clouds/ And you're gone.'

But by then, as this man I was about to meet again would soon attest, you may have been given the chance to make your mark.

Chapter 2

Every day he waited for the letter that was going to reshape his life, take it to where it should be, and still now, 60 years since it finally arrived, he could ransack his well-ordered house and show you in some corner the words that came under the imprimatur of Chelsea Football Club.

They said he should pack away the dreams he carried each day to the building sites of his home town of Bath. There was, however, no need for a search. The letter will always be imprinted deep in the mind of Tony Book. It was brief, stark and did not allow for appeal as it delivered one of those short punches which catch you off guard and are thus re-doubled in their impact.

'I was 20 and it was a very hard rejection,' Book says. 'I was recommended by the sergeant major in charge of my army team and I played three or four games for Chelsea in their London Combination side, and I thought I did all right. I was quick and I knew that I understood the game. I believed it was something I was born to do, it always felt right. Then the letter came from the manager Ted Drake, the great old player who had a reputation for having a good eye for young talent. He said he was sorry but he didn't think I'd make the grade.'

There is a small intake of breath and on the lean, weathered face beneath the neatly cut thatch of grey hair the slightest flicker of an ancient pain. This, though, is a man for whom the gnawing of recrimination and self-pity had always to be stoically rebuffed. It was because it is addictive, destructive and not only could it damage what was left of your hopes it could also corrode every aspect of your life.

These days this determination of Book to try, however discouraging the circumstances, to measure the good things he has enjoyed rather than linger over those which he may have lost, or was perhaps never granted properly, is seen again and admired each time he joins his old teammates at the Etihad stadium as they gather to chart the progress of another, infinitely wealthier Manchester City and such massively rewarded successors as Yaya Touré and Sergio Agüero.

They see it in the easy exchanges and occasional hugs he shares with Francis Lee and they wonder if, in similar circumstances, they might be quite so willing, or able, to return so comfortably to the best and most equable of their past – certainly a feat beyond the powers of their hugely admired colleague Colin Bell who, like Book, had the last of his working connections with the club broken under the chairmanship of Lee.

Both were aggrieved not only by their sackings from a youth system to which they believed they were making an important contribution, but also by the rough, impersonal style of their delivery. The word came down the line and the man with whom they shared the greatest days of their lives was, at least to them, a suddenly distant figure. Yet if Book drove away with a rare anger in his heart – he was particularly, almost peculiarly incensed by the fact that the news came to him not in the old stadium where his deeds would one day see him elected an honorary president of the club but in an anonymous, rented business office – he was, when the first pain of the severance eased, able to review the ledger of his days in the company of a great and inspiring teammate and decide that he could forgive. Colin Bell couldn't and insists that he never will.

Book confirms his understanding of the unbridgeable chasm between two men who once shared so unreservedly in each other's glory, saying, 'Unfortunately, and this is a great sadness, one of the deepest felt by the team, we know that whatever we do we will never put back the relationship between Belly and Frannie.

'I went the other way after falling out with him when he was chairman of the club. I was very hurt by the way I was dismissed. He got the secretary, Bernard Halford, to tell me – and that was poor. But I thought about it for a little while and I decided that you are just too long dead to harbour grievances over the years. I thought about all that we would always share, as men and footballers, all those days when everything seemed so perfect and we respected each other so much, how we were part of something which would always be so important to us, and in the end I decided that was what I was going to dwell on.'

It is, you are reminded again and again in even the most cursory re-examination of his career, the motif of Book's life. It is, all available evidence insists, a benevolent pragmatism born in a man who will always believe that once he was touched by a kind of miracle, one that not only redirected his ambition but the very way he thought of himself.

He is very precise about the day it happened and how the meaning of it so quickly unfolded. He tells you with an emotion startling because it is so undisguised, 'Still today, and more often than you might imagine, I wonder what might have happened to me if Malcolm Allison hadn't come to see me that day when I was working as a bricklayer, and he climbed up the scaffolding, this fabulous-looking figure, and said that as the new coach of Bath City he would make sure everything changed for me – and for any of the other lads who cared to come on a different kind of journey.

'We would no longer be pale imitations of pros. We would be doing the real thing, we would be training not two nights a week but four; we would be making the kind of commitment, doing the work that made winners. Instead of climbing up the scaffold, he might have been arriving on a magic carpet. He was, you see, telling me all the things I had yearned to hear from long before Ted Drake wrote me that letter, and of course I had come to believe I would never hear them.

'Back in those days before Malcolm came, I did play with lads who had come out of league football. I played with Charlie Fleming, a big star at Sunderland, and the great Stan Mortensen, who scored a hat-trick in the Stanley Matthews Cup final of 1953, and if he had lost some of his speed he still had the swagger of someone who had seen it all and done it all. There was the legendary Tommy Lawton playing out the last of his days – and though it is difficult in these times to reconcile, even imagine the fact that after such a career he still had to string out his earnings as a footballer, he had such a bearing and you could see in a flash or two what had made him such a terror to the greatest of defenders.

'Ian Black, the old Fulham goalkeeper who played once for Scotland, was pushing 40 when he came down to the West Country and he was another who when he talked gave me a sense of the life and the experiences I might have enjoyed as the years rolled by.

'At one time my fellow full-back was Lou Bradford, who had had a run with Bristol Rovers, and I couldn't help asking myself, even as I kept my head down and played with everything in my possession, "Why have you never had a chance in the big league after striving so hard all your life, ever since you played barefoot in the dust with the local Indian kids at your father's wartime army camp when he was away fighting in Burma?" I tried to avoid bitterness, but the truth was I wasn't comparing ability so much as opportunities, getting a little chance to prove yourself in life, and I suppose that was inevitable. By then I had had quite a few knock-backs.'

This made the deliverance to days of fresh hope and sure-fire achievement by the new coach of Bath City all the more exquisite. He reveals that hardly a day passes without some at least fleeting consideration of the fate that would have awaited him down the years ('I know I would have been laying bricks until I was 65') if his foreman had not called out, 'Bookie, there's someone here to see you,' and he laid down the mortar trowel with the care of a fastidious, resigned practitioner of an honourable but ultimately unfulfilling trade.

'When I joined him at City three years later,' he says, 'I felt like an 18-year-old with life just opening up before me. I was 32 by then but I might have been a teenager. Had he not come into my life, no doubt I would have played on into my thirties but not as long as I did in the first division, playing with and against great players. I couldn't have done that because I would have been doing two jobs, and one day the pressure of it would have been too much and I would have been left with the trowel and the mortar and the bricks.'

Instead, all sense of an oppressive fate, of an inexplicable injustice, lifted from his shoulders: he was the man, the professional he always wanted to be, and there is a catch, and still a little wonder, in his voice when he describes each successive stage of the underpinning of a reopened world with its entirely fresh prospectus.

As Book talks of arguably the most spectacular individual renaissance in the history of English professional football, I remember a call I received from the famous sportswriter Desmond Hackett on the spring day in 1969 when a piece of news-agency tape had been handed to him at his Fleet Street desk, beside which a hatstand was adorned by the brown bowler that had become a symbol of his celebrity as the best known, if not most scrupulously accurate, sports scribe of his day.

The news flash said that the Footballer of the Year award would be shared between Dave Mackay, the great star of Tottenham Hotspur and Scotland, and Book. Mackay had long been lionised by Hackett and his peers, and for the most impeccable reasons. He was a force of nature as much as a great footballer, a fact most tellingly illustrated by the dramatic photograph of him lifting his ferocious compatriot Billy Bremner off his feet with one hand in the heat of a battle between Spurs and Leeds United.

It was an eruption that portrayed all of Mackay's vast physical authority but he was also a player of wonderful touch and intuition. Bremner's midfield partner John Giles once neatly answered a question concerning who was most important to the workings of Bill Nicholson's superb Spurs team, the iron-clad Mackay or his silky, Irish captain–philosopher, Danny Blanchflower. Giles said he could only answer the question with a question, one that asked, 'If you could have two Blanchflowers or two Mackays, which pair would you take?'

'In my opinion,' he said, 'there can only be one answer because Mackay gives you everything you want in a footballer, he gives you the class of a master player and also the steel.'

Such was the level of critical appreciation to which Tony Book, the erstwhile bricklayer from Somerset, was now elevated, and for Hackett it was a story guaranteed to set his old Remington typewriter clattering. What was also true was that among his more experienced colleagues Hackett was notorious for massaging the facts in the interests of an eye-catching headline, perhaps the most unshakeable being his description of the ill-tempered 1954 World Cup quarter-final between Hungary and Brazil as the 'Bloodbath of Berne', an account which included a spurious reference to blood spattered on his Savile Row suit.

But now, before Book was briskly added to his gallery of heroes – and he retired to one of his favourite watering holes, the Bell, to knock back his preferred tipple, a 'Black Velvet' composed of Guinness and port wine – the old wordsmith had to assemble a modicum of facts, and thus the call to a colleague in the northern office. 'Now, my young colonel,' he said to me, 'tell me about this fellow Book, how is it that he stands beside Davie Mackay, and now let's get one thing straight right away – what age is the old bugger?'

I said, fairly enough, that not too many people in football had ever been quite sure. Indeed, he was rather like the great fighter Archie Moore, whose quoted age of 39 was widely doubted when he went in against the bludgeoning, merciless Rocky Marciano. The rest of the conversation was brief and perfunctory and I shouldn't have been surprised at the headline which blazed in the *Express* the following morning above Hackett's vivid prose: TONY BOOK – THE ARCHIE MOORE OF ENGLISH FOOTBALL.

Book saw it too and now he smiles at the memory and the coincidence that he too, and officially, was 39 when he went out to perform for the last time at the highest level of his game. He says, 'The issue of my age did rear up again when I won the award but I was home and dry then, I had my first division medal and was heading for the FA Cup final at Wembley with this player of the year honour, which down the years had gone to men like Tom Finney and Stanley Matthews, Bobby Charlton and – just the year before – George Best. I was told later I was in the running for it that year after leading City to the title, but then a few days later Bestie played brilliantly in the European Cup final when United beat Benfica and that was that, or at least it seemed impossible not to believe so.

'One of the first things Malcolm did when he joined Plymouth was come back to Bath to sign me. He said that he had told Plymouth I was 28 when in fact I was already 30. Luckily, I didn't have to doctor my birth certificate. In those days you kept things like that in a shoebox, folded in four, and fortunately there was a big crease in the line that said I was born in 1934, making me 30.

'At that age you have to be thinking, "It must be over now." I was coming into the big league as an apprentice, one who had been given a long-service gold watch by a non-league club. And so, of course, when we all went to Malcolm's funeral, I had to think to myself how much goes out of your life when you lose someone like him. I would never have played in any of those great games. Never won a title on the last day of a season at Newcastle. Never had that night in Vienna when we played through a rainstorm to win our fourth major trophy in three years. Never had my name placed in a list that included men like Matthews and Finney.'

Nor would he have arrived, gripped by apprehension, at Heathrow to make his first flight in the early summer of 1964. He had been summoned by Allison, whose reward for a successful first season at Bath was the close-season appointment as coach of Toronto City, a team owned by the rich, extrovert Greek immigrant Steve Stavros.

The owner saw in his new coach a man perfectly suited to the job of exciting passions in a city league which split ferociously along tribal lines, with strong support in the Italian and Portuguese and Greek communities. Toronto City had in Allison someone with the swagger of Zorba the Greek and in Book, the coach believed, they also had a player who could not have been more determined to make a success.

Book recalls, 'I was supposed to fly out with Johnny Brooks of Spurs but he hadn't got a work permit and I was on my own at Heathrow. I had never been near an airport before, and yes, I was very apprehensive. I'd come back from India with my family on a troopship, passing through the Suez Canal, and my fears only increased when we ran into a storm before landing in New York. There were storms around the field, too, when the fans got so excited, but mostly it was a dream – a very fulfilling dream.

'In the days I had very little to do, so of course I trained at every opportunity. I began to realise what it was to be a full-time player, and it was a great experience. My confidence soared with my fitness and after one game Malcolm came into the dressing room, sat down beside me, put an arm around my shoulder, and said, "You do realise, don't you, that you can play?" Around about the same time, Nigel Sims, the Aston Villa goalkeeper, called out to Malcolm, "Where have you been hiding this fellow all these years?"'

The football story might have ended around this time with solid, professional achievement and the confirmation that down all those years Tony Book had never been foolishly over-reaching his true potential. He was a player, all right, and every time he went out on the field in cosmopolitan Toronto, and then back among his own people at Plymouth, where he finally became a fully contracted and astonishingly consistent performer in the Football League, he tirelessly re-stated the new reality. He missed just one league game in two seasons for Plymouth, played with a speed which later persuaded his City teammate Freddie Hill that he was so quick he could 'catch pigeons', and it seemed his game gained a little more authority each time he went out on the field.

When Allison recognised a residual weakness at right-back at City after the first season which brought the second division title, he told Joe Mercer that Book had to be signed, not just as a defender of the highest quality but as someone who would add hugely to the sum of the club's ambition. His leadership would be of the least complicated kind. It would be that of the purest, most instinctive example.

Tony Book was not only an accomplished, proven footballer, he was a progressive force, a man who had fought so hard to establish his strengths, and would fight down the coming years to maintain them at the highest level. Rather, as the coach slyly put it to the sceptical old football man, as Mercer, the captain of Everton and England, had done when he was transferred to Arsenal at precisely Book's age.

'How old were you when you left Everton?' Allison asked impatiently when his boss continued to demur. 'You were the same age as Tony is today – and it didn't work out too badly, did it?'

It was Allison at his best, aggressive, utterly convinced that he had recognised in Book someone of massive intrinsic value to the development of his team, and prepared to go out on any necessary limb to get his way. The coach saw clearly that Book would set a level of performance that would radiate through the team. He was a superb defender, blisteringly quick, sure in the tackle and as a natural-born leader he brought the gifts of both authority and inspiration. The result was, quickly enough, historic for Manchester City and the culminating move in the life change of Tony Book. For him the significance of Allison's winning argument with Mercer was monumental and, fittingly enough, its conclusion came on a day of great significance for English football. It was the one in June, 1966, when England launched against an obdurate Uruguay the campaign which ended with the victory over West Germany that delivered their one and only World Cup.

It is another one of those days Book re-inhabits for a little while when he feels the need to lift his spirits.

'Playing in the first division was always my deepest ambition and here I was travelling to Wembley for the big match in the company of one of the great figures of the game,' he recalls. 'I had a good feeling because I had had two very good years at Plymouth. There had been quite a bit of talk about City signing a full-back for their return to the first division and it had been a thrill to see my name linked with them. Another who was being mentioned was Peter Rodrigues of Leicester City. After Malcolm made the deal at £17,000 with Plymouth, I went up to London to meet Joe Mercer. It was quite hard making sure I wasn't a bit overwhelmed by the situation. We had lunch at Churchill's Hotel before taking the tube up to Wembley. We talked generally for a while and then we got round to the contract. I was on £35 a week at Plymouth in the second division, and Joe said, "Tony, I've got to tell you the well is empty. I can only offer you a fiver on top of what you're getting." I had had something a little more in mind coming up from the West Country, something that would make life a little easier for Sylvia, who was a wonderfully supportive and patient wife as I pursued my football dreams, but, I have to honest, I was still exhilarated on the ride up to Wembley. At last I would be playing among the top men, and if I hadn't been offered a pot of gold, there were a few little incentives. I would get an extra £4 for a win, £2 for a draw and there would be crowd bonuses at the 20, 30 and 40,000 mark. So if we were successful my income would grow well enough.'

Book and Mercer encountered an observer on the way to Wembley, a quizzical but on this occasion uncertain sports reporter, the late Frank Clough of the *Sun*. He sensed something was afoot but Mercer's companion, whoever he was, didn't look young enough to be a player targeted by a club seeking to remake itself in the first division. Clough rued his missed scoop when the story broke but he wasn't short of company in his miscalculation. Book had to ride a lot more than the doubts of Mercer (and now Clough) as he fought to establish himself in the top flight.

He remembers, 'My first game for City was a 1–0 win at Southampton. We were up against two very good wingers in Terry Paine and John Sydenham but we dealt with them very well. I marked Sydenham very tightly, and after the game Peter Gardiner, who covered City for the *Manchester Evening News*, told me he had made me "the Monday Man". It was an encouraging start and I also benefited a lot from the voluble support of Malcolm on the touchline. In those early days in the first division a lot of opposing coaches and managers stood on the touchline and shouted to their wingers, "Run the old bastard," and Malcolm's response was always the same: "Two-to-one the Book," he cried.

'I had a wonderful run of fitness before breaking down with an Achilles problem in training before the 1968–69 season. They wouldn't do an operation, citing my age, and kept trying to treat me on a piecemeal basis. In the end I went to Christie's, the cancer hospital in Manchester, and got a shot of chemo. It was not a perfect cure but it certainly eased the problem. I came back in the January in a Cup tie, where we got a draw, and then we ran through to the final at Wembley.'

Ran, indeed. No one did it harder or more sharply or with more exhilaration than Book and when now he thinks of that winning sweep to Wembley, a year after the drama of the title charge at the grounds of Tottenham and Newcastle – and then, in just another year, victory at Wembley for the League Cup, and the European Cup-Winners' Cup in Vienna – he returns to those feelings which came to him so strongly at Allison's funeral. 'I keep thinking,' he says, 'of all the good fortune that wouldn't have come my way if Malcolm hadn't showed up that day in Bath and changed my life. No one else would have taken such a chance on someone like me. To tell you the truth, I'd really given up on it, deep down. You are thinking, "Why don't you face up to it, you're a bricklayer and a part-time player, and if you don't believe it look at the gold watch you got from Bath City."'

That, certainly, was the impetus behind Book's decision to so swiftly overcome the disappointment of City's terms and tell Mercer – around about the time the leading TV analyst Jimmy Hill was announcing to the nation that England's goalless draw meant that it could forget winning anything 'with this lot' – that he was accepting his offer of a £5 rise.

It took him just one training session at City to confirm that he had made a wise choice. 'I could see straight away,' he says, 'that I had become part of a group of players who complemented each other perfectly all over the park.' His eyes have an old gleam as he recalls his sense of one strength piled upon another: 'I could see all the possibilities, they just leaped at me. Playing behind Mike Summerbee, for instance. It was a dream. He never wanted me to run beyond him. All I had to do was get the ball and give it to him. He used to say, "Don't go past me because that's my job." I would go forward but only when the system called for such movement – and never to take any of Mike's ground. When you gave "Buzzer" the ball you knew he wasn't going to lose it. He could hold his own with anyone; even the big beasts like Norman Hunter of Leeds and Tommy Smith of Liverpool would think twice about trying on anything with him. He was strong as an ox and you knew he could run past people all day long.

He was also one of the best crossers of the ball you would ever see. When he came inside, Frannie would go outside and cause just as much trouble. Wherever you looked there was someone willing to take responsibility, and someone who could do damage. Glyn Pardoe and Alan Oakes came of age in the team, you could see them growing up together as great players, and Neil Young was so elegant, and Mike Doyle so strong.'

There is still awe in his voice when he speaks of the speed of the team's development. 'It was as though we had taken on a life of our own, a belief that sent us smashing through barriers which just a year or two earlier would have seemed insurmountable. You had to feel that a little bit of telepathy was at work when Malcolm sent us out and Joe was there in the background, beaming his crooked grin and obviously enjoying some of the best days of his football life. We were moving forward at a staggering pace, and then something happened which would always affect the way we thought about ourselves – and what we might be able to achieve.'

It was a day in the life of a football club that those who lived through it and created it, and those who were merely around to see it, will always recall with a mixture of pride and wonder. It was a glorious invasion of imagined possibilities, a performance which a member of Manchester's Hallé Orchestra said, many years later, might have been set to the music of Tchaikovsky.

It happened on a Siberian day at Maine Road on 9 December 1967 – and it said that here was a football team which had found in itself something quite stunning. A fine Tottenham team, containing men of the quality of Cliff Jones, the superb Welsh winger, Jimmy Greaves, possibly the best pure, natural-born, lethal striker in the history of English football, the immense Mackay and the most formidable of goalkeepers, the big Ulsterman with the barrel hands, Pat Jennings, were not merely beaten 4–1, they were reduced to absolute futility – and this after Greaves had skipped across the ice to give them the lead.

The game could not have happened in these days of immaculate, heated pitches, when a snap in the air is enough to make so many players pull on their gloves and yearn for a balaclava. No one wore gloves on 9 December 1967.

Book remembers the sting of his breath and the exhilaration that came to his spirit. 'People who played in it, and saw it, will always speak of "the Ballet on Ice",' he says. 'But the fact was we had already begun to go to Old Trafford, which for us was the ultimate yardstick, and get results that were telling us we had indeed joined the elite. We had begun to believe we could compete with anyone, it was the way we had come to think about ourselves and it came partly from the knowledge that we had become the fittest team in England. We had done the work, extraordinary work with scientists and great athletes, and that poured to the surface in the ice game against Spurs.

'I have to say that though the football we played was tremendous there was another factor, and it was something that I contributed, something that made me feel that my background was really stronger, had given me more knowledge and practical insight into the game than sometimes I imagined in those days when I had been forced to believe that I would always be on the fringes. My influence on the ice game came from something I remembered from when I played for my wife's home-town team of Peasedown Miners in Somerset. It was something an old codger of a trainer named Charlie Neuth told us when the pitch was frozen as hard as flint and the east wind was coming down from the Mendips so hard it seemed as if it were cutting your body in two. He pointed out, in those days when the referee's pre-match inspection was never more than cursory, that it was possible to adapt your boots to the conditions. What you could do was take the top layer of leather off the old studs and leave a bit of nail exposed. Of course, if you went down somebody's leg you would have had him in trouble, and maybe yourself, but it did give you that much more chance of a foothold.

'When we looked at the pitch before the Spurs game, which the BBC were desperate to cover for their *Match of the Day* show – ironically the only one in which we would feature that title-winning season – the words of old Charlie came flooding back. Against a great team – and Spurs were a team and a half in those days – we were able to stand up and dominate. The longer the game wore on, the better we were and the more we confirmed our growing stature. We had such an appetite for the game and in his commentary Kenneth Wolstenholme declared, "Manchester City have become the most exciting team in England."'

Spurs were stunned and after the match their old Yorkshire manager Bill Nicholson, whose Double-winning team at the start of the decade would always be one of the glories of English football, believed he saw a moral dimension.

A few years later Nicholson was so outraged by the conduct of the Tottenham fans before and during a European tie against Feyenoord in Rotterdam that he went on the stadium's public address to declare, "You people make me ashamed to be an Englishman." At Maine Road he could not disguise the fact that he felt another degree of shame, for that day at least, at being manager of his famous club. He said, "It was one of the most remarkable things I have seen in football. One team wanted to play, the other didn't."'

In the smarting that came with such a massive, unforgettable defeat, it was as though old Bill Nick was writing an enduring epitaph for that City team which erupted so astonishingly. 'They wanted to play,' he said, and in the mind's eye his words are underpinned by a score of memories. Of a Cup tie at Stamford Bridge when Bell ravaged Chelsea, whose celebrated fans, the great actor Richard Attenborough and the TV entertainer Lance Percival, shook their heads in the guest room and mourned in advance the reviews that, as Nicholson did, would speak of two football teams operating on separate planets. Of Summerbee and Lee matching each other in their imperious belief that they could not be denied. Of Neil Young sweeping in unstoppable goals with both power and beauty. Of Book snagging pigeons before they could gather pace, and the relentless work of the Cheshire yeomen, Oakes and Pardoe, sapping the life of all but the most obdurate opponents. Of a fine Nottingham Forest team, skilfully assembled by the old Manchester United master full-back, pipe-smoking Johnny Carey, being demolished, piece by piece, at Maine Road.

There will be a time to discuss what went wrong, how the dream eventually was broken, but for now Book is happy to talk about how it was on those days when Manchester City operated in what seemed to be an impregnable state of grace. He drifts back, as so many of us do almost involuntarily in this story, to that afternoon of farewell to the fallen coach at Southern Cemetery. 'There was a really strong feeling, almost an excitement that day at Malcolm's funeral,' he says. 'I think it came with seeing so many people to whom he meant so much, and I think that brought out the feeling in everybody. It seemed to recreate, or at least refresh, the pride in what we had done when he was on top of everything.

'He had assembled a brilliant set of lads and every day we spent together was a bonus. We had little groups forming, but that never affected a feeling that when it came down to it we were all together, all working for the same thing. Glyn, Oaksie, Doyley stuck together; Mike Summerbee and me were roommates. We shared the West Country background, but Mike was his own man, he knew everybody, and wherever we went there was somewhere for him to go, there would be the shout, "Mike," and he would be off. He was very close to Bobby Moore and when we were in London he would spend a lot of time with him. But as a group we really worked quite beautifully.

'A lot of what Malcolm was about, his love of a good time, rubbed off on the lads, and it always showed when we went off for a change of scene to somewhere like Southport or Blackpool. We did our work, very hard work, on the beaches and the training field, but in the evenings we really enjoyed ourselves. There was never any bad feelings that grew down the days, the kind of thing which in the end can wreck a team. No, that was never going to be the fate of our team. There would be other problems which would surface in a few years, and almost all of them were to do with Malcolm's ambitions, and maybe the way in the end he misread his own strengths, but the team was, I have to say, like a rock in its respect for what we were doing, and how we were doing it.

'The supreme moment was winning in Newcastle, taking the title, and I think a lot of our exhilaration was to do with our rivalry with United. They were in with a shout that season and they might have pipped us if we hadn't won our last two games at Tottenham and Newcastle, so of course at White Hart Lane and on Tyneside we were playing for our lives. The atmosphere in Newcastle was unbelievable. We would score, they would score, and then our hearts would be in our mouths, but in the end it didn't matter, we played through all that, we were too strong for them, we wanted it too much, and coming home we were part of a great cavalcade – there was a tide of blue flowing back to town. We had a few beers on the coach and then, all of a sudden, we were among the fans in the social club, and that's how it was in those days. No one needed to tell us that what we did was for the people, that they were the point of it all.

'It was another reason why it was so heartbreaking when you could see Malcolm and Joe Mercer moving apart, because until then we could feel that we had formed a perfect circle. It broke your heart because it was so clear what they had achieved together, and it was because their relationship was so strong and balanced. You had to wonder how something that seemed so complete could fall apart, but the trouble in the end wasn't so hard to diagnose.

'Malcolm was hell-bent on stepping up and the tragedy – yes, I will always think of it as that – was that he was never going to be a manager. He was a great, yes, unique, genius coach, but at the end I have to say he thought he was the only one who mattered, and there are not too many football chairman who are going to stand for that. I never tried to counsel Malcolm because our relationship wasn't pitched like that.

All I could do was try to support him the best I could, because no one in my game had ever owed anyone more than I owed him.'

Nor had anyone so strongly related the way you saw life to the way you played football. Most vital was the degree of courage you brought to the challenge.

'He made you feel you could do anything. He not only changed the way we played but the way we thought. When I consider how after all those years of frustration I was able to progress in the game, I'm always reminded of how it was with Alan Oakes, one of our greatest players, who still holds the record for City appearances. He was a strong man with a great left foot but he was also a bit like me before I had that summer in Canada. He had to be persuaded he was a very good player but, as is so often the case, when he began to believe in himself things started happening for him quite dramatically. You could see him grow as he walked down the tunnel.'

Book revisits the seasons of his team with the precision of a traveller who remembers every change in the weather, every different shade of the leaves on the trees, and he is best, like so many of his surviving teammates, on the great surge that came in the spring of City's days in 1968, the change in the air and the growing warmth of their self-belief.

'We began to be a really strong team when Frannie and Mike started tackling defenders early doors in a game. They used to get among the defenders and that was the start of it because all of a sudden the defenders were thinking, "Jesus, what's happening here?" Defenders used to have a bit of an easy time of it on the ball in those days, but these two were withdrawing privileges, taking them on and making them rethink everything they did. You can't really tackle today, not in the old way. I go to City regularly and watch a lot of football on the box and there are all these different nationalities, and some very skilful players, but then you remember how it was when Frannie and Mike were going at it with the likes of Smith and Hunter and you realise how much the game has changed. Some might say it is the difference between night and day, but about one thing there is no doubt. It is another reality, a different set of rules.'

There is a confirming flashback as Book speaks of the ruthlessness of those old football days. It is of standing outside the dressing room of the visiting team at Maine Road with a newspaper colleague and suddenly the door being flung open and a trainer dragging us by the arms into the medical room where a Portuguese defender was lying on a bed with the inside of his thigh resembling a piece of raw beef. 'Your man Francis Lee did that,' yelled the trainer. 'He is an assassin.' All you could say was that you had seen a few of his wounds, too.

Book is a most important witness in the story of his team's great emergence – and to the later years that sometimes mocked, but never finally obscured, the greatness of what had been achieved. He had six good years as City's manager after Ron Saunders was fired for his failure to maintain the level of the Mercer–Allison era; he won the League Cup in 1976, and he brought in some players of high quality. But he carried a burden he had helped to create for any manager who followed, and in 1979 he was asked to share command with the man who had saved his career. It was a vain attempt to recreate the past and for Book it brought the excruciating discovery that the Malcolm Allison who had made his career and, effectively, un-made his own 'was a different man – and I cannot tell you how painful that was to see.'

The pain of it, of course, was only compounded by the memory of how it had once been. 'We had so much going for us [in the mid-sixties],' Book says. 'We had a wise old manager, some great players and so many people who longed for such a coming together, but we knew right from the start the basis of our strength, the force which would carry us forward. Of course it was Malcolm.

'He cottoned on to things so quickly, he was so clever. Someone could say something to him which was in itself not so profound, at least not to the rest of us, but it could cause a spark in him, one which would prove to have a much wider effect. That was him. He could see around corners.'

As I leave, Book puts his hand on my arm and says, 'You know, it wouldn't have surprised me at that funeral if he had suddenly sat up in the box.'

Chapter 3

But then on some men the box is never closed, not quite, at least not beyond the certainty that something they did or said to make you laugh or to cry, will flare again so vividly it might have been yesterday.

It happens frequently to David Allison, the coach's elder son, who for some years has been both the patriarch and the unifying force in a family which for so long needed such a healing and gently philosophical presence.

He has broken into his rounds as a district sales manager for a power company and we are on the terrace of my local pub, taking the kind of working lunch – toasted sandwiches and mineral water – his father would brusquely eschew when he occasionally arrived in the village still carrying the swagger of a man committed to the task of extending his colourful past – like that day in Langan's Brasserie in Mayfair when he was discovered alone but cheerily buoyant, advising the head waiter, an Italian, on what precisely he might expect in the forthcoming World Cup in his homeland.

David Allison is telling me how it was to be Big Mal's son and, inevitably, we are travelling in a wide swathe of pain and sadness and quite a bit of confusion, but now, suddenly, there is a smile on his face and a shake of his head. 'Yes, it is true, like all the kids I felt neglected,' he says. 'He was never around. But I do remember very well the time, when I was 15 and just before I signed as a pro at Blackpool, he was going up to scout a game at Newcastle and he said, "Why don't you come with me?" I was surprised but also delighted.

'He was driving a nice Jaguar. After the game he had a few drinks in the boardroom and when we were coming back he asked me, "Can you drive?" and when I said I could, that I certainly understood the principles of it, he said, "Well, why don't you drive along this motorway, I really need to take a little kip." So there I was, 15 years old, gunning the Jag down the motorway, which was just as well because if I hadn't we wouldn't have got home that night and I would have missed school in the morning. When we came to the end of the motorway, and the driving was less straightforward, I pulled over and said, "I really think you should take over now." No, he wasn't a normal daddy.'

Yet long before he became a constant source of worry in the last reaches of his life, albeit one lifted from time to time by flashes of the old, biting humour, he was (against so many odds) an immense source of pride. He was the kind of father another kid, in more normal circumstances, might have fantasised into existence.

'Whatever happened, whatever stories I heard, including the notorious one my mother tells of his going out for fish and chips on a Friday night and coming home the following week, I was always proud of my father.

'This was despite the fact that I spent so long away from him. I played at Blackpool, had a spell in Australia and was in Hong Kong 27 years. After the initial Manchester City days, I wasn't involved when he went off to Crystal Palace. I missed the fedora hat period when all the publicity he generated couldn't disguise the fact that fundamentally his career was unravelling, but the City days will always be unforgettable for the pleasure and the pride they brought to a lad like me.

'In my whole school year there were no more than three or four City kids against 300 to 400 of United. For me that meant that it was very hard to go to school in the early days. One of my greatest moments was when City beat United 3–1 at Old Trafford in their championship year, and Dad had predicted it very loudly all over the press and television, though he wasn't picking scores at that time. That came later after he met Muhammad Ali. They met when Ali was on a tour of Britain. My dad had just published his autobiography and they collided at a book launch and I still have a fantastic picture of them together. Imagine that, a picture of the greatest sportsman of the age and your father hugging each other like old mates who had just been reunited.'

He remembers also a newspaper picture of his father in a horse-drawn carriage in Turin when he was summoned to Italy by the president of Juventus and offered the then fabulous sum of £20,000 a year (tax free) and the use of a private aeroplane to fly his English friends to Italy each weekend. 'We had the picture framed and sometimes he would look at it, shake his head, and say, "Turning down the Italians was one of my biggest mistakes."

'It was something I thought about a lot and I have to say I think he was right. I think they would have loved him in Italy, as they did his great friend John Charles. It could have been that sort of thing: John was the great player, the gentle giant, and Dad could have been the great coach, carrying his team and his people forward. With some success there, I'm sure he would have acquired mystique. He never told me the real reason he didn't go. Maybe he worried about shaking the Italian obsession with defence. It was completely against his nature and way of thinking, but of course it went very deep into the Italian football culture.

'Then again I also wondered what might have happened if he had thought about it a little more deeply. Perhaps he might have considered the possibility that the brilliant victory of Jock Stein's Celtic over Inter Milan in the 1967 European Cup final had created a chink in the Italian armour, and that it was because of the way his City played Juventus had come to him in the first place. And now they were offering a great stage, and huge resources, to make it happen at Italy's most famous club.'

There is more than a hint of an old yearning in the voice of David Allison as he considers what may well have been the pivotal wrong turning in the life of his father. 'He certainly loved it in Lisbon, where he won the title and the cup with Sporting and was hugely popular with both the players and the fans. I visited him several times there after breaking my knee in Hong Kong, having to come back to England for treatment. In Portugal he was probably at his best since the City days. He had shown again how he could organise a team, get them to play beyond their hopes, and this knowledge filled him with some of that old confidence.' For a few moments David is working back more than 40 years for the most telling reminder of those days when his father still had the strength and the nerve – and the credibility – to build on a superb career foundation.

Maybe this memory of a time of unexpired opportunity softens, to some degree, the bleakness of what he is about to say. 'Alzheimer's is a horrible disease. My wife and I came back to live in England around the time he was taken ill. He had come to Hong Kong when he was still in an in-and-out stage. He had the start of dementia. He was staying in our flat when I realised, finally, that he was losing his bearings.

'He disappeared in the middle of the night. He had only a raincoat on, nothing else, and the police picked him up. He didn't know where he was. They took him back to Happy Valley police station and all he could tell them was that he was Malcolm Allison. They asked him if he knew his telephone number and of course he didn't. So they looked in the phone book and saw there were only two Allisons listed. I was one of them and another was a Dr Allison, who I happened to know. Eventually, they called me and I went through the deserted streets to pick him up. He was fine the next day, but I knew then that he would never be the same again.

'Once he was diagnosed with dementia he went into a care home in Sale – and frequently he would escape. He was still dressing smartly then and he became quite crafty. He would hang around the door and wait for someone to open it as they came in or went out, and then he would slip away.

'I can't tell you the number of times my younger brother Mark and I went in search of him. Always when we found him he was in a pub. He would walk into a pub without any money and then everyone would buy him a drink. He was the life and soul of the party even when he had dementia.

'He was, you see, a bit of a character at every stage of his life, but really, in the end, it did get very, very sad. He got worse and worse and, to be perfectly honest, I was glad when he passed away. It was an agony to see him in that state, and the more so when you thought of who and what he had been.

'Some of the people in the home were very old and badly affected by dementia, but the nurses were very good and he got on with them very well, especially the women.'

A half-forgotten image comes back to mind. It is of visiting the home and being led into the lounge, where the coach was taking an afternoon nap. As I waited to speak to him, and by this time with no certainty that he would remember quite who I was, an old lady, clad in a nightgown, whirled up to his armchair and then performed a quite alarming arabesque. She was rescued by an attentive nurse but not before the coach stirred and opened one eye and said, with a familiar, rumbling chuckle, 'Well, Jim, at least I can still pull.'

Now there is a smile of recognition from his son and he says, 'Yes, you found yourself laughing at some of the things that happened, and that is the thing about Alzheimer's. If you don't laugh you cry, and there were times when I did have to laugh. When I walked into the home one day I saw he was wearing something that resembled a cricket sweater. I asked him, "Where did you get that from? I've never seen you wearing anything like that in your life." He said he had been playing cricket – in Derbyshire. It was one of his days for making up stories, and I never found out where the sweater came from. Even in those circumstances, he still showed flashes of that old appetite for life, and, no, I don't think he will be quickly forgotten.'

This, you have to believe, is an ultimately forgiving account of a life that was lost – especially when you remember that if Alzheimer's came upon it as a late and hideous assault, there had been so much earlier, and persistently self-inflicted, damage.

There were, David Allison is obliged to point out, quite a number of victims, and at the head of the list inevitably he places his 81-year-old mother, Beth. 'Yes,' he says, 'my mother was a saint. I think that when it was all finished she was hurt, quite a lot. She came to feel that the heart-ache would never go away, there was always something new happening, something to tear at her.

'She was always happiest in the quiet periods and, God knows, there weren't too many of those. In all the years of being left alone she never had a relationship with another man, not seriously, and in the end the maelstrom of Dad's life just got too much for her.

'I suppose you can go on only for so long. Then you must feel you are beating your head against the wall. She went back to him when he moved from City to Palace, living for a while in his flat in Cromwell Road in Kensington, then later in Selsdon near Croydon. But then soon enough it was all happening again, the same old headlines, the same old stuff. Of course it was sad for the kids as well. Dawn and I were about the same age, Mark a bit younger and Michelle was the youngest. She took it all very hard.

'I was the luckiest because I went away to Blackpool, and then overseas. I never saw close up the worst of his years – the playboy years, the relentless stories about what he was up to and with whom. Nowadays I suspect it would be even worse with the internet and mobile-phone cameras in every bar and restaurant and nightclub, and newspapers in the market for every sleazy titbit that comes their way. You saw the changes down the years, you saw increasingly how people were set up.'

There is another flashback as he traces those days of his father's most vertiginous decline.

It is of my finding him in the bar of the Baltimore Hotel in Middlesbrough on a June day in 2000. He was 72 and largely beaten. His devoted last partner, Lynn, had been made increasingly desperate by his erratic behaviour and had changed the locks on their home in the nearby village of Yarm. A few days earlier the *Daily Mail* had ransacked the last of his celebrity, paid him £600 and announced in a double-page spread, 'He was one of sport's most flamboyant figures with a penchant for Bunny Girls. But now Malcolm Allison reveals he is on the point of suicide.'

It was the parading of a broken man, the modern equivalent of a day in the stocks. For his £600, Malcolm Allison was required to sing out his agonies, and for his family and friends there were painfully intimate details of where his excesses had carried him. In one excruciating paragraph he described how he sought the aid of Viagra in a desperate attempt to save his last relationship.

Here was the crushing denouement of the man who had not been shy about his affair with Christine Keeler, the courtesan who helped bring down a government. There had also been the beautiful daughter of a Brazilian diplomat, when he was at the peak of his national fame as a TV analyst of the 1970 Brazilian World Cup. They met at an embassy party celebrating Brazil's magnificent triumph and inevitably he was the centre of attention.

His second wife, Sally, was a Bunny Girl, and she followed Serena Williams, who was a convent girl when they first met in Plymouth and was still decorating his life in the early seventies when he flew to Madrid on a football spying mission – and a nightclub club encounter with the great player Alfredo Di Stéfano. Michael Parkinson wrote that he was 'possibly the least tranquillised Englishman alive' – an impression he did little to stifle when in 1974 he announced to a gathering of Fleet Street sports writers attending the launching of his autobiography that he was a little tired after staying up all night in the company of the singer Rosemary Squires.

Yet if the *Mail* wrote about the possibility of suicide it appeared to some, at least those who wanted to believe so, that he might just be on the point of rescue. There was certainly a significant reaction to the broadcasting of his plight. His old players rallied to a cause that had so deeply stretched the resources of his family and which, in the run of their daily lives, they had not grasped had reached such a critical point. I called Francis Lee from Middlesbrough and confirmed that if the *Daily Mail* piece had one value it was that they had made it so clear that the walls of his old coach's life, such as they had become, were indeed falling in.

It had been a short but desperate and chaotic journey from a no longer supportable life in a quiet village to the Baltimore Hotel, where the cost of his stay was being covered by the proprietor. He was Tony Zivanaris, a Cypriot-born property developer who had briefly served as a Middlesbrough FC club director and had been deeply impressed by the style and imagination of the new manager who seemed, on his best days, to have brought to the North East all the colour and excitement of the big world of football. He was thrilled by Allison's vision and tolerant of his excesses, but now he had inherited the dog days of that brilliant career.

When the coach left the Middlesbrough club amid controversy in 1984, he had retreated to the Baltimore and one day the manager phoned Zivanaris to say that their guest had built up a bill of £11,000 and was about to check out without any sign of payment. 'Let Malcolm go,' said the owner, who a year later received a cheque for the precise amount owed. It was posted from Kuwait, the latest staging post of what would prove, but for the swiftly truncated breakout in Portugal, an irreversible ordeal of collapsing hopes.

Now, at this critical moment in 2000, Zivanaris was the man who stood between his old hero and the street. His staff prepared meals and served them privately and when some guests, seizing on the last of his celebrity, insisted on buying champagne they attempted, though not always successfully, to ease him away from the bar.

Even as the *Mail* were preparing their shocking piece, Zivanaris came to the hotel for a last attempt to persuade the coach that he couldn't go on like this. He was around about the end of the game. Zivanaris told him he had a friend, but one who had a duty to point out certain realities. Malcolm Allison could still be a good man, one who people were attracted to because of who he was and what he had to say, not for some old image that for some time had been falling apart. The headlines and the Bunny Girls belonged to his past if he was to have any kind of future.

It was a message reinforced when men like Lee and Mike Summerbee, Colin Bell and Tony Book became aware of the degree of a decline which had sharpened so forebodingly two years earlier when he'd lost his job with a local radio station having uttered an obscenity in the heat of a match commentary – and yes, he had been drinking. There was a three-week hiatus in Romania, where he coached youngsters, initially with pleasure and optimism, but disillusionment came quickly and soon enough he was seeking the consolation of the cheap local brandies.

Back in Yarm, he broke into his old house, where on a happier day his friend and devoted disciple Bobby Moore had made a charming speech as the godfather of his last child Gina – and joked that it was the only christening he had attended when most concern was not attached to the behaviour of the baby. On this more forlorn occasion, the coach found a bottle of wine, drank it, and was then arrested by the police.

Two weeks earlier he had travelled to London for the annual dinner of the Football Writers' Association, ironically as a guest of the *Daily Mail* writer Jeff Powell, but unaware that a group of friends, including his coaching protégé Terry Venables, finally alerted to the severity of his situation, were preparing to take him into a private room to discuss his future. Before that could happen he took a very liquid lunch – he didn't remember where – before finding himself back on a train to the North East.

There was trouble on the train and he might well have been ejected but for the calming intervention of an acquaintance. He was dishevelled and dislocated when he hammered on the door of his old home and was again arrested by the police. He told friends that he spent four days in custody. It only seemed like that. The police kept him for 24 hours. And then he arrived at the Baltimore.

I told Lee that it seemed to me there was only one place where the reclaiming of Malcolm Allison could begin. It was in detoxification and rehabilitation, in a place like the Priory, which had an establishment in the Manchester suburbs where he would be close to his family and old friends and players. But then, of course, the Priory costs money, rather big money.

Lee said to arrange his transport to the Priory immediately. He would call the place at the end of our conversation and leave details of his credit card. He would also phone Gordon Taylor, chief of the players' union, to see if some long-term help was possible.

Taylor was encouraging, saying, 'We know that when a player's career ends it can often have the effect of a cold shower. Malcolm had so much success as a coach, was such a great man in the game, you have to imagine his shower has gone on for a long time.'

Within 24 hours Zivanaris had his driver take the coach to the Priory. He also had a new dressing gown, pyjamas and slippers packed into a case.

There was, though, a certain price to be paid for these attempts at deliverance from the most serious crisis of a tumultuous and so often perilous life. It was a series of role-reversal lectures from the players he had once influenced so profoundly. One by one they arrived at the Priory, bearing fruit and Havana cigars – but no champagne. The most trenchant speech came from Lee. He said, 'You made Belly and Mike and me and all the others do a lot of things we didn't want to do. You made us work so hard we spewed up. You never stopped kicking our arses, you made us achieve things as footballers we never dreamed were possible. You were bloody incredible. I don't believe there has ever been a better pure football coach. You changed our lives. Now you have to change your own. We're here, all of us, to help you, but you have to do the real job.'

Summerbee, who still had the bespoke shirt business he launched at the peak of his success at City, went along to take some fittings – and to say, 'Even now, after all you've been through, I don't believe there is anyone in football with a sharper brain, a more complete understand-ing of what is most important in the game. It's a tragedy you're no longer involved in the game and maybe that's partly football's fault – but it is also your own.

'You have to come out of this place in charge of yourself, with your pride back, and if you can do this I wouldn't be surprised if someone said, even at this very late hour, "Wait a minute, maybe this guy could help." Not as a manager, Mal, because let's be honest, you were never a manager. You were a coach, a glorious coach, the best there was. When I arrived at City I was proud to wear that pale blue shirt, but I was also scared of what was in front of me. And then, in no time at all, you had me running around full-backs as if it was my right.'

Summerbee noted that after the title had been won so brilliantly in 1968, the coach had declared, 'Next stop, Mars.' He never got there, of course, but as we all knew so well now, he nearly died trying. Perhaps you could at least hope, Summerbee suggested, that he had finally settled a little nearer to earth.

Before the end of that first week at the Priory there were some encouraging portents. The coach had taken under his wing a youngster fighting drug addiction, one who displayed some impressive football skill. 'I feel good helping this boy,' said the coach, 'because if anyone can understand some of his problems it has got to be me.' He also won the clinic's weekly quiz, a success which provoked a reassuringly immodest claim. 'I'm going to make a record recovery,' he declared.

It was a heart-warming resolve but soon enough there was evidence that it could not be fulfilled. Summerbee reported, 'One day I got a call from Frannie saying that Malcolm had escaped from the Priory and needed some money. "How much have you got on you?" he asked. I told him I had about £70, but I also said that if I gave it to him it would mean only that he would get badly pissed.

'But Frannie persisted, saying, "He says he needs the money and he sounds desperate, so go and find him and give him the money." I did a tour of the pubs and eventually found him in one in Altrincham. It was filled with cigarette smoke and seemed to be a real boozing den. He was in a corner, surrounded by people, and sitting next to him was the most beautiful inebriated woman I had ever seen.'

David Allison augments such accounts of mislaid hope from what seems like a bottomless well. He also goes back to his attempt as a young man to fashion some identity of his own. 'As a son in such a situation,' he says, 'you just try to take the best and live with the rest. Dad loved all his kids, I'm sure about this, but he never gave any of us much time. For instance, he didn't come to my wedding. It was because while he was in America he went on a night out with Rodney Marsh and they finished up in the cells. There had been a bit of an incident which took a little time to sort out. But then, to be fair, he did write a letter to apologise.

'Michelle didn't come to the funeral. Now she realises her dad did love her and she wishes she had gone along. She had some hate in her for all that happened, and that was reflected in the fact that she was the only one of us not to attend. We all said to her, "You will regret it later." And she said, "That's my problem, isn't it?"

'But she does regret it now. I think the problem was she was the youngest and, while the rest of us had our separate lives and relationships, she felt isolated. It was always Mum and her. Maybe it was that she felt she had been closer to it all for a longer time and there was just too much pain to put down all in one go, simply because he had died.'

He rummages, briefly, in his past – and declares, 'I do have some good memories. I remember going to the charity games the Variety Club staged in little grounds like Knutsford on a Sunday. He would always take me along and I remember Kenny Lynch, the singer and comedian, was always there. I would have a kick-around with some of the older players, which was brilliant.

'Later everyone would be in the pub and I would be sitting outside with my bag of crisps and Coca-Cola. In those days people didn't think anything about drinking and driving, so it was about coming home at 10 o'clock and going off to school in the morning. But I always loved it, the atmosphere around it, and being able to tag around after my dad.

'It was a forerunner of the kind of thing they do with pop stars today, but it was very low key, and I could see something in my dad that was always impressive. He did a lot of work for charity and I was always proud to see he had a lot of good in him – and how he had all that power to inspire people and make them feel happy. But then, of course, there was the other side.'

Which left his eldest son struggling to prove that he could make a life outside of his father's huge and often troubling shadow. 'One reason I went abroad was that in England I never felt me. I was always Son of Malcolm. I was never just David, a kid trying to make his way, and that did my head in.

'I played in Blackpool reserves for two seasons and I was never going to get into the first team. When the manager Bob Stokoe released me I thought, "I'll go to Australia, I'll be myself." One thing I had learned was that you have to lead your own life, you can spend so much time in somebody's shadow that it is half over before you have any idea of who you are. I have talked with the son of another big football personality – Michael, son of Tommy Docherty – and it was uncanny how our experiences and feelings were so closely related. He said, "It was the same for me, I had the same curse of a being a "Son Of".

'My father didn't really coach me. He saw a couple of school games when I was 11 or 12. He was, though, very proud when I got a letter from Manchester United asking me to go for a trial. He blustered, "You're not going there." But the letter had been signed by Joe Armstrong, United's famous chief scout, and it was clear enough to me that he appreciated it was something to have.

'I was a midfielder, an old-style wing-half, and back then Altrincham and Sale Boys beat Manchester Boys three times in one season. We won one game 5–1 and we beat them at Old Trafford. So we had quite a good team and five of us went on to be pros.

'It's true that many professional footballers find it hard, if not impossible, to escape from a time warp that leaves them psychologically forever young. I was 30 when I broke my knee in Hong Kong and I remember saying to my wife, "You know, I still don't really know what I want to do when I grow up." I never played at a high level but I made it to that age as a pro, and this gave me a certain satisfaction. After Blackpool, I went to Australia and played there for a couple of years, for Wollongong, south of Sydney, in the New South Wales competition before they set up a national league.

'In 1974 Australia qualified for the World Cup in Germany, and because of the different seasons it was decided the domestic league would be scratched that summer and my club said I could go somewhere else on loan if I could find a deal. Brian Harvey, brother of the fine Everton midfielder Colin, was in Australia and he landed a job in Hong Kong and asked me to go with him. When I was there I scored a goal in a semi-final just before I was due to return to Australia. The Hong Kong club talked to Wollongong and signed me for £7,000. So I never went back to Australia, I got the knee injury and that was the end of my football story.

'I took a pub in Hong Kong for a couple of years and then I got a job with the San Miguel brewery looking after their major hotels and supermarkets in Hong Kong, a corporate kind of job. I worked for the brewery for seven or eight years and then I went into finance and brokering. I had a good time and my dad paid several visits, the happiest and least complicated [of which were] when he came out to work for Hong Kong TV on their coverage of the 1990 World Cup in Italy. He particularly enjoyed the fact that our flat overlooked the Happy Valley racecourse and we could watch the racing from our balcony.

'He was covering a lot of ground then. He was all over the place – Kuwait, Turkey, those stints in Portugal with Sporting and then Vitória de Setúbal, where he met the goalkeeper's young son José Mourinho, and who knows what kind of chemistry that helped put in place.

'After that incident when he went missing in Hong Kong we knew we were heading for a nightmare because it was clear things were only going to get worse. He would lose his keys, things like that, when he was living in sheltered accommodation in Manchester and he would have to break down the door or smash windows to get back into the house. He did get a little bit violent but that's part of the disease. It comes from frustration.

'Some of it his wife, Lynn, probably wasn't aware of – she was thinking it was almost all to do with alcohol. It was a combination of alcohol and, progressively, the effects of dementia and, of course, it was a tragedy for both of them. There is certainly no doubt that the drinking had gone out of control.'

Who can say where it all first started to go wrong, when it was that the luminous trajectory began to trail into the clouds, but David Allison is still another who believes that momentum began to fade, fatally, when his father stopped listening to Joe Mercer. 'I don't really know what happened in the relationship between my dad and Joe – he never confided beyond a few generalities – but when I was young and all the turmoil in his career began I would never hear a bad word about Joe. He was good for Dad. I'll always believe that and I know certainly that it was only when Dad got out of that situation with Joe that things really started to go wrong in his career, and not least when he went against Joe's advice and signed Rodney Marsh when another league title was all but won. Joe could see the Indian signs, all right, but of course by then he no longer had Dad's ear.'

All David Allison can do now is draw the best from a fractured legacy, both for himself and his mother and his five wounded but now (he is happy to believe) uniformly proud siblings. He tells you, 'My mother is in her eighties and has problems with her knees, but she is still a beautiful woman – still all there with her wits, which is a great thing for all of us because it was so terrible to see Alzheimer's happening to somebody we loved who had been so full of life.

'I still keep in touch with Lynn and Gina and Alexis, my dad's daughter from his second marriage with Sally, who died. I remember coming back from Hong Kong to see Dad, and Alexis was very young, sitting on his knee. He was [also] teaching her tennis and she loved it – she would smash the ball at him and he would smash it back. She was no more than three years old but she tells me she still remembers those days.'

By the time of the funeral David Allison had good reason to be satisfied by the way he had been able to gather together, the steadfast defection of Michelle apart, the strands of his family. He had nourished all those instincts of pride and, of course, forgiveness, and when the ceremonials were concluded he was both moved and relieved.

'To see so many people at his funeral was unbelievable,' he says. 'We drove around the Eastlands stadium with the coffin, then Maine Road, before finishing up at Southern Cemetery, and there were people everywhere. Tommy Docherty, at whom my father had made some shocking public swipes, was there, and his old Crystal Palace star player, Peter Taylor, who went on to play for Tottenham and England, said some very nice words.

'Dawn and Alexis spoke in the chapel, along with the City secretary Bernard Halford and an old football friend, Lennie Lawrence.

John Bond, his old West Ham teammate, came along. They were great mates at Upton Park, and they were never really enemies even though they had some differences when John followed his second stint at City and took the team to the 1981 Cup final.

'Wyn Davies was also there, and when I saw him I thought that he was probably the reason we went to Newcastle the time he had me drive the Jaguar. Dad always loved Wyn, the way he hung in the air and was such a great, brave header [of the ball]. Dad loved players like that. He was, of course, a big guy himself – and good in the air.' In all the circumstances, you had to think as David Allison drove away, it was not the worst of epitaphs.

Chapter 4

The coach loved them all, but none so much as the one in whom he invested a passion and a faith that was, right from the start, almost haunting.

He extolled all their virtues. He cherished the competitive furies which were always so near the surface of everything that Lee and Summerbee did. He adored the commitment of men like Doyle and Pardoe and Oakes, the understated yet unswerving leadership of Book, but it was only when he spoke of Colin Bell that he might have been performing an incantation. The lift in his heart could not have been more apparent. It was as though he was celebrating not only a great player but also a great spirit, and if this sounds like a fancy assessment it is hardly ill-served by this April morning I'm spending with the man who provoked that first reverence and now, as he grows old, inhabits an aura of respect which as a shy, dislocated boy he never imagined he would attain.

We are in the corner of a clubhouse out of which he can no longer, at the age of 68, take his golf bag because of the accumulated effects of arthritis in his hands and the injury which so cruelly, and prematurely, ended his career. But all this is at no cost to the impression of a man deeply content with what he was able to achieve – and the manner in which he did it.

This is because when you sit with him and listen to his sometimes tortured explanation of a lifelong diffidence, an endless battle to exert himself in, perhaps more than anywhere else, his own mind, you too are drawn into the sense of an aloof but mighty presence. Bell is someone who has, along with accumulating trophies, absorbed the regard of those who have always seen and acknowledged not only an extraordinary talent but a huge professional integrity, and has accordingly assembled a set of the hardest certainties about the value of his life and the part in it football will always play.

He tells you, for example, what he would want to read on his own gravestone, saying, 'I would like it said that he had two families, his wife and children, and Manchester City, family number one and family number two, and that the respect he won for himself with these two connections was for him unbelievable.

'I sometimes see people I first knew as young kids and they say things like, "You're my dad's favourite player." Or, "My mum sends her regards," and that gives me a very warm feeling. It also makes me feel very lucky to have been part of those brief, wonderful years when everything was so simple, so perfect and I always felt there was a guiding hand on my shoulder.'

He is also affecting when he talks of the void that has to be occupied when the rhythm of a footballer's life is broken, as his was ultimately when his knee ballooned grotesquely after a tackle by Manchester United's Martin Buchan. 'The thing that is hard to convey is quite how much your life works by Saturday when you are a footballer. The whole week revolves around that day: you play, you express yourself; you make a success or a failure of the days that preceded it. You only know what day it is in relation to Saturday.

'When you are fit everything falls into place – you played yesterday so today you relax before going back to training. Maybe you play a round of golf, take the kids to the park, but always there is Saturday, looming up, dominating your thoughts. And then when you are injured the calendar goes haywire. The days no longer run through seamlessly.

'The fact that my son and daughter did so well in their education, and got such good jobs, is a credit to my wife Marie. I never felt any compulsion to stay in football when my playing days were over, but I did know I could recognise exceptional talent in a youngster. I also know that I can always spend time weighing up something in football – a player maybe, or a situation – in a way that I couldn't in any other sphere of my life. I suppose for me football was always a case of all or nothing.

'As I always say, football is a learning trade and the best players never stop learning. The truth is that apart from family, football is the only thing I have lived for. Nothing else has been so compelling – or made me examine so much my deepest feelings.'

At first the game merely helped him pass lonely hours but soon enough it was the driving force to a personal vindication. He goes straight to the heart of the widely perceived dichotomy of a masterful footballer and a withdrawn personality who was once grabbed by his City and England teammate, Lee, and asked, 'For Christ's sake, Belly, don't you realise you can take any game apart?'

'Throughout my time in football,' Bell says, 'I've been a shy person. I don't do television. I'm not capable of doing it. It is something that comes from my childhood. When I was one my mother died and I was given to an aunt for eight or nine years. And then my father took me back when he remarried.

'So that was quite a long time to be without a mum or dad in a stable situation and I think that was my downfall in any pursuit of a confident personality. The truth is that apart from my time on the football field I've always hated being in the public eye. I suppose it has left me a bit of a Jekyll and Hyde character.

'I would plead not guilty, though, to a charge that I've used "shyness" as cover for a desire to be aloof, to not bother with people.

I would love my personality to be better, to be more outgoing, so that I could talk to people more easily, even if it was just a bunch of old rubbish, but unfortunately I don't have that ability. I'm just not like that. I hate drawing attention to myself, and it was like that in school. I still remember the agony I went through when, like all the other kids, I had to read some sentences from a story we were studying before the whole class. Each of us had to pick up the story and read nominated sentences but I just marked down my lines and kept reading them over and over before the story was handed to me. My teacher used to have me with her in front of the class, by the radiator, and when my turn came she would put her arm around me and say, "Come on, Colin, love, you can do it."'

It is, when you hear such an account of boyish uncertainty, less of a surprise when he tells you of his admiration, and natural affinity, for another great product of North-Eastern football fields, Sir Bobby Charlton. 'There is no one in football I respect more, or closely relate to, than him,' he says. 'And I suppose this may have something to do with the fact that not only do we come from the same part of the world [but he also] has quite a bit of shyness in him.

'I remember once when I was here on a golf day I saw him walking away down a hallway and I chased him to say hello. He seemed to be aware that someone was coming behind him and he quickened his steps, as though he wanted to get away, almost as if he was running for cover, but then as he gathered speed he did glance over his shoulder and recognise me. He stopped immediately and said, "Hello, Colin lad." Suddenly, he had switched off completely. He was back as one of the lads, one of the boys who played in so many kickabouts on the streets and wasteland of the mining villages. He's a lovely, modest person and when he comes to watch a game at the Etihad stadium he always says hello. He's invited me to Old Trafford a million times.'

These meetings of two great players, and the meaning of them, takes me back to the time I found myself sitting next to Charlton on a flight from Chicago. He was connecting from a trip to Los Angeles and I was returning from the annual pilgrimage to Augusta and, at the end of the long conversation with a man who still flies uneasily all these years after the Munich tragedy, I was told, almost as an aside, 'The publishers will contact you about the book.'

'Which book?' I asked.

'The autobiography you're going to help me to write,' he said.

Also recalled is the opening statement of that book, one which might have been uttered by the man who once chased him down the corridor. It said, after all, 'Now, when I look back on my life and remember all that I wanted from it as a young boy in the North East, I see more clearly than ever it is a miracle. I see one privilege heaped upon another. I wonder all over again how so much could come to one man simply because he was able to do something which for him was so natural and easy, and which he knew from the start he loved to do more than anything else.

'None of this wonderment is lessened by knowing that when I played football I was probably as dedicated as any professional could be, though I claim no credit for this. Playing was, in all honesty, almost as natural as breathing. No, the truth is that although I did work hard at developing the gifts I'd been given, the path of my life has truly been a miracle.'

It might be Bell speaking as he recalls those first days in Hesleden, County Durham, on the muddy school field and then as an 11-year-old for East Durham Under-15s before bursting, with stunning stamina and acute ball skills, into the colours of Horden Colliery Welfare Juniors. For Bell the miracle took a little time to form – and was set back by a rejection by Arsenal – but quickly enough it was inexorable.

And if the wider world of football was much slower than Malcolm Allison to recognise extraordinary potential – before signing him in the spring of 1966, for £45,000 from second division Bury, Allison threw off rivals by severely disparaging the young player when he watched him while sitting amid a gaggle of rival managers and scouts – in the end the consensus was thunderous.

When Bell was forced finally to concede defeat in his fight to recover from the knee injury, at the age of 33, the litany of praise came down from some of the highest peaks of football achievement. Sir Tom Finney, of whom Bill Shankly once said, 'He was so good I would have played him in his overcoat,' declared, 'Colin Bell was as good as anything I have ever seen.' Charlton placed him in the ultimate category, announcing, 'Colin Bell was unquestionably a great player.'

These tributes are still held close to Bell's heart but he tells you that if he had the power to recreate a single moment of the acclamation which built around his football life it would be when he ran down the Maine Road tunnel for the second half against Newcastle United. It was his first appearance in a comeback that he feared, presciently, would never truly take flight; never return him to the level of performance which his former teammate, and then manager, Book, swore he might otherwise have maintained until he was 40. 'I realised soon enough that the comeback wasn't really going anywhere but what it did bring – and I can never forget this even as I sometimes fret over what else I might have achieved but for the injury – was the single most unforgettable experience of my career. The whole of Maine Road seemed to shake with the noise when I ran on the pitch. It is about 50 yards down the tunnel and by the time I was on the pitch the atmosphere was astonishing. There were kids hanging over the wall of the tunnel. The word had swept around the stadium, "Belly is coming on." I wasn't aware of it at the time but there were people with tears in their eyes. Something like that affects you for ever. I still feel tears coming to my eyes when I think of it. These were grown men reacting to what you had done as a footballer, what you had come to represent to them as they went about all the struggles of their own working lives. So you see, the connection between me and those supporters is, after my family, second to none.

'There was for me, of course, an added poignancy that night in that I couldn't be sure I would ever play again in that way which had created the public response. It was a bad injury and it never got better. In football you get injuries like a pulled hamstring and, though it is an inconvenience, you can tell yourself, "I will be back in four or five weeks." I had nothing like that certainty, only the grinding fear that I would never come back, at least never whole, never confident that I could do the best of my work.'

In his autobiography, published in 2003, Bell is scrupulous in dismissing suggestions that he was the victim of skulduggery, saying, 'I don't blame Martin Buchan for the injury. I know there are players in the game who set out to kick you and injure you if they can but I don't think he was that type of player. I was a little disappointed, though, that he didn't visit me during my time in hospital. If it had been me who had done that to him, I'd have gone to see him, as long as I knew in my own mind that I hadn't done it on purpose.'

There may be a subtle implication in that last sentence but, for his part, Buchan is emphatic about his innocence: 'I have never had any problems sleeping at nights over that tackle. The injury was caused by the fact that his studs were in the ground at the time of impact. The referee never stopped the game.'

So there it was, according to Buchan, and to an extent Bell: the ultimate curse of football, the split-second miss-step which can take away the last of your years in an arena you have come to dominate.

However he dresses it, however much he celebrates the extraordinary achievements which preceded that moment of the life-changing tackle, when his knee filled with blood and later doctors advised that the stress of the resulting physical trauma might have brought on thrombosis, part of Bell, he admits, will always be rooted in that shocking passage of fate.

He says, 'Now I struggle up and down the stairs, taking them one at a time. I don't get pain in the knee, just the disability and, of course, I sometimes think of how it was before the injury, when the end of my career seemed so far away.

'In the end I had to accept my fate for the most practical, unavoidable reason. I couldn't bend my leg any more. Many years later the club physiotherapist, Fred Griffiths, said he thought they should have gone into my knee in the old-fashioned way with a big incision rather than the keyhole surgery which had come to be favoured.

'The keyhole surgery just didn't work, the knee refused to bend. For two or three years I fought the good fight, refusing to accept that I was finished, hoping against hope that one morning the nightmare would be over and I could do as I once did, run with the confidence that I could win back all that I had lost. I wasn't in a situation where someone with far greater knowledge than me looked at the damage a few days after the incident and said, "Your career is over." That would have been a terrible shock but I suppose, in retrospect, it would have made me face up to my situation, and certainly it would have meant that three or four years of my life were not spent in a kind of limbo.

'My first game back was against Blackpool reserves, and after the match I went to see Tony Book, who was now my manager, and I said, "Look, Bookie, even in a reserve game I couldn't pull my weight." There were too many situations in the game where I knew that if I was right, if I was heading in the right direction, I would have got there, but the truth was I just couldn't do it. With the knee so rigid I got there only to find that the opponent had gone. I was thinking, "I have to cut this guy off, I have to do this or that in a way I didn't have to before" – and this in a reserve game against Blackpool. I said to the manager, "If I'm in a reserve game and not pulling my weight, well, I'm sorry, I just can't do it."'

Bell's face, which is still the finely chiselled one of a pure athlete despite all the years of enforced and dismaying inaction, is suddenly set along the grimmest lines. And then, the ghost of a smile. 'It was a hard speech to make but then I was always a bad loser, I just could bear the idea of defeat, personally or collectively. When I lost in the first division I just put my head down and went off along the tunnel as quickly as possible. Shaking hands with people after we had lost didn't do too much for me. The whole process was a horror, something I needed to put behind me even before I got into my car to drive away.

'Fear of the big injury had been, as it was for so many footballers, the shadow over my life, and of course it came in the end. At the peak of my career, as I played for a winning City team which was so brilliantly motivated and organised, and a powerful England team then among the elite of the international game, I could tell myself that everything had worked out for the best – the Arsenal episode, the acquiring of good experience in the warm East Lancashire atmosphere of Bury and the good luck I had in my wife and children couldn't have been better. And then there was the injury which still, even today, brings me pain when I look at the record books and I'm reminded of quite how much more I might have done.'

But then, as he tells himself often enough, there was not a lot more he could have done in those years of ebbing hope. He says he fought the good fight and a whole club and its following attached itself to every flicker of hope. The trouble was that there was never enough of them, and when Maine Road erupted so emotionally when he came running on against Newcastle the flame was, in truth, nothing so much as another candle spluttering in a cold wind.

Bell sighs and agrees that he knew it in his bones. 'I went to the ground every day, trailing my hopes – and my fears. Roy Bailey, Freddie's assistant, drove me to the ground every day because I couldn't work my knee while driving. Freddie and Roy were great as they pushed me along, around the ground, up and down the terracing.

'The shame was that when I first started using weights I could hardly pick them up, but by the time I finished I could lift a full block of them on the machine. I had worked so hard on my strength down the years, and you can imagine how it felt, feeling so strong but also crippled whenever I went on the field. I had some bad days, bad nights, because I hated so much the idea of it all coming to an end. You look for every bit of encouragement, you do your work, but in your heart you know it is a losing battle.'

Another battle was lost 17 years later when he was fired from his job in the City youth system, and when that happened he had, along with the Buchan tackle, the second great and lingering regret of a career that in all other respects had fulfilled the hopes he had conjured as he kicked a ball along the Hesleden kerbside on his way to school.

He needs to address it in the strongest terms still now as old colleagues like Summerbee and Book attempt, with declining optimism, to mend the broken relationship with the man he will always blame.

Frannie Lee was the chairman who authorised the firing and, Bell claims, made himself elusive when the wounded player demanded an explanation. It is the one shadow playing back over the fierce, often phenomenal unity which was such a foundation of the great City team. And it is one that Bell swears will never be dispelled.

First he tells of his shock and anger when the news was delivered. Then he retraces his own football boyhood and the lessons he learned about the vulnerability of kids and the need to nourish even the most obvious of talent. It is the exploration of an old but still vivid wound.

He says, 'One thing with me is that I'm stubborn and I'll never make up with Frannie – not after what he did to me and my family. It is a crying shame for everyone involved, including the supporters, and I will always believe it just shouldn't have happened. I always feel that I have to insist it wasn't my fault. It made it worse that the ordeal – for that is what it was – was so prolonged.

'Frannie washed his hands of it, said he wasn't involved even though he was chairman of the club, and I had been eased out at the youth level. It was something he could have sorted out if he had chosen to but, to be perfectly honest, I have never really known how the situation began to develop in the first place. I imagine that, deep down, he regrets it because it surely wasn't good for the image of the club. It was terrible for both me and my family contemplating the possibility of an industrial tribunal. I would never have believed my relations with Manchester City would have come to that.

'The point I must make is that beyond anything else my love for family comes first – always has, always will. I couldn't stand what my family was put through in those days under the shadow of the tribunal. I'd never done harm to City and if I had bad feelings about anyone there I would not have told them to any Tom, Dick or Harry. I'm not that type of person.

'I heard that Frannie had people digging around for negative reports on me. I heard he called a couple of scouts in Scotland, but they were absolutely on my side, and they had nothing to tell him about me, nothing negative anyway. I couldn't believe any of it because I had never tried to rub the club up the wrong way. I kept asking myself, "Where did all this come from?"

'Earlier you asked me about money and its place in my life. Well, I can tell you if Frannie came today with a wagon filled with twenty million pounds and tipped it on my front garden, I would fill the wagon back up and send it on its way. I might be short of cash, I might need it very much, but I wouldn't touch a penny of it. I see him at City games but we do not speak; occasionally he gets up from his seat and says, "Excuse me, Mr Colin Bell, can I get past?" and I just let him go. I have nothing to say to him.'

Eventually Bell believed there were problems with the youth system concerning the style of recruitment and the payments that we're being made and that he had been treading on difficult – and delicate ground – when he protested about the treatment of some of the boys.

He says, 'I heard that Neil McNab, who was in charge of the youth system, was sending kids home crying, and I was finding this out from parents. So, yes, I kicked up a bit. Kids come into a club and, all right, some are better than others but you treat them all the same until their time is up and then you say, "We're keeping you, you and you, and we're sorry but there's no place for you others." It's bad enough when you have to part with kids in the end, but you do not give them a rough time when you have them. It's a difficult thing telling a kid that he's not going to make it, but it has to be done honestly and as kindly as possible. They know when they come in that they have two years to prove themselves, and you should know at the end of that period which two or three are going to make it and which ones are not. Then it is just a question of considering the feelings of the kids who have to get on with life after a dream has been broken.'

You can see on his face that he has been revisiting the terrain that shaped his life, and it is very easy to imagine that every time a boy collected his kit and put it away with his hopes of being a professional for the last time he took a few steps back along his own past – and speculated all over again what might have happened to him if he hadn't survived his own disappointments. If he hadn't persuaded himself that football wasn't so much his vocation as the opportunity to make sense of his place in the world – and his best chance of underpinning it. He goes back to his boyhood quite seamlessly because he knows that it is somewhere he will always inhabit in his deepest thoughts: 'It was very early in my life, from the age of four or five, when I decided I was going to be a footballer. I used to kick a ball along when I went to school or do errands or walk the dog. I kicked a tennis ball along the roadside. I spent so much time in the backyard with my most precious possession, my football, kicking it and chesting and heading it, keeping it up, volleying against a fence, lobbing it against the roof. I went everywhere with the ball. It was part of me.

'There were difficulties in my family situation, it wasn't a normal life for a young boy, but I don't think that was why I immersed myself so deeply in football. More than anything it was that I felt I was born to play football, that it was both my release from some of the more painful realities of my life, but also my expression. I used to join in any game I saw. Back then in the village men played even as they came out of the mines, and there were always a few kids to make up the numbers. The men would start a one-on-one coming up out of the pit and then, in no time at all, it would go from two-on-two, to five-on-five and often it would finish up something like 18-on-18. It would never have happened in Hale Barns, where I live now. It wouldn't happen anywhere now, not with the shopping malls, the game arcades, the places where they sell iPads. The way my world was it was the most natural thing to play football.

'Looking back, everything I did as a young footballer seemed to be written up in the sky: going to Arsenal for a trial while nursing a bad back and not telling anyone and then coming home and the doctor telling me not to kick a ball for six months; settling down in the homely Bury club; before making my way to City. Really, the big injury is my only bugbear when I look back on my life as a player. If my career looked the way it should, if it had everything I worked for, it would have everything it has – and five or six years tagged on.

'I certainly wouldn't have rushed to play God when it came to deciding on a kid's future. I used to tell the scouts at City, "Look, I've seen the kid once and I wasn't so impressed, but you have to see a kid more than once: he might be not quite physically right the first time, there might be trouble at home or he might be in the middle of a growth spurt." I had that problem myself between the ages of 12 and 14. I grew about eight inches and there were times when I could hardly break into a walk. I felt weak, I could hardly rouse myself.'

You do not interrogate Colin Bell, no more than you do his friend and kindred spirit Bobby Charlton. You tell him how you remember him out on the field, how you noted the intensity of his purpose and the consistency of his effort. And how he built around himself an extraordinary level of respect but no real understanding of what was going on inside . . . and then you wait for the tide of the feelings you know, sooner or later, will again swirl over the walls of the dam he felt it necessary to make for himself. You do not have to wait so long.

'Money,' he says, 'never had much, if anything, to do with my football. I rarely if ever thought about it while considering my future. The club would say you were on so much, and I just accepted it. You were just so grateful to be a footballer on a three-year contact. Three years! It was an age, a lifetime back then. For three more years you would be paid to keep yourself fit – and do something you'd rather do than anything else you could think of. I always felt, like Bobby Charlton, that if you did your job well and honestly, if you never hid away when it was time to play, you would be made a new offer.

'You were never run by money, only by your ability and your form and your fitness. And then you were in the hands of the manager. I never thought that with my success on the field, when I was called up to the England team, that I had created my own security. You were always only as good as your last performance, and I suppose that was why I so much hated to lose. It was more than a match you had lost. Maybe it was a foothold on being somebody you would never cease to want to be.

'You knew the manager would come to you in the last six months of your contract and offer you a deal, and you never thought there was anything you could do to affect the situation, no threats, no pressure, because by then you felt you had done all that you could. I never thought I was bigger than the club, or anyone else in the dressing room, and when I got my contract I always felt the same. I was playing for a big club and I was somewhere down the ladder.'

There was always someone to tell him that he should be more assertive. The coach said that he should look in the mirror and see a giant. He just didn't realise how good and how strong he was, Allison said, in an almost daily mantra.

Paul Doherty, the football journalist and son of the great City player Peter, was especially frustrated. Doherty was both a confidant of the coach and he got closer than most to the great but doggedly introverted player.

'Paul Doherty wanted to be my agent, officially,' says Bell. 'But I never had an agent in those days of modest finances, though he was the nearest thing to one I ever had. At one point he urged me to go down to London to see a hypnotist. Someone who might help me build up my confidence off the field for such things as TV appearances and ads. But I said, "No, Paul, you know that's not me." I think he got very frustrated with me because after I'd built my reputation as a player, and City had achieved so much quick success, he was unable to exploit the commercial possibilities.

'He came to me with so many ideas, but I was always resistant, always stubborn, and it was the same when he reported a chance meeting he'd had with the Manchester United manager Sir Matt Busby on a London train. They talked about this and that and then suddenly Busby said, "Does Colin Bell fancy coming to Manchester United?" Doc was honest enough, saying, "I don't think so, but I'll ask him." I said to tell the great man that I was extremely flattered by the question but I was happy where I was. I was part of a very happy family. Yes, we were a band of brothers.'

As Bell talks, you are forced to imagine how that scenario would play today – as indeed it did a few years ago when Bell's old club made it clear they were interested in United's then disaffected striker Wayne Rooney. The player and his agent Paul Stretford applied immediate pressure on United. Rooney, who had just emerged from a catastrophic performance in the South African World Cup, where he had complained of the boredom of England's training regime on the Highveld – and had suffered a trailing through the media of lapses in his private life – publicly lectured his manager Sir Alex Ferguson on the failings of his transfer policy. Angry United fans gathered around the Rooney mansion in the Cheshire stockbroker belt, yet, progressively, the player has had his way. He won a new contract and a large rise and by 2014 he was reported to be earning around £300,000 a week.

Bell rolls his eyes and says, 'When I go around the grounds people are always asking me about stories like Rooney's and all I can say is that it isn't really the player's fault. If someone comes to you and says, "Will you take £300,000 a week?" you're not going to pass on that, say, "No, that's too much." But having said that, of course, sooner or later the danger is that it will destroy the game, do something to its nature and change, completely, the attitude of the people who play it.

'When I was a player I always thought there should be a ceiling on both transfer fees and wages, and this struck me particularly when Joe Jordan moved from Manchester United to Milan. I just felt it was fundamentally wrong that a club could just come along and throw some money on the table. How much better if everyone had a decent chance of competing, building their teams, applying their skills and experience as coaches and managers and then seeing who did the best job? Why did it always have to come down to money?

'I know that in today's climate that probably sounds like the ultimately naïve question, but there it is, deep in my bones. And this is so even as I go along to the Etihad stadium and cheer my old club, who have become one of the richest in the world and have one of the biggest wage bills. But then even the most one-eyed fan has to recognise certain realities.

'The basic one is that only the teams with the most money have a decent chance of taking the big honours. It means that you have to feel sorry for the managers who don't have the money and therefore, despite whatever talent and vision they might have, cannot seriously compete. No, let's face it, they really haven't got any chance at all.'

You are reminded that just a few days earlier City had taken over the contract of a 14-year-old prodigy who was being groomed by Malaga. The cost ran into millions and when you mention this Bell again shakes his head, more in bewilderment than anger. 'If you're that kid,' he says, 'something like this has to change the way you see not just football but life. It must change something inside you.

Somebody was telling me the other day about all the lads who have come through the Arsenal system without sniffing a first-team place who have become millionaires and are now virtually retired without a single memory of how it was to play at the highest level, how it was to see how you stood up to the challenge. I couldn't help thinking about this when the Arsenal manager Arsène Wenger was insisting that City should be hammered under the European football authority's Financial Fair Play regulations. It seemed to me an unlikely source for any argument on the need for level playing fields.

'I heard another story about a lad going up to Norwich City from the lower divisions and being embarrassed by the scale of the offer he received. He had a culture shock in a place not widely seen as one of the power centres of English football.

'I have to admit I find it difficult to celebrate the fact that players should have so much in the world of today when so many people have to struggle to cover the basics of housing and feeding their families. It is as though footballers have become a separate species, utterly detached from the people who come to cheer them on – and pay their wages. In my day the players' wage was a relatively small percentage above the national average, and that was why I went into the restaurant business before my playing days were over. I realised they would come to an end when other people in other walks of life were still climbing up the rungs of the ladder. There are no work guarantees when a player reaches 30, and back then there were not stockpiles of money to guard you and your family against what the future might bring.'

So it has meant that Bell has been a fiercely alert sentinel of his family's well-being in the prosperous Cheshire suburb where he lives, so far from the old played-out coalfields of his youth. His son Jon is a surgeon, one who reacted swiftly when a senior colleague read that his father's mother lost her life so early through bowel cancer and suggested a precautionary examination. The result was the prompt and successful removal of a tumour. His daughter Dawn went to Oxford and got a degree in maths and became a player in the City of London. Nowadays, he says that his main job is to listen attentively to the orders of his wife Marie, towards whom his devotion is intense.

He is proud of his family, his MBE, the Manchester City stand named for him, and also his ability to grow beyond those early fears that he might never be able, because of the constraints of his personality, to truly exert himself. That was an apprehension devoured in the greatest years of his life and that, as we will see and hear, still carries him through each day. Would I like to return with him and hear precisely how all of that felt? Yes, indeed, I say.

Chapter 5

Still they course through the mind, hundreds of playbacks reminding you why it was that Colin Bell was called Nijinsky after the Derby-winning thoroughbred. How it was he could tear open a game as easily as he might some flimsy package. Once more you see him forcing great players like Dave Mackay to face for the first time the spectre of old age. You see him devouring the heavy ground in a few strides. You see him invading the most hurtful places. You see him turning and wheeling, whirring away with barely a dab of sweat on his brow and a pulse rate so low it would regularly astound the scientists who hooked him up to their machines.

But then maybe the most telling image of an athlete made separate by the sheer scale of his physical gifts, is conjured by Bell himself when he relives those days when it seemed that he could run for ever. When he felt that all the steps of his life had brought him to the right place at the right time and, just occasionally, the feeling was so strong, so uplifting, even he had to give it some public expression.

It is an extraordinary picture he paints of the end of a routine recital of the demands of the regime put in place by the coach. Bell is standing in the middle of a group of sweat-stained teammates at the conclusion of an especially ferocious training session. They are shouting abuse, including the kind of rough language he has always abhorred. Inciting their rage has been a rare case of Bell affirming and celebrating the powers his teammates had long judged to be something from another world. While they had dragged themselves back to the changing room, their limbs and their lungs on fire, Bell had performed a strutting, and it seemed to some aghast colleagues, callously provoking proto-version of Michael Jackson's famed Moonwalk dance routine. In their eyes he might just as well have declared, officially, his alien status, his easy enjoyment of what for them was an ordeal that dragged them to their limits, if not beyond. And in that flashpoint of collective frustration, it was as though every taunting step, every triumphant gyration, was a rebuke to their own inadequate physical powers.

'It was not like me, really, and I suppose that's what took the other lads by surprise and caused their reaction,' he says. 'For me I suppose it was mostly the exhilaration of feeling that I was so on top of what I was doing, that I had plenty of effort to spare. It was, no doubt, a privilege I had but it was also a testament to the vision of Malcolm Allison about how to get the best out of his players on the training field.

'A lot of people paid most attention to his grand gestures but they missed what was most important about him. He brought people into Maine Road to talk to us about so many different things that he considered relevant and helpful to our work. We were lectured on our eating, sleeping, training, movement and psychological strength. His objective was to shape our thinking and he succeeded.

'He wanted to know everything about our physical and mental potential, how far we could be pushed and how quickly we could recover from the really big efforts. We used to go to a science lab at Salford University to have our ears pricked and our blood taken. We had monitors on our backs and, on occasion, we would have to put on gas masks as we worked, and in that situation you could hardly get air. But always we got through the tests pretty well.'

No one was doing such work in English football, no one was assaulting the barriers to full-on, 90-minute-plus performance with such energy or imagination. For Allison it was a deeply satisfying enactment of an instinct which he had felt so strongly as a national serviceman while watching the Red Army team training in the Viennese woods one morning on his way back from a romantic foray into the Soviet-ruled sector of the city. They were doing their work in big army boots but there was a freshness to it, a life and a bite which he could only compare favourably with the desultory sessions he had suffered with fast-rising frustration as a young player with Charlton Athletic.

For Bell it was not so much a trial as a liberation. He says, 'It was around about this time that my ability to do so well in these tests persuaded some of my teammates that I hadn't come from the North East but a different planet with a whole different set of physical parameters.

'I went to the 1970 World Cup in Mexico, joining men like Bobby Charlton and Alan Ball and Bobby Moore and Geoff Hurst, proven world champions, and though I was sick before I left, when I came back I had never been so fit in my life. In that pre-season, when we really should have been building towards another league title, I was simply flying. It was the most brilliant feeling to know that you could get to the last 20 minutes of a match and be certain that you were the strongest man on the field.'

He says it lightly, without a hint of hubris, because he remains one of those men who regard the neglect of any gift, and especially one that comes to you in the cradle, as a crime wilful beyond any excuse.

Yes, he says, he was the strongest man on the field but he will never forget the good fortune that placed him in the care of the coach. 'People often talk about how they felt at Malcolm's funeral,' he says, 'and some are a little bit confused about their feelings, how they remembered the good and the bad, but I was not in any doubt. I felt as I have always felt. I said again that people simply didn't know how good he was. They knew the wrong side of his life – they read all about it – but they didn't know how he was when he did his work among footballers. As a trainer, a coach, a motivator, he was surely the best. He had the job of shaping and driving the team, which he did so well, but his genius was in grasping the different needs of every player. He would pull players to one side when he felt they needed a bit of special attention, and this was completely across the board, it didn't matter if you were Tony Book, Mike Summerbee or Frannie Lee. He called me into his office a few times and whenever I left I felt 10 to 20 per cent better as an individual player who understood the needs of the team.

'He did that along with driving the team forward in a general way, and in training he was fantastic. He read books on the theory of it all, and his eagerness to pass it on to his players was inexhaustible. It was thrilling for me that he gave me so much encouragement, called me Nijinksy and all that, because he was held in such high regard by all the players. He was our prophet and our leader.

'He was always picking up players, pointing the way forward if they had run into a few problems, a few doubts. OK, sometimes you might have thought, "Maybe Mal is bulling me up a bit here," but there was always some content in what he said, and I know every one of us benefited from his putting his arm around us from time to time and telling us we were good players.

'He always saw the strengths of individuals, was as quick to praise a brilliant tackle by Mike Doyle as a run by Summerbee or me, or a superb strike by Frannie Lee or Neil Young. He could so easily separate the different qualities each player brought to the team, the ability of Book to stifle a winger, or young David Connor to do a marking job.

'Above everything else, he hammered home the value of supreme fitness. From match to match, week to week, he reviewed the progress of individuals and the team, pointed out things that were being done well and those that could be improved. I keep telling people in business that if someone isn't doing well for them, it is their job to lift them, point out where they are going wrong. If a boss earns respect he has a tremendous power to influence the people who are working for him, and it doesn't come with kicking someone in the teeth when they are down.

'I've known a few managers, and a few at City, who have dropped people and knocked them after doing so, and then a month or so after handing out stick expect them to come back and help a struggling team. That was never Malcolm – he could make his point brutally, but then he would soften it before it destroyed someone he needed to go out to perform much better in the next game. That was his great lesson. He saw the whole picture of the team, he saw the individuals who needed a kind word rather than a kick up the backside, and he saw the others too.

'I've always believed a boss has to keep his players happy because he never knows from one day to the next when he might need them. You have to nurture players, keep them ready for the day when you really need them. You cannot believe a certain eleven is going to be fit all season and that they are the only ones you have to keep sweet. You have to keep everyone sweet for as long as you can, and that was another of Malcolm's gifts.'

Yet in all that sweet chemistry, Bell was forced to see along with his teammates a central and killing paradox. If the coach could keep his players sweet, if he could nurse them with great skill and humour through their days of doubt and bleakness, it was a task he could not perform for himself, and the sadness of that reality is something Bell will never cease to regret.

'It is only when you consider how effective he was in those years between 1965 and 1970, when you remember the extent of his influence over all of us, that you can truly know the extent of our loss when it all began to fall apart. Before it happened, we saw him in the best possible light, and when we look back now it is so easy to see that those were the days when he listened to Joe Mercer, when they were like a brilliant but sometimes reckless son and a protective father.

'When you think of that it brings you back to the realisation that all you can do is thank God for the fact that we had those good days, those exceptional days that were always going to live beyond the disappointments that followed.'

Bell, like all his old teammates, offers such thanks on a daily basis. And what it brings is not just extraordinary pride in his team, and his place at the heart of it, but a swelling of satisfaction in that they were days which demanded a level of relentless performance. It was not a time of fleeting inspiration, a passing phase of confidence and some accompanying swagger. Those were days when all the details of team effort were attended to so fastidiously there were no longer excuses for any lapses in performance.

'It is only in hindsight that I realise how certain the team was about what it was doing, how clearly it saw the path ahead, and how good it was. It had to be that good to win so much, and with such style and authority and to do it all so quickly, and sometimes now when I'm watching a game at the Etihad it strikes me how many good teams, how many outstanding players, there were in that old first division.'

He is back in the time which will always be his idea of ultimate football competition. It was one, he insists, when every game was a battle which came without guarantees, wherever you went in the land, because there was always somebody with the power to perform something so startling that it made you draw from yourself everything you had worked to attain: 'If you played the bottom team in the league on their own ground you always knew they would take some beating as they fought for their lives. From one to eleven you were facing a good team. Most vividly, I remember playing Leicester City in the 1969 FA Cup final. They were already relegated, heading down to the second division we had escaped from so recently, and they had players like Allan 'Sniffer' Clarke, Peter Shilton, David Nish and David Gibson. You looked at the quality of such players and you thought, "How can they be going down?" Think of a group of players like that and if you are old enough you will surely take my point. Clarke would become one of the most celebrated and feared players in the game after moving to Leeds United and gaining international recognition. He didn't earn his nickname 'Sniffer' lightly. He was deadly around the box, seizing on any little scrap of encouragement. Peter Shilton was a phenomenal goal-keeper, a prodigy of a kid who would go on to the win the highest total of England caps. Nish was a target for Brian Clough and would break the British transfer record when he joined Derby County for £250,000. He was a beautifully balanced player. He always had plenty of time even in the most pressing situation. David Gibson was in the classic tradition of creative Scottish players, chipped from the same stone as the great John White. A team might be near the bottom of the first division but would still be favourites to win on their own pitch. If a contending team won three or four times away from home, and threw in a draw or two, they had a very good chance of landing the title.'

The more he immerses himself in that old arena, the more you sense his dissatisfaction with so many of the values and the assessments of today's football. He concedes we are bound to acknowledge the brilliance – and athleticism – of some of the titans of today, the phenomenal power and skill of such City successors as Yaya Touré and Sergio Agüero, the spells cast by Lionel Messi and the astonishing virtuosity of Cristiano Ronaldo. But he is talking about competitive depth now, the sheer weight of both exceptional talent and the numbers it embraced.

So there is more than a hint of defiance in his eyes when he declares, 'It's true. When I look back at those teams and those players it is another reason to say that I would never change my moment in time, though of course I wouldn't have turned my nose up at the money if it had been so readily available – or the perfectly manicured pitches.

'I find myself in conversation with old players and names are mentioned and repeatedly I find myself thinking, "Oh, I forgot about him. I forgot what a terrific player he was." There were just so many good players then. We talked about Nish and it made me look at him again and think what a fine player he was. At Derby there was also Roy McFarland and Colin Todd and you could go right through that team without finding a point of weakness. Todd's tragedy was that he was around at the time of Bobby Moore – and the same was true of Norman Hunter.

'Look again at that Liverpool team, how somebody like Kenny Dalglish came in on the heels of such players as Ian St John, Roger Hunt and Ian Callaghan. What a player Dalglish was – you had to play against such men to know their quality, you had to try to cope with the range of their talent. But then it was just another degree of the ability that you came to take for granted.

'And then, of course, just a few miles across town was United, the team who when we first started loomed like a great mountain range – Law, Best, Charlton, they set their own standards.'

He glows in his memory of how hard the battles could be. 'So many times when things hadn't gone as well as hoped, you had to say, "Well, that was a really incredible performance from so-and-so today." It was also true that the defenders you played against invariably had two functions: one was to let you know they were there at the very first opportunity; the other was to get on the ball and show you how good they were going forward. If you throw up names like Norman Hunter and Tommy Smith the first reaction is, "Killers, wreckers, destroyers," but they could play beautifully on their own account. They could be playmakers of the highest quality. The game was more violent then, much more physical, and so many players were shoved into the category of destroyers, but it is too easily forgotten that they were also highly skilled; they were living in their own time and operating in some very loose rules of the day. Of course, they also knew that if they didn't, there was no shortage of people who would.

'Joe Baker, a quick, dynamic forward who at one point was in the running for the '66 World Cup, is someone who sometimes pops into my mind when I think of the range of the talent in that old first division. I remember playing his Nottingham Forest at home and going three-up by half-time. We were all over them in the first half, hitting them in waves, bursting with the aggression that was so wonderfully expressed by Frannie Lee and Mike Summerbee. But then early in the second half Forest got a goal back and it finished 3–3. We were at home, we made a flying start, but in the end we were waiting for the referee to blow the final whistle in the knowledge that if anyone was going to get a winner it would not be us. We went back to the dressing room completely drained and asking ourselves, "How could we blow a three-goal lead?" The truth was that we had been playing a great team, one far too good not to notice, and exploit, the fact that we had switched off early in the second half. Then, of course, they were back in the game with everything to play for.'

What Bell is underlining is the scale of the challenge Allison accepted when he first answered the call of Joe Mercer, and how astonishing it was that the task he set himself and his players was accomplished so quickly and against such formidable rivals.

By 1966, when City achieved their first objective of returning to the first division with the help of the key signings Summerbee and Bell, United, Liverpool and Leeds United, the last under the austerely motivated and cynically inclined Don Revie, had formed what seemed like an iron-clad elite. I travelled across Europe with those teams and came to take their excellence for granted. It was, looking back, an extraordinary intimacy granted a callow reporter, and it was only later that one came to put a value on the company that had been kept, the weight and the accessibility of it. Giles and Bremner, Charlton and Law and the young Best, St John and Yeats and the young Tommy Smith, were mostly forbearing giants of their hard business when dealing with the casual familiarity of an unknowing kid. They were at the apex of the league which Bell will always insist was much better equipped to deliver an ambush than the Premier League which succeeded it in the gold rush of the early nineties.

'So, yes,' he says, 'we had to be more than good, we had to be exceptional to cover so much ground, so quickly.'

The threat that City represented, coupled with Allison's needling, provoked heavy resentment among their more established rivals, especially from Revie. When Allison was banned from the touchline after one intemperate performance too many, the Leeds manager, and former star of City, declared, 'That man is an embarrassment to the game.'

At Liverpool Bill Shankly was no more forgiving of the City coach's excesses and this was notably so one very early morning when he called my home in a rage that, even by his pyrotechnic standards, could only be described as incandescent. In those days a football writer was never too far from managerial rebuke. Today, with the retirement of Sir Alex Ferguson, the threat of a ferocious eruption against an individual miscreant is largely subdued by an army of media advisers. Back then the scolding was routine, and no one delivered one more ferociously, and with a deeper sense of personal betrayal, than the man who called me so angrily that morning.

My crime was to have ghostwritten a classic Allison football polemic a few days before City were due at Liverpool for an FA Cup tie. It was a typically inflammatory piece and, as always, its effect was only heightened by a vein of the kind of truth that in football those days was so often lost in a tide of euphemism. Yes, said the coach, Liverpool had built a fine tradition, were a strong side, but they had lost the power to intimidate in the old way. 'Tell me,' he asked, 'what have they won recently? They have become, for a team like mine, just a bunch of trial horses.'

At the other end of the phone Shankly's voice had the soothing properties of a road drill. 'You should be ashamed of yourself,' he roared. 'Why, Bill?' I asked meekly, obtusely, and after a short pause he told me it was for 'consorting with a maniac'.

But the madness worked, City fought a hard draw at Anfield, then saw off Liverpool in the replay at Maine Road. The second game would be remembered mostly for Francis Lee's belly-flop dive in mockery of what he judged to be a dive by Kevin Keegan, but it was also evidence that City had graduated into a front-rank force happy to compete at the highest level.

John Giles was the intellectual force of Leeds out on the field, as well as an enforcer of some of the harshest punishment delivered in that age of ruthless and often utterly ungoverned violence. But he was generous when he considered the speed of the City advance: 'We eventually believed we were as good, if not better, than anyone around, but we did not reach that level of self-belief as quickly as City under Allison. He did a lot of grandstanding but there was no question that he had created a team of genuine quality. What they had, supremely, was the ability to surprise you. They came on the field believing they could do anything and, very often, they could.'

Bell also saw it that way; each game was a new test, a fresh adventure, and so many times the team came off the field with the sense that all barriers against winning performance had been pushed aside. 'Being out on the training field with us, seeing his players respond to his ideas however tired they were and covered with sweat, and knowing that he had won us over, was, I will always believe, the happiest time of Mal's life. He was a born teacher and leader and achiever, and if that part of him could have been detached from all that was wasteful, and at times silly, he surely would have been knighted. I say this because if he hadn't been so distracted by that other part of his life, if he wasn't so hungry for the reassurance of instant acclaim and the glamorous life, I think he would have won everything.

'When I was driving along the other day I heard some very experienced football men talking on the radio about the impact of Malcolm at the national coaching centre in Lilleshall when they were early in their careers, working on their first coaching badges. They talked about the electricity he generated, the current that seemed to be sweeping around the place, and I found myself nodding. They were saying how much they had learned from being around him and, yet again, it took me back to those first days at Maine Road when all of us finished training thinking that a great gift had come into our lives. We all agreed how lucky we had been to be touched by his ability. If you were 80 per cent decent there was no doubt that he would give you another 20 per cent.

'Someone once said to me that after an early spell at City Ryan Giggs went to Old Trafford to be coached into being a great player. I said that you cannot coach anyone to be a great player, but then it does help if you give him the right environment to develop all of his strengths. But, of course, there has to be something there in the first place, there has to be a spark, a devil, a belief that you can really make an impact.

'Our coach's genius was to recognise quality however it was presented to him and then develop it, hone it, to the highest degree. Not even Mal could give a kid something that wasn't down deep in his nature, but if it was there, he could see it more quickly, and bring it out better than anyone I've ever known in football.'

When Sir Matt Busby made his overture, Bell said – just as his coach had when Juventus owner Gianni Agnelli had dangled some dazzling gifts before his eyes – that he couldn't prise himself away from Maine Road. Allison cited the work that he could not abandon, the attachment he had to the players who had helped him achieve so much; Bell spoke of his band of brothers – and he will always do so because even the rupture in his relationship with his great teammate Lee can be seen as one of those hard and unfathomable developments that sometimes occur in the most tightly bound families.

If in this case the bonds have been damaged, almost certainly irreparably, their existence will never be denied. 'Frannie was wonderful to play with,' he says. 'He was always so full of life and aggression and you could see the opposing defenders looking at him with wary eyes. When he attacked them so early, they always knew he would never relent.'

Bell picks out the names of all his old teammates as though he is intoning a litany. They leap back into his memory and each one them has a special place, a life that in four wrenching cases goes beyond death and is as vital to him today as it was more than 40 years ago.

There are, inevitably, special places for the men who had fallen: Neil Young, Mike Doyle, George Heslop and Harry Dowd. All of them suffered hard times before they left the pantheon: Heslop was mired in financial difficulties after an unsuccessful attempt to be a publican before suffering a heart attack; Young was a victim of cancer and of a long and painful withdrawal from the club which had been at the centre of his life since those boyhood days when each morning he drew his bedroom curtains and saw the thrilling bulk of Maine Road across the Fallowfield rooftops; Doyle, the greatest of partisan teammates, could not win his battle against alcoholism. Harry Dowd spent his last years trapped in dementia.

For Bell they are the departed brothers. Heslop came from Everton and out of the shadow of England centre-half Brian Labone. Allison liked his promise of unflappability, a knack of getting on with the job under any kind of pressure. 'George,' says Bell, 'was a quiet lad who never shouted the odds but came into the team and gave us a good solid feeling. He was what we needed at that time and you knew he would never let you down. If he made a mistake, as everyone does from time to time, he would just get on with the game.'

Neil Young will always be a vision of grace and the most easily summoned power. 'He had such a beautiful talent,' says Bell, 'but the only thing he lacked was a bit of natural physical bravery. He loved to play head tennis in the little gym beside the tunnel, and he was very good, but on the field you rarely saw him head the ball. He didn't like the possibility of serious contact. But then as a striker he brought the huge compensation of the sweetest timing and technique. He was a joy to watch. His ability to adjust to the position of the ball and to get his body lined up instinctively was just sublime.

'I remember joining the team at the Lilleshall training centre soon after moving from Bury. I was keen not to make a fool of myself in any way and I was thinking of this when I found myself in a one-on-one situation with Youngy. I was saying to myself, "You've got to win this one," as I looked him in the eye. But then he dropped a shoulder, just perceptibly, and he promptly sent me the wrong way. I was facing thin air. He did something he was born with and I knew I would never be able to do it. He had just swayed his shoulders for an instant and he was gone and I thought, "Where did he get that from? How did he do it?"

'Before I joined City I used to get the *Manchester Evening News Pink 'Un* on a Saturday night and it seemed that every week I was reading the name of Young in the black type of the goalscorers. I used to think, "Dearie me, does anyone else ever score a goal for City?" What a sweet passer and finisher he was. Had he been a little braver about 20 per cent would have been added to his game. Even without that natural physical courage, he was a great player, and when things went wrong in his career no one could take that from him.

'He was the first of the big names to leave the team, and he took with him a sour feeling about not getting a testimonial match from the only club he had ever wanted to play for. I think he was promised a testimonial match before leaving for Preston, which as far as he was concerned might have been on the other side of the moon. He never wanted to leave, his heart was so deep in the club. I have to say I didn't really see his form slipping. You could always see his talent, it never disappeared to the point where you said, "What's going wrong with Neil Young?" Form slips but it comes back if people, and not least yourself, keep faith in it.

'I was surprised when he left – I was also saddened when, after those great years, it suddenly seemed that everything for him was falling apart. In those days players stayed at a club if they were happy – it seemed the most important thing was not the financial rewards success might bring but the environment it created.'

For Doyle the decline of his spirit and his health was more gradual, a private ordeal known mostly only to his family, and certainly Bell observed it only spasmodically – and at some distance. 'I was aware from time to time that Doyley might have a problem with alcohol, but for a while it seemed – or at least it was nice to think so – he had come through it. I was never really close to Mike but I valued him as a great teammate and a great lad, and I suppose the truth is that however well you know someone you cannot be aware of all their feelings and their weaknesses in the face of difficulties and changes that come into their lives.

'For a time we shared a room for away games and I was always happy to be in his company. Apart from his being an extremely fit lad, you were always pleased to see him running out on the field with you because you knew how much he would contribute, physically and psychologically. He had a wonderful engine and he could never wait to get at the other team, verbally, physically, any way that might undermine them.

'It's also true, and ironic in the final circumstances of his life, that he was such a good professional who never lived it up excessively, and always prepared well for the next game. Like the rest of us, he knew it was a short career and that he had to look after himself. This was especially so in the regime that the coach imposed, one where great fitness was a basic demand. Under Malcolm you just couldn't get away with anything less than that.

'No doubt Mike had a problem which is quite common among ex-players. It is that one which asks, "What do I do with the rest of my life?" If you hadn't shown much interest in gaining coaching badges, you had to face another question: who wants an ex-footballer when he is washed up in his early thirties? What profession do you break into as an extremely late starter? What is going to make you happy after the simplicity and constantly recharged excitement of the footballer's life?

'These were big questions for all of us but deep down we also knew that we were doing what we always wanted to do, and when you were a kid you knew how many would have happily traded places with you. And then, of course, when we started winning the trophies, when we grasped how good we had become, for a while there was no other life that beckoned, no other place we would rather be.'

Watching players like Glyn Pardoe and Alan Oakes move on to an entirely higher level of performance, shedding their uncertainties so quickly they might never have existed, was just one of a series of excitements which seemed to grow a little stronger, more arresting each day on the training field and then in the big games. Pardoe always had skill as a potential centre-forward, a touch so easy and precocious he remains the youngest player ever to wear the City shirt, at the age of 15, but it was when the coach moved him to left-back that it was so clear so quickly that only the gravest misfortune would prevent him occupying many years as a defender of wonderful facility and international stature. The misfortune came, as it can do so arbitrarily in terrible injury, but not before the making of a reputation that in Bell's eyes will never fade away.

'Here,' he says, 'was another case of people not immediately seeing how a good a player we had on our hands. The best guide to his ability was the way he performed against Mike Summerbee in training. Mike was fantastic, so strong and sharp and always looking to seize on a defender's weakness. He made our hearts beat faster. He was also fearless, which is not always the first attribute of a winger. When I think of what Mike did, I have to say that if David Beckham hadn't played for who he did, I can't believe he would be the phenomenon of wealth and celebrity he is today. I remember him coming out of an international game and the TV commentator asking in panic, "Who's going to take the free-kicks now?" When I look back on the qualities of my old teammate playing in Beckham's position, when I think of what he represented in strength, competitive character, the ability to go past his man, and remember that Beckham was considered to be worth more than a hundred England caps, I'm at a loss to know where that leaves Mike. Today he would be picking up cap after cap. He was such a hard man it became a little suspicious to us that Terry Cooper, the extremely talented left-back of Leeds United, seemed always to be out injured when we rolled up at Elland Road, and we certainly heard word on the grapevine that the same question was being asked in the Leeds dressing room. Certainly it is amazing to me that Mike won only eight caps.

'However, none of this had the slightest effect on Glyn. At the end of training we always asked the same question: "How is it that each day he takes Summerbee to the cleaners? How does he do it?" He did it with control, great skill and wonderful timing. This was all the more stunning because he didn't have the natural build of an athlete. In fact, he looked a bit podgy, but then he started to play and you saw how much talent and nous he had.'

If there are parallels in today's game, if such young English players as Jack Wilshere at Arsenal and Ross Barkley of Everton have sent up flares of signally similar natural-born talent, Bell worries about their chances of developing to their full potential in a new football culture of vast reward and imported, instant stars. It is certainly less taxing to run back through the old comrades that will always surround him, ticking boxes in which he finds all the essentials of a perfectly rounded team.

Oakes in some ways was a mirror image of Bell: the same clean looks, the shock of fair hair, and a sometimes pressing need for the coach to put his arm around his shoulders and tell him that he was a great player. Indeed in the early days of their relationship, Oakes's shirt was covered in sweat before he went down the tunnel. Bell confirms, 'I own up to being shy, sometimes quite withdrawn, but there was no doubt Oaksey was worse than me. He wouldn't say boo to a goose. He was a lovely lad off the field but he became utterly committed on the field; no footballer ever covered his shirt in more honest sweat. There will always be a player like this in every team, but I have to say that City were particularly well blessed in this respect. One to eleven, there was no one who could ever be charged with not pulling his weight.'

He might be his old schoolmistress ticking off the class register and handing out stars. The goalkeeper rivals, Ken Mulhearn and Harry

Dowd, who would have to give way to the eventually refined colossus Corrigan after winning, respectively, the medals of title and FA Cup winners, are remembered as bastions of congeniality, keynote figures in the creation of a buoyant, amiable dressing room.

'They were both great characters who seemed, amazing as it is to say, to think about each other as much as their own ambitions. My first game for Bury was a 1–1 draw with Manchester City in those days before substitutes. Harry got injured and could no longer keep goal and an outfield player took his place. Harry moved into the forward line and was their most dangerous player. I had opened the scoring and Harry got the equaliser. What was remarkable about the goalkeepers was that, unlike most of the rest of us who were pretty well assured of our first-team places if we were fit, they always had a selection issue. Yet it never touched their relationship, and in its way it was a symbol of what we had come to represent. There was no edge, no resentments, we pulled for each other in every possible situation.'

If anyone was going to test this level of camaraderie though, it was surely Tony Coleman, the tearaway Liverpudlian who appeared to have ruined his career when striking a referee while playing for Doncaster Rovers. Coleman's disciplinary record filled Mercer with misgivings but Allison was insistent. Yes, he needed curbing but he could play in a way that made his knocked-down price of £12,000 potential larceny.

He was, like Summerbee, another winger for whom the concept of hiding did not exist. Bell says, 'Off the pitch he was a bit of a strange lad, you weren't always sure what he was going to do next, but once he arrived at Maine Road he got his head down and played a full part in our success. Like the rest of us, he enjoyed the sense that we were covering new ground, that for the first time in our lives we could taste the prospect of great success.

'One of the best things about TC was that he was never a soft touch. In those days you couldn't so often say that about wingers, not with defenders like Ron "Chopper" Harris stalking the land, and our bonus was that we had two of them, Summerbee on the right, Coleman on the left. I never saw either of them back down, however ruthless the opposition, and there was no more reassuring sight than seeing them among us as we got off the bus at somewhere like Elland Road or Stamford Bridge.'

Not everything worked out as Colin Bell, in his most euphoric moments, would have ordained. But when he invokes his old teammates, when he thinks of such comrades as Coleman, last heard of in Thailand after a truck-driving stint and divorce in Australia, and those like Joe Corrigan and Tommy Booth, who could never abandon their roots, it is only to confirm the inevitability of his decision to stay within the colony of footballers whose careers, and lives, became so interwoven. When he moved to Manchester City he was another who was making a permanent and inviolate home.

Chapter 6

When Neil Young realised he had only a little time left, perhaps no more than a week or so, he asked a last favour of his great ally and admirer and former youth teammate Fred Eyre. The request would always carry an almost unbearable poignancy but Eyre is a tough-minded, eloquent man bred in the unforgiving, unsentimental streets of north Manchester. If he knows the hard side of football as well as any man alive, he is also aware that what Young said to him that day went to the heart of the meaning of Manchester City for the two friends who first met as opponents on a school field more than 50 years earlier.

'He knew it had come down to a matter of days, maybe a week or two,' says Eyre, 'and he asked me if for the West Bromwich game at Maine Road at the end of the week he could be wheeled out to the centre circle. And would I be the one to push the wheelchair? Obviously, I said yes, and I kept thinking about it during the week, wondering if I could just lift him out of the chair in the centre spot and support him so he could wave to the fans. I was worried that he was so weak his legs might go and that without any kind of support he would just fall down there in the middle of the pitch on which he had always been so controlled and, yes, elegant. I could hardly bear to think about this possibility.

'But then as it was, it didn't come to that. I kept my worries to myself, didn't discuss them with Neil or anyone else that Sunday before the Saturday game. Then when I came into my house after covering City's FA Cup tie at Notts County for a local radio station – it had been a freezing day and I was removing layers of gear – the phone rang. It was Neil calling from Christie's cancer hospital, to where he had been moved from Wythenshawe, and he got right to the point. He said, "Fred, cards on the table, I'm not going to make it to the West Brom game. In fact, I think I've probably got just a couple of days. I'm ringing to say goodbye."

'Lifetimes, his and mine, passed before my eyes and all I could say was, "Neil, is it really that bad?" Yes it was, he said, and he wanted me to promise I would always be kind to Carmen, his third wife, who had been such a comfort to him when his life became most difficult. He said, "If Carmen ever wants to go to a game, even though I'm not there, will you take her and look after her and never refuse her, and can I have your word?" I said that of course he could. It was the least I could do, and when I said that my mind raced back down all the years, from our first meeting and all the time we stayed so close after our paths had parted and he went on to achieve all the things that I had longed for.

'He died on my birthday, which was three days later, and so he never got to say that last goodbye to the fans who loved him as much as he loved them. When he made his first request to me he thought he had left maybe a couple of weeks. But it narrowed down to three days. I was sat in my house with an old friend, Tommy Gore of Wigan Athletic, when I got the news. It was 1.20. He died at one o'clock. Naturally, I played back all the years.'

Fred Eyre was a crack player in one of the most outstanding teams in the history of Manchester's schoolboy football, and he would become, by a quirk of changing regulations, Manchester City's first apprentice professional. He signed on the same day as Young, along with two other teenaged contenders for the professional life, but if he failed to match the progress of his friend down the next few years, or that of Mike Doyle, his story is no less remarkable for that. He became a highly successful businessman, wrote *Kicked into Touch*, a memoir of his struggle to break into the game so filled with humour and insight and borderline endurance of pain that it has sold more than a million copies, and he remains a lion of the after-dinner circuit. It is also true that the circumstances of his life, indeed almost every single heartbeat of it, make him a superbly informed witness of the days which shaped the City team that exploded so spectacularly and in which his fallen friends Young and Doyle played such vital roles.

'I played for Ducie Avenue, which at that time was a brilliant example of every team, every school and every dog having its day,' he says. 'We had a great intake at Ducie. There were five of us in the Manchester Boys' squad, which is traditionally one of the most powerful in the country, and for one school to have virtually half the team, well, you're going to be very good. The whole time I was at Ducie I was never on a losing side but we did draw one game, against Heald Place, which like Ducie was just a stone's throw from Maine Road. We hung on for a 2–2 draw and the reason we were under rare pressure was solely because of a gangly, six-foot kid. It was Youngy.

'We were in the middle of our run when I first met him. I started playing for Ducie as an 11-year-old in the under-16s and I came across him when I was 13. It was a shock because he was so good. Most people first remember him from the time when he had developed into a number 10 or 11, but in his school team he was a centre-half who played all over the place. He played us virtually on his own and we were stunned. I was thinking about it only this morning. I remember coming off the field with him, shaking hands, and I don't know whether it was a sign of a bit of respect but the first words he ever said to me were, "Do you support City? I do." It was all one sentence, the words linked together, and it tickled me, and I said, "Yes, as it happens, I do." He then said, "I always get there early because I only live across the road.

So I might see you at the game." And I replied, "Yeah, I'll look out for you." I remember thinking, back in the changing room, "That's the first great player I've ever seen in another team."'

It was a rare onset of humility in the Ducie ranks but to be fair to Eyre and his teammates they had reasons enough for a high opinion of themselves. A leading force was Bobby Smith, who joined United as Eyre did City. Smith would have a long career in the lower divisions before becoming the youngest manager in the country when he was appointed by Bury at the age of 28. He went on to run Port Vale, Swindon, Newport and Swansea and was David Pleat's assistant at Sheffield Wednesday when the club signed Paolo Di Canio. Smith looked destined to become one of the marquee names of football in the sixties but, as Eyre recalls, 'It didn't take long for us to realise that it was Youngy who was the star, the one who would go the full distance. He had something beyond any of us. He was star material, you could see that every time he turned on the ball.'

Eyre watched his friend's coruscating progress and even as he re-made his life – which in so many ways achieved a security that Young would find elusive (not least when he was at the peak of his success and popularity) – and analysed his own failure to fulfil his boyhood promise as a player. 'Possibly it was a case of peaking too early,' he sighs. 'I can't really explain it. There are players who do not make it and you can say to them, "Well, what did you really expect? You were out every night, you never trained properly." But that never applied to me. I went back to do more work in the afternoons. I made sure I got all my sleep. Looking back, though, I might have been too perfect. When I consider this I think of Mike Doyle, who came to City two years after me. I used to look after him a little bit, but then all of a sudden I'm standing still and players like him are much better than I am. I couldn't get to the next level. Nor did I realise that while this was happening my confidence was really suffering. I know now what I should have done and the reasons I didn't are all down to me.

'At my next club, Lincoln City, I had another negative experience under Bill Anderson, a veteran manager who doted on his dog but scarcely said a word to me. I never came into the reckoning when he went off with his dog to pick the team. Really, I suppose I shouldn't have let things happen to me in the way I did. Maybe I was little weak, more mentally scarred than I imagined when I was shown the door at Maine Road.

'I shouldn't have automatically taken on board everything anyone ever said to me. I was too steeped in obedience. When the City trainer Jimmy Meadows gave me orders I would follow them without any questioning of what might be best for me. This takes me back to Neil and a game we played together in a junior City team in which the former star Johnny Hart, who would later become coach and, briefly, manager, was included with the brief of pushing along the kids.

'During the game he said something very sharp to Youngy, who was normally the quietest lad in the world. But a few minutes later Neil turned to Hart and shouted, "When are you going to do some fucking work?" I was astounded, because whatever Hart said to me I followed it to the letter. Looking back, I can see Johnny wasn't suited to the task of bringing on the kids. He was a bit dry, he had been there all his life and never lifted us. I could never find the nerve to challenge this hero of my early boyhood – and I took the same docile attitude to Lincoln. I should have just got on with what I was doing but the problem was I thought I had to listen to everybody. It also happened that Anderson was the longest serving manager in the Football League. So when he tells me something when I'm 19 I just do it – and then I look back and see that most of the things he told me were just not right.

'Perhaps I should, even belatedly, have followed the example of Mike Doyle. He would talk back to anyone, including the great icon of the club, Bert Trautmann. Of course, I'm not saying that if I had adapted my approach my football career would necessarily have been better, just that I might have given myself more of a chance of making it.'

But then if Fred Eyre didn't do that, if he didn't march to the level his boyhood dedication and natural authority had once promised, he did achieve something to be envied by anyone who cares about football, who craves to know how it might have been to have, for even a little time, the life of a professional player. He spent more than 20 years fighting for that status, and no doubt it brought him much pain as he moved from club to club, but it also gave him a deep knowledge of the life he most wanted – and so many of the bittersweet tears that irrigate his cult-creating book. First published in 1981, it has rarely been out of print. It is a tale of one man's dogged refusal to give up on his most pervasive dream. You smell the sweat of the rickety dressing rooms and the grit of his old, tough but large-hearted city to which he always returned for the treatment of his wounds. Self-punishing laughter punctuates almost all those tears.

Maybe most notable was the combination of both that came at the end of a friendly match in which his teammate was the legendary John Charles. Back in the dressing room, the great man put his arm around Eyre and said, 'Fred, you're a smashing bloke but you may be the worst fucking player I ever played with.'

It wasn't always like that, and certainly not the day he signed his apprentice forms at Maine Road and then waited for three young colleagues to complete the brusque ceremony, the last to do so being Neil Young: 'We were together that day and I did have reason to believe that down the years we would share so much at the club we both cared about so deeply. Our friendship developed quickly after that first match and, soon enough, we were playing in area trials for Manchester Boys. I lived in Blackley, north Manchester, but my school was just one bus stop away from Maine Road in Moss Side. This was because I'd won a scholarship to Ducie Street. It wasn't a grammar school, it was in the middle, but if I hadn't gone to Ducie Street, I might have been in jail like a lot of people from Blackley. My school was close to Youngy's, and in the Central Area, and we both made it into the under-14s team.

'Neil was the star even though Bob Smith went on to play for England Boys. Neil was the quality and I was amazed when he didn't get an offer to join the City groundstaff. They said they wanted to sign him but not to the staff. They got him a job with an electrical firm, and I thought, "Jesus, if Youngy has only got a part-time arrangement, what chance have I got?"

'We were playing together for the first part of the season and training two nights a week in Urmston. Then City took me on to the groundstaff and I worked at Maine Road for a couple of months before Neil arrived. We were groundstaff lads for a year and then one day we were told, "You lot have got to go up to the secretary's office." When we got there we saw loads of forms out on the desk. We were told, "You're all being converted. There's no such thing as groundstaff boys any more." We were standing in our kit, and they said, "Sign the forms and you all become apprentice professionals. Nothing changes, you don't get any more money."

'There we were – Eyre, Flecky, Loftos and Youngy. I was told to take the pen first, then Kenny Fletcher, captain of Manchester Boys, Peter Loftos and Neil Young. Flecky had become a bit notorious because when he was signed to Manchester United he was approached by Wolves (all the lads had been approached by other clubs except me). When he had the Wolves approach he told his headmaster. Wolves got fined and Flecky received a lot of publicity for blowing the whistle. He played with me in non-league football for years afterwards.

'Peter Loftos, who was always complaining, "They've spelt my bloody name wrong again," died 40 years ago. He was released by City the same day I was. While I was always going to give football another go, Peter became a milkman. One day a lady I didn't know came into my office supply shop and collapsed, sobbing. "Fred," she said, "Peter's died." It was his wife.'

So Young became an apprentice approximately a minute after his friend but there would be many occasions when such a fleeting time lapse seemed to be the flimsiest possible measurement of the gap between them. It was a disparity of football achievement and nature that saw one ride his talent as though it was a gift that could never be withdrawn, except perhaps in the most unjust of circumstances, and another who knew that he would always have to fight for his place in this world he found so compelling.

So often Youngy would let the plot of his life unfold against the certainty that he had been given an exceptional ability – and that it would always carry him through to the experiences he had always desired.

Eyre provides a striking example of their different states of mind. It came just a few months after the Maine Road signing ceremony: 'We were sent down to Lilleshall, along with some older lads like David Wagstaffe and Paul Aimson, for a massive coaching session put on by the Football Association and attended by all the major clubs. It was a huge event in the lives of young professionals. All the top clubs sent their kids. It was run by the great coaching guru, and first England team manager, Walter Winterbottom, and he had with him some of the brightest coaches of the day, men like Jack Mansell, Jimmy Adamson and Phil Woosnam. It was a great experience for youngsters and the highlight of the week came with the climax, a five-a-side tournament. As the days ticked by, it was all the lads talked about, and this included some very big prospects, lads like George Graham, Brian O'Neil and Tommy Smith. All the top players were there. Each club entered a five-a-side team. City had taken eight of us down there and all the others were more experienced than Youngy and me, so we didn't really expect to play. There was no problem with this. We were the new kids and maybe we would get our chance next year. But then I heard something – and did something that reinforces my feeling that I was quite a bit different to a lot of the other lads, including Neil. I heard that a kid called Alan Baker was going to play for us. He was a fine player, an ex-schoolboy international, and Waggy and the other older players really liked him.

The trouble was that he was attached to Aston Villa. However, he loved Waggy and his mates to the extent that he slept in our dormitory every night rather than Villa's.

'Waggy and his mates badgered Johnny Hart into picking Baker for our team. None of us younger lads doubted he was a good player and a good lad, one who eventually played in the Villa first team. But we also thought it was diabolical that he was going to take one of our places in the City team. I said to Youngy, "Look, I normally wouldn't mind not playing but this is a different situation. How can Harty play a kid from another club?"

'As I was saying, Neil was not like me, and he just said, "Yes, it's awful but I don't see how we can do anything about it."'

Eyre could. He went round the other dormitories looking for players who knew they would not be playing for their clubs. He found Ian Cairns of Villa and Ray Whittaker of Arsenal, who would later have a good career with Luton Town. Eyre asked them, 'Do you want to play in the big tournament?' and they replied, 'Yeah, of course we do.'

Eyre told Young that he was going to see the great man Winterbottom and try to win a place in the tournament for his patchwork team. 'Come on, Youngy,' he said, 'We have to stand up for ourselves on this one. What's happening is just not right.' Young said no, he didn't have the stomach for the mission and all the fallout it was likely to bring.

'I have to admit,' says Eyre, 'the door of Winterbottom's bedroom was getting bigger and bigger as I marched down the corridor. When he opened the door and said, "What is it?" and looked every inch a formidable headmaster, I didn't go into the Alan Baker situation, I just told him that a few of the lads who hadn't been picked by their clubs wanted to play in the tournament. Would it be possible? He said right away, "Yes, why not? What do you want to call yourselves?" When I said I didn't really know, he asked me my name, and when I told him he said, "Well, what about Fred's Boys?"'

In fact the story of Fred's Boys, which gathered force so quickly in the next few days, is really about the stunning potential displayed by Young. 'The team carried my name but it really belonged to Neil Young. He made it so from practically the first kick of the ball,' says Eyre. 'Our team was Flecky, Eyre, Cairns, Young and Whittaker, who as a very promising goalscoring forward was not absolutely delighted to be playing in goal. We got a bye in the first round, at which stage the official City team was knocked out. We then beat a very good Southampton team and went on to take the final against Villa. The person who presented us with our medals, and me with the trophy, was Joe Mercer, the man who eight years later would be manager of the City team which won the FA Cup through the sweet left foot of Neil Young.

'Our triumph was based on Young's ability and the strategy I worked out with Ian Cairns. It was a very basic one. Ian and I ran around a lot, Flecky patrolled the circle in front of our goal, and Young would stay up front on his own. We scored 16 goals to win the tournament. Guess how many Youngy scored? Yes, he got the lot, and if he wasn't going to make a footballer, a really top one, the world was also going to slip off its axis.

'The following year we went back to Lilleshall and we were now the Waggies and the Aimsons. Before the tournament, Johnny Hart said to me, "Who do you want in your team?" We won it again. This time I scored a couple of goals, so did Flecky, but Neil knocked in another 14. We entered it twice, we won it twice and Youngy knocked in 30 goals. There was never much reaction from Harty, but I think he was quite pleased we won and that I was named captain of the team which played Woosnam's Coaches team.'

Eyre's good standing in the regard of Hart was as transitory as he might have feared. Just a year later he would be gathering up his gear and walking away from Maine Road, banished by the kind of dismissive verdict which once seemed to signal the end of Tony Book's ambitions.

'Not for me,' Hart had scrawled against Eyre's name on the report card which went to the City hierarchy as a brusquely administered death sentence.

By comparison, Young's progress was meteoric. 'As my days at City closed, Youngy's simply took off,' Eyre says. 'He was 17 when he made his first-team debut. They played him on the right in an away game at Villa because Waggy owned the left wing. But Neil had showed so much promise they felt they just had to play him. They stuck him on the right wing and told him to get on with it. That's how it was in those days. A young player was required to swim – or he sank. Today they are nurtured so carefully, at least in the successful clubs who know what they are doing.

'But then soon enough Wolves bid £35,000 for Wagstaffe and there was no doubt City thought, "Well, we don't really want him to go but that's an awful lot of money and we do have a ready-made replacement."

'Right from the start the City fans recognised Youngy for what he was: a very talented young player who passionately identified with the club and its fans. He walked to the ground every day, and you can't get much more *Boys' Own* than that.'

The story flowed on for eleven years, during which time Young scored 86 goals in 334 league appearances and made decisive contributions to the great final successes at Wembley in the FA Cup of 1969 and, a year later, in the Cup-Winners' Cup in Vienna. From time to time his physical courage was questioned, and sometimes this was heavily implied in the partly derisory, partly affectionate cry of 'Nelly Young', but there was never any doubt about the authority bestowed at crucial moments by the high level of his skill.

At Wembley he scored the only goal with one of those classic flourishes which marked his best, most smoothly devastating work. Later, he recalled to Ian Penney, author of *Manchester City, the Mercer-Allison Years*, 'When I was a little lad I used to dream of playing for City and when I achieved that the next one was to play for them in a Cup final.

To play and to score was even better. It was undoubtedly my day; a dream come true. If you can't play in front of 100,000 on a Saturday afternoon in a Cup final then you will never be able to play. About five minutes before I scored the goal I had mishit a chance and thought to myself, "I'm 25 years old and if I get another chance that one's going in." Mike Summerbee rolled a great ball back to me, right into my path, and I was running on to it. I knew as soon as I hit it, it was going in. I could tell by the sound. I caught it perfectly. The ball was in the back of the net before Peter Shilton took off.'

In Vienna, against the rugged, hard-running and skilful Polish side Górnik Zabrze, he was no less decisive, snaffling up a rebound from a Lee shot, and then winning a penalty when the goalkeeper was lured to him like a missile programmed for the man rather than the ball. 'We were soaked to the skin,' he reported, 'but the cold never reached our bones. We celebrated one of the greatest nights of our lives.'

In the gaiety of the old Schönbrunn Palace hotel, where under the chandeliers the champagne flowed and Lee commandeered the grand piano as the platform for a striptease which reached down to his Y-fronts, it seemed that the dream that first formed in the mind of Neil Young when he looked out across the south Manchester skyscape had never been so deeply ensconced in a glorious reality. He was just 26, his powers had been restated in a great old arena of the European game, and there was every reason to believe that the future stretched out with the promise of still more nights like this.

Yet within two years Young was banished from his beloved City, the foundations of his life were broken apart. It was a shocking denouement which Eyre still says can only be retraced in the terms of a personal tragedy.

'I don't think there was any reason for his career to nosedive so quickly when City decided he had to go,' he says. 'I think it was a case of someone, and it was almost certainly Malcolm Allison, deciding that something had to be done to develop the team in a different direction, that it was going to be painful, so it might as well be done straight away. Malcolm had the Rodney Marsh idea and it wouldn't go away and so, I believe, he dreamed up a quick death for Neil at City. He probably did it in some nightclub over a glass of champagne and while smoking a Havana cigar. Mal had a decision to make and he made it, but the way he did it suggested to me that he knew the person he was dealing with, and how it would affect him, and that's what made him think, "Well, I've got to get it done, it's going to be hard, so I'd better get it over with."

'It was all very quick, and by this time [City signed Marsh in March, 1972] there was nowhere for Neil to go at Maine Road. In the old days they might have shoved him back on the right wing, but Mike Summerbee was there. Everything was taken. His career had rocketed but we were still close despite the fact that we were no longer in the football trenches together. I tried to help psychologically when he became obsessed by City's refusal to give him a testimonial. And I don't think I succeeded.

'As time went on it became increasingly clear how just driving from his home in Handforth in Cheshire to his new club, Preston, brought him so much pain. In those days he had to go via Princess Parkway, so he practically had to stop his car turning in the direction of Maine Road. In football everyone has to move on, but it was killing him. I suppose in some ways it is the same for everyone. I felt it going down the Parkway, where I used to run when I thought everything was before me, just waiting to happen, but there's no doubt that for Neil it was harder than most people could imagine.

'In one way I think there was a misunderstanding about Neil's anger and frustration over the lack of a testimonial, and I have a theory which I don't think is an oversimplification. Indeed, I believe it was probably borne out in the last days of his life. No doubt the money a testimonial would have brought would have been handy – it would be stupid to say it wouldn't have been. But I think the thing he wanted most, the thing he pined for when his place in the team was gone, was the acknowledgement of the fans. I think he wanted most the last hurrah. Maybe it would, to use the popular term of today, have brought closure. Certainly when he talked over his last years, he never said anything like, "That bastard chairman Peter Swales didn't give me the testimonial that would have changed my life. I could have opened a business, I could have paid off my mortgage, I could have done this or that." No, it was never anything like that; it was always, "I never got the chance to say goodbye to the fans." And when he said that he always filled up with emotion. I'm not saying for one moment he couldn't have done with a few quid. But it wasn't the overriding thing, not even later on when he did struggle to make ends meet. His earnings went down sharply when he left top-class football, and like most of us he had no real qualifications to do anything else.

'Sometimes I would hear from someone – "I've just seen your mate, he's a milkman now" – and I would say, "Yes, brilliant, isn't it great?" And they would ask, "What do you mean?" And I would say, "Well, he's not on the dole, he's not on benefits, he gets up at 4.30 every morning and he delivers your milk." And then they would say, "Yeah, yeah, I know what you mean."'

Eyre has spent much of his life rebuilding the broken place left by his football experiences and has met with extraordinary success, but this never blinded him to the difficulties of those who would always be left wounded, and in this category he has always placed his friend highest among the victims. Yet if he often despaired of Young's ability to emerge repaired and content – apart from the time when he was lifted by a brief spell coaching youngsters – he was also frequently touched by evidence of both an unbroken dignity and some natural humility.

'Neil worked for Attack Sports, a big sports shop in Urmston near my office supplies business, and so all of a sudden we were seeing a bit more of each other again. He was dealing with sports equipment in the day and he got a job at night stacking supermarket shelves.

So he was prepared to work in the day and go out at night to keep things together – and he was absolutely fine about that. It was difficult, obviously, when compared to the glory days at City, and the biggest problems were psychological. I tried to boost him by inviting him to dinners, but he would always say, "No, they will not know me there." And I would say, "Give over, Youngy, they would love to see you." But he kept saying, "No, no, no." He didn't like to capitalise on his fame, and I don't think he ever quite realised how well liked he was.

'His first wife, Margaret, used to have a boutique around the corner from the ground. She was a lovely girl from a lovely family, and they had lovely kids, but looking back you have to say they were probably both too young to get married. She was a beautiful young lady and, of course, Neil was very handsome – and all the way through his life, right to the end, he was always well turned out. Even when things were toughest, and his health was going, he was never dishevelled, he never let himself go. He liked a Bacardi and coke, but I never saw him drunk. I wished he'd smoked less. I never packed up trying to get him to stop, and when he finally did I said, "Well, it's only taken 40 years." Cancer was written on his death certificate, but in any wider obituary of Neil Young it was impossible not to include the dwindling of the flame that, right from the start, had always sustained him when so much else in his life had brought pain and a diminishing optimism.

Eyre recalls, 'The funeral was at Altrincham Crematorium, the most local one, and he had already said no to a plot in the garden of remembrance near Maine Road because he wanted to be near his brother James, whose death at the age of 31 had been a terrible shock he never got over.'

Joe Corrigan has an enduring memory of his old teammate from his later years. He says, 'Neil Young's early death was our great tragedy – along with Mike Doyle's. I remember him walking beside my granddaughter Victoria after a City match, putting his arm around her shoulder and asking, "Who are you?" And when she pointed to me and said, "That's my granddad," he said, "Let me tell you he was one of the greatest goalkeepers who ever played the game." And he had a big smile on his face I will never forget.

'Nor will I forget the great goals he scored, so easily with a wonderful stroke of his left foot. Another memory of him is on the long flight to Australia and looking back on the plane, in those days when smoking was still permitted, and seeing the glow of his fag as he sipped his Barcardi and coke.

'I remember going to the Ritz ballroom in Manchester with Neil and Doyley and having a few drinks, of the unfamiliar Bacardi, and how they got me to a taxi and poured me into my house. Neilly was someone who cared about people. Amid the team he was a great example of someone who would never leave anyone to their own devices if they were struggling a bit. For him it would always be a priority to make sure someone was safe, but then I suppose we all had a bit of that in us. It was the environment we were brought up in.'

Five years after Neil Young had been a star of Vienna in 1970, the destructive force in the kind of European triumph which 45 years later his plutocrat City successors still strive to replicate, he played his last professional game. It was before a thinly scattered crowd at Spotland, the home of third division Rochdale. They were playing Swansea, which was not a game guaranteed to draw a football aficionado. But, inevitably, Fred Eyre was there, as he had been at Maine Road 14 years earlier when his friend made his debut against Aston Villa.

'But for Neil, and the fact that it was a nice spring night, I would not have gone to see Rochdale and Swansea playing their last game of the season,' Eyre says. 'In the last minute of the game a Rochdale player broke along the left and cut it back, as Summerbee did in the 1969 Cup final but from the other wing. As the move developed, my interest heightened. How many times had I seen Neil Young finish off a move like this, and now I expected it once again. I expected Neil to go ping as the ball came across – and see it billowing in the back of the net.

'Instead, it went over the goal, the crowd and the stand and it went bouncing down the road that runs beside the little stadium. That was Neil's last kick of the ball as a professional. There was no last *coup de grâce* delivered by a beautifully elegant footballer, and as the ball went down the road I might have been looking into the future of my friend, catching a glimpse of his frustration in the years that lay ahead.

'City sent a beautiful floral tribute in the shape of a football. Colin Bell was there, along with everyone who mattered. Waggy came, not knowing he would be attending his own quite soon after. I went to that one too. Neil's funeral was played down. The family agreed on one thing. They wanted it quiet, and so it was held away from where his life had been.'

But then it was also true that when Neil Young sent the ball flying over the bar and down a Rochdale road, it was more than the anticlimax of his least encouraging season. It was, effectively, the end of that part of his life that had made him feel entirely whole.

Chapter 7

In another group of men, the characters of Neil Young and Mike Doyle might have been surefire points of friction. As some of his greatest admirers have already pointed out, Young could at times be gentle to a fault. Doyle, by comparison, was about as equivocal as a fighting bull. Yet in City's swift ascent to the peak of the English game there was a quite remarkable lack of dissonance. The team built an extraordinary rhythm and unity of purpose, and perhaps nothing reflects this quite as completely today as the utterly indivisible nature of the mourning for two comrades of such contrasting styles and instincts. Young, so diffident off the field, followed the impulses of a refined, even delicate football spirit. Doyle's command centre was rather nearer his intestines. Yet their effects were as complementary as caviar and vodka. In their separate ways they made the team's competitive urges soar.

Now there is maybe one last paradox lying in the fact that these men who in so many ways were quite separate shared the same non-negotiable sadness when the football and, it almost seemed, the meaning of their lives ended.

It wasn't the best kept secret that Mike Doyle was drinking, and sometimes on his own, when his playing days were over. However, it was scarcely nudged upon when his old colleagues and friends gathered at those occasions intended for celebration of all the triumphant certainties of the past. It was something mentioned from behind a hand, with that reluctance borne by the hope that the subject under discussion would prove less permanent than a bleak and irredeemable fact.

This meant there was no lessening of the shock felt by his former teammates and the great following of Manchester City when he died, of liver failure, five months after Neil Young.

If to some extent all men make their defences against the worst the world can bring, Doyle more than almost anyone you could think of, needed to believe in himself. He was the kind of man for whom the possibility of failure could disappear in one hard stare into the middle distance. The drinking wouldn't beat him, those who knew him best insisted, because he was just too implacable for it to happen. He was too sure that he could handle any situation, too certain about who he was and what he represented. He was like that from the start. As a boy, he inflamed Steve Fleet, the experienced goalkeeper and understudy to the great Bert Trautmann, so intensely during a five-a-side game in the gym that he lashed out a kick, missed, and badly injured his foot against a wall. Doyle had wound him up quite relentlessly, then wore a look of injured surprise.

Even more shocking was an incident involving the legendary Trautmann. No man had ever enjoyed more deference at Maine Road than the former German paratrooper. His presence in the dressing room was God-like. Yet even the football deity have their off-days and Trautmann was certainly not at his best while conceding six goals against West Ham one Saturday afternoon. On the following Monday morning, Doyle, the groundstaff boy, broke off from his cleaning chores – he was 16 at the time – to ask Trautmann, 'How's the back this morning, Bert, after bending to pick the ball out of the net so many times?'

Fred Eyre, who was foreman of the apprentices and beginning to occupy in the life of Doyle the role he had been playing for some years in Neil Young's, could scarcely believe what he was hearing. He ushered his friend out of the dressing room as a heckler might have been ejected from the Queen's Speech – but not before the great goalkeeper had Doyle against the wall by his throat.

'I'll never know what Doyley expected, maybe something relatively amiable like, "What did you say, you cheeky little twat?" But what he got,' Eyre recalls, 'was being rammed against the wall – with the rest of us thinking, "Fucking hell, imagine what it must have been like when Bert was fighting with the Wehrmacht. It was done in a second."'

Alf Wood, the hulking centre-half, was another Doyle enjoyed inflaming. 'They were always going at it,' says Eyre, 'but I have to say that right through his life, and in all circumstances, he was totally respectful to me. Whenever I saw him after I was released by City he was always friendly. In the first days of my new career, working in a stationery store in St Peter's Square, around 10 in the morning [one day] a car came into the square and double-parked outside the shop. Doyley and Vic Gomersall came in and told me they were playing at Cardiff that night. "I thought I'd come round to tell you," Mike said, though why he thought I would want to know this at that particular point in my life, I wasn't quite sure. It was pure Doyley, marching on, operating almost entirely in his own world. Of course, I said, "Well done," and they jumped back in the car. They won in Cardiff.'

'Naturally,' thought Eyre when he heard the news. He now sees some of that extraordinary single-mindedness in Doyle's grandson, Tommy (whose other grandfather is Glyn Pardoe). 'Tommy is at the City academy and there's no doubt he's got a chance,' says Eyre. 'He just oozes confidence. Very early on I asked him what kind of season he was having, and he rapped back, "Good." Then I asked him what position he played and he replied, "I'm all over, really – it's my job to help the poor players." I said, "There's not a shadow of a doubt about it. You're definitely Mike Doyle's grandson." Tommy was aged 10 when he spoke at his grandfather's funeral. His parents were concerned that it would be too much of an ordeal for a young boy to withstand. But he was adamant. He couldn't have been more resolute as he marched up the church and spoke so clearly. It was a stunning performance, a statement that seemed to come from his blood.'

Like Colin Bell and most of Doyle's former colleagues – except, most notably, Pardoe because of the family connection that came with his daughter's marriage to Doyle's son – Eyre was shocked by the rate of the final decline: 'I was stunned for a while because he was another one like Neil Young who always looked smart, always in control of himself. When he first quit playing I had absolutely no indication of bad days ahead. Some people would say to me, "You know Doyley's on the piss, don't you?" and I would say, "No, I don't. What do you mean? He got pissed one night?" And then I was told, "He's on the piss all the time." I was told he was going to Redditch Golf Club every day and hiding bottles behind trees. I said, "You have to be joking." But they weren't, and soon enough I was seeing him at functions when he seemed to be struggling a bit, fighting to get his brain into gear, and then I began fearing the worst.

'Going to golf clubs was his job. He worked for Slazenger on the golf side and I thought he was absolutely fine when he slipped into his new role. Unlike Youngy, he hadn't fallen off the football cliff-edge when he left City. He played more than a hundred games for Stoke and then he had a useful spell at Bolton. He was a very good golfer, played off scratch, and seemed to have every reason to believe that another game would replace football in his competitive needs.

'But then he was soon told that he shouldn't really play golf because it was aggravating his old knee injuries and, who knows, maybe that was the final stroke, the thing that broke down his belief that he could find some of the old contentment in this new phase of his life.'

Glyn Pardoe, who proved remarkably philosophical when faced with the trauma of serious injury at the end of his playing days, is less speculative about the cause of Doyle's decline. He says, 'Some people found Mike a bit abrasive, but I always got on with him, and I used to go with my wife to stay with his widow, Cheryl, and her mum and dad. It was very sad the way it happened. He lost his way a bit after he stopped playing, and it was very hard to see him going down. It was such a change, and you couldn't help thinking how strong he had been in the old days, how very clear he was about how he saw his life and how it was so rooted in the game. We were so close at one point, and seeing him suffer made me think that in life you can either do things or you can't. You get on with life or you let things get out of hand. Really, it's up to the individual.'

Pardoe is a remarkably balanced and congenial man – Eyre, a very close and trusted friend describes him as 'adorable' – but it is a state of grace which he acknowledges is not automatically bestowed on foot-ballers at the end of their careers. As he speaks of Doyle his mind also turns to one of the most brilliant of the young players who came in the wake of those great City days. He thinks of Tommy Caton, a stunningly precocious centre-half who at 19 became the first player of such age in English football's highest division to play a hundred games. He was selected 14 times for the England Under-21 team and a big future in the club and international game seemed utterly assured.

He was still short of his twentieth birthday when he appeared in the 1981 FA Cup final at Wembley, and when his teammate Tommy Hutchison gave City the lead over Spurs he believed that one of the dreams of his brief life was about to be fulfilled. But then Spurs came back into the game – and won the replay. Caton, a father of three, died when he was 30, of a heart attack and, those who knew him well believed, the aggravation of suffering injury and a slide from those early peaks he enjoyed first with City, then Arsenal. His career dwindled away at Oxford United, then Charlton Athletic. Pardoe says, 'Tommy couldn't handle going out of football, and before that he found it very difficult dropping down from the level he enjoyed at City and Arsenal at such an early age. He had struggled with an injury that brought the first big crisis of his life. Suddenly a lad who had been completely uncompli-cated in his thoughts about what lay before him had a hard time getting through his days, and this is tragic when you think of what a brilliant talent he began to see slipping away before he reached the age of 30. He had shot to fame so quickly.

'I don't think Mike's problem was so obvious, at least not at first. Things started to go wrong in various ways. It was harder for him to drum up the old self-belief, and he started drinking a bit. And then it got out of hand and, of course, when that happens it gets very hard to control.'

Joe Corrigan was shocked when he first saw that his old teammate, and such a point of certainty, was in trouble. He says, 'It was only in later years that I became aware Doyley had a drink problem, and this was partly because it had developed when I was away working at Liverpool and then West Bromwich. It became more obvious to me when, at one of City's Hall of Fame dinners, my wife and I sat next to Doyley and his wife. I had lost a lot of weight, after getting up to 21 stones, and he turned to me and said, "What's the matter with you?" And I told him, "No, nothing. I needed to do the weight." And then I took a closer look at him and felt that maybe something was not quite right. I talked to a few other people and heard what was going on, and it was like getting a slap in the face – it was just tragic.'

Eyre recalls, 'I came back into Mike's life more regularly when he joined Bolton. I was covering their games for radio, and the Bolton manager John McGovern let me travel on the team bus. Invariably, I sat next to Doyley and I didn't get any indication that he was heading for a bad place. Once when we were going through London and passed the Iranian embassy, which had just been besieged, we talked about that episode and what it might have meant, and there was nothing flimsy about his conversation. He also talked very sensibly about his situation in his mid-thirties, how he had to deal with it. But then when time moved on, and his life unravelled, I had to think that everything changed when he no longer got up in the morning and went training – and lived the only life he had known.'

Eyre remembers the bleak process vividly enough. You could be listening to any of the Forever Boys of City, with the possible exception of the supremely self-programmed Francis Lee, who crave in some corner of themselves to be young again. 'It's not easy if it happens when you are 20 or 35,' says Eyre. 'It can be so hard, so heartbreaking. I cannot really know what's easier in the end: scoring a hundred goals, getting a Cup-winners' medal at Wembley, winning a great game in Newcastle to win the title, then gaining a European trophy in the pissing rain in Vienna. Or not having any of that and having to leave the game as a kid. I had no choice, no options, I had to do something, so that makes me wonder if the longer you're in football the tougher it is to leave it.

'So that also means I don't really know if Johnny Hart did me a favour when he wrote the dismissive note that I was not for him, when he bundled up all my aspirations and chucked them in the rubbish bin and wrote my football obituary in three or four words. Who knows, Johnny might have been thinking in the same way that Mal did when he got rid of my mate Youngy. He might have been saying, "What's the point in dragging this out?"

'I'll never forget the scene when I walked away from Maine Road. It was the summer. The ground was almost completely empty. Two people were playing snooker – Glyn Pardoe and Stan Goddard, an extremely promising youth player who, like me, would fail to establish himself at the club. My laces were dragging along the corridor. I was going down it for the last time. The lad Jim Fossard popped his head out of the office door and said, "I'm glad I've seen you." He wanted to say goodbye. He said, "It's been awful seeing you these last few months, struggling for a place here and still not knowing what was going to happen." I asked him, quite sharply, what he meant, because for a second I thought he meant that it had been hopeless my thinking I could make it as a pro and everyone else knowing I wasn't going to do it. It was then that he went back into the office and came out with the final report: "Not for me."'

Eyre's great friends Young and Doyle had flourished and survived at the highest level of football, but their time came. So who really won – and who really lost? There is no final answer to such a question, of course, but if Eyre celebrates his success as a tough and enterprising businessman – if he knows that no one could have worked harder, or with more wit, to mend a broken place – he also remembers vividly enough what lay behind him when he trailed out of Maine Road for the last time as a professional footballer. It was a day-by-day rejoicing over the way of life that had fulfilled so many of his boyhood hopes – and nothing he would achieve would ever separate him from this view. It was that place in his existence which he had been required to fill with new challenges, and one for which Neil Young and Mike Doyle could never find adequate substitution when it was taken away from them so many years later.

Apart from the thrill of playing and training, it was, above everything else, the companionship of men like Harry Dowd, the goalkeeper who would have, even when he was lodged in the dementia which finally claimed his life in the spring of this year, won any poll among the players as the one among them who was always least affected by the strain of competition – or any sense that he needed to enjoy his life on any terms other than his own.

I happened to sit next to Dowd on the City team bus on the heady ride to the West End from Wembley after the winning of the FA Cup in 1969. At one point he was handed the great trophy and noticed, as the dedicated maintenance man that he unswervingly was, that the silver lid was insecure, and he handed it to me for safekeeping. I mentioned this to his friend and rival goalkeeper Ken Mulhearn, and he nodded and said, 'You might have thought Harry was enjoying one the greatest moments of his life on that bus ride, but he would probably have told you that it was the time he fixed a problem stopcock.'

'Harry struggled for some years with dementia in a care home in Urmston,' Eyre reports. 'His wife got it when she was 55. She was a beautiful, striking woman, one who made you turn your head and say, "She is a beauty." For about 10 years Harry went every single day to see her. From around 11 in the morning to eight at night he would watch over her. He was so devoted to her, but in the end he was in a worse condition. So eventually they were both in homes, for some time in the same one, but in the end they had to move Harry because they kept losing him. When she died, Harry didn't know.

'Before he went down, we used to say, "Harry, take a day off." But he always replied, "Oh no, I can't do that. She looks forward to me going."'

But then if Harry Dowd became enclosed in his own world there was no question that his brief time at the top of football would not always be remembered as much for its unbroken humanity as for the flaring of personal success.

'The striking thing about Harry was that he really didn't have any profound interest in the game, or more than a most basic knowledge,' Eyre says. 'Harry used to give us lifts from training when we were kids. He was older than the groundstaff boys and, in fact, he was the proper groundstaff. He was the general handyman, the plumber, the joiner, the man who would do any job that cropped up.

'Sometimes you would hear someone say, "Hey, Harry's in the A team," and someone else respond with something like, "Yeah, you know, the one that does the plumbing." But it was also a knocking bet that when Harry came out of goal during Belly's first game for Bury (when they were playing City) he would score. I heard an account on *Sports Report*. I'd left City by then and when I heard he'd been moved to centre-forward after injuring his thumb, I said to myself, "It's a certainty he will score." And, of course, he did. He was always the first pick for five-a-side games. We called him Harry the Horse. He was a galumphing figure tearing about the field, he was all over the place, and he also had a bit of skill. He probably wouldn't have believed you if you had told him on that ride through the West End that he would never go out again as City's first-team goalkeeper – but then what a way to finish in the top flight, it surely doesn't get much better than that. It was, I suppose, another case of Mal making a big, career-changing decision, and in this case it was in favour of Joe Corrigan.'

You hear it on everyone's lips. 'Everybody loved Harry,' they say. They loved his easy presence, the sense of an everyday perspective about what mattered most when all the shouting and the cheering was over. You saw Harry and you wanted to smile, see that life shouldn't always be a desperate struggle and that sometimes you should stop and enjoy the little things, like the wind blowing in your face when you went out to train, and you felt good, full of running. You loved the intensity he brought to something as routine as hanging up a light or fixing a plug. No one was ever less likely to be consumed or diminished by the football life.

Ken Mulhearn remembers the times he enjoyed a relaxing drink with him after training, but quite often he would be told, 'Sorry, Ken, I'll have to give it a miss today – I've got a little job on at home.'

For Eyre, Dowd embodied so much of what was most enduring in the ebb and flow of the football life, and if you talk to him long enough he will tell you a little story – an inconsequential one he is ready to concede but still, in his opinion, a good example of how it was to be a young footballer laughing, often with great exhilaration, at both yourself and those around you. It unfolded one summer day when Harry drove some of the young lads back to town from the Urmston training field. 'It was a steaming July day and the work was very hard,' says Eyre, 'with a lot of running in the morning, a bit of a break and then back to it in the afternoon. The two people who always gave us lifts were Harry and Roy Cheetham. On this day we were in Harry's Ford Consul. It had bench seats. Alongside him in the front were Waggy and Vic Gomersall. In the back were Paul Aimson, Kenny Fletcher and me. We were all very hot and tired after the hard day, and someone said, "Harry, pull over so we can get an ice lolly or summat." Obliging as always, Harry swung the car over and stopped in front of a shop. "Aimo", who was everybody's friend, got out of the car and said, "Harry, what do you want?" Aimo was a great lad but he tended to be the butt of everyone's jokes. Harry said, "Ice lolly, orange." Aimo then asked Vic and was told, "The same: ice lolly, orange." Flecky and I said that we too were orange ice-lolly men. Then Aimo asked Waggy, and this, we all knew, was unlikely to be so straightforward. "Get us either a strawberry or raspberry, I like the red 'uns," he said. Aimo came back with the orange ice lollies, then he turned to Waggy and said, "They didn't have strawberry or raspberry, so I got you a pie.'"

Every football team, every army platoon, has an Aimo and a Waggy and a Doyley – an innocent, a provoker and a hard man – and when they grow older, one of the things most cherished down the years is the amount of enjoyment that was drawn from such differences within a group of men trained to think of themselves as one.

A sense of this came to me again one spring morning when I went to Maine Road to stand and remember how it was before the town houses and condos were built where the old pitch was, and so long before the corner shop, where on my way home I would buy the evening sports paper, became a halal butcher's shop. I remembered the swell of expectation when Bell, Summerbee and Lee came onto the field, how it seemed to move up a notch with the passing of each week of rising expectation, and I recalled, too, how the young Joe Corrigan, reporting for his first trial with the club, said how he walked around the big old stadium with new eyes.

All that was round me again when I joined some of the survivors from that time – Pardoe, Cheetham, Eyre and Fleet – in the canteen of the City academy, a short walk down Platt Lane.

They were having their weekly meeting to discuss the dates of their assignments as part of the social apparatus of the new mighty City, which on the other side of town is now so keen to keep in touch, and still cultivate, the old tradition and these men who experienced so deeply one of its most vibrant phases. Inevitably, the talk over the morning coffee soon enough swings back 50 years. Mostly they talk of the astonishing trajectory of City's rise from the founding of the Mercer–Allison regime and then the wrenching pace at which it raced to the precipice.

Most sombre in his memories is Steve Fleet. He says, 'When I saw what happened to Malcolm I felt I would never wish success on anybody. Because, of course, success can be a monster. There was no doubt about it, when he first arrived at Maine Road he was God's gift to coaching. He was lucky enough to have some very good raw material at his disposal, but no one could have had a more dynamic impact. He was a great coach, and in Joe Mercer he had a great manager who was able, for a few years, to draw a line between giving him his head and letting him run away with himself. Success came and it was fantastic, but it can be a heavy burden to bear, and not so many people have the equipment, the character, to cope with it. Sadly, in the end, you had to say that Malcolm didn't. He lost touch with reality and so it became a long descent. I had returned to the club when Malcolm came back for a second time in 1979, and by now he seemed to be living in his own world. It was a terrible shame because if it had all carried on as it started, with such a hard concentration on the basics of success, who knows how gloriously it might have ended?'

Roy Cheetham, a midfielder of impressive skill, was never a central figure in the Mercer–Allison revolution, but between 1956 and 1968 he played 127 times for City and, when he left as a 29-year-old for Detroit Cougars, he could see the great strides which would be confirmed in the league title success. He also had a small but honourable place in the club's records as its first substitute, when he replaced Mike Summerbee in 1965. He speaks of the change that came to the club when Mercer and Allison arrived as you might define the difference between the most dispiriting night and the brightest of mornings: 'You just cannot exaggerate the fact that Joe and Mal were the best things that could have happened to the club. I played under Les McDowall, saw the Revie Plan and all that, through to the George Poyser period. Because George had always been under McDowall nothing changed when McDowall left.

'It was a dead club. There were loads of talented players, like Glyn here, but they weren't being used, or nurtured, as they should have been. Then all of a sudden George was out and Joe was in. Joe wasn't active, he wasn't that well, but he had so much respect in the game that everything he said was taken on board. Somehow, and it was an incredible feeling, you always felt that what the manager was saying was right and it was what you had to do. Joe was a wise man and he was certainly smart enough to know that he needed a good young coach out there working for him. I don't know for sure whether it was a masterstroke, evidence of Joe knowing more than anyone else, or just good fortune, a lucky break when he settled on Mal. What was clear almost overnight was that he couldn't have done better in lifting the place, giving it a new purpose and excitement and belief.

'My first personal recollection of Mal is of him after he had been around for about a week. I was working in training and all of a sudden he said, "Roy, have you got a minute." Now, on the face of it, that might not sound so important, but the fact was that he had hardly met me before and there were people around Maine Road who had been there 10 years and still didn't know my name. This told me that Malcolm was making a connection with me, as he was with all the players. He had taken the trouble to remember my name, and you just had to have been around the place all those years to understand the impact of this. It was also clear straight away that between Joe and Mal there was a wonderful chemistry.

'Mal was so sharp in training, and along with this [had the] knack of making everyone feel they were part of what was happening, [that] they had something to contribute which he valued. Above everything there was a feeling that this was the start of something and that a lot of lethargy and resignation and failure was just being swept into the street. You just knew everything was going to change because you could see it happening before your eyes. You didn't need any sixth sense. Unfortunately I flew away to Detroit when things really took off in 1968, but I had played a few games under the new regime and I have always felt I was involved in something remarkable, and that I knew how it had been made to happen – and certainly I agree totally with all those who say that it should have gone on from that first brilliant burst of success between 1968 and 1970.

'I don't know the detail of why that did not happen, but it was more than surprising; it was shocking that it didn't after seeing the momentum that had been created, and going into training each day and seeing the look of contentment and enjoyment on everyone's faces and feeling the rush and hearing the buzz. That should just not have fallen away. Whenever you think of it you find yourself shaking your head.'

As the canteen coffee is replenished, and the kitchen staff prepare for an invasion from the training field of another hungry generation of putative football stars, Glyn Pardoe repeatedly nods his head as Cheetham speaks. He is the gentlest, least intrusive presence in any exchange of views, but he feels bound to make a point. He says that it comes to him with some poignancy, and not least here, so close to the old battleground.

'It really was like being a family, a happy one in which everyone is pulling together,' says Pardoe. 'We all knew each other very well, it was as if we were being pushed closer together, and every day it was a good experience because there was so much respect around despite all the mickey-taking and the noise of training and the larking around in the dressing room. And none of this unity was touched by the fact that we all had our particular mates. I was more or less inseparable from my cousin Alan [Oakes], who I always referred to as "Our Kid", and Doyley and Belly, the quiet one, tended to be in our group, but that didn't mean we were not very aware of all the different characters. There were the extroverts – Francis Lee and Mike Summerbee – and someone as easy-going as Harry Dowd. But when it mattered it was really as if we were one. We knew each other's wives and children, and it is like us sitting around this table now and being able to talk to each other at every level. We all understood what we were being asked to do and we were all travelling down the same track.

'I broke my leg in 1970 and I was fighting to get fit, so I was out of it to a large extent when things started to go wrong between Joe and Mal, but I saw and heard enough of it to realise that the big issue was that Malcolm wanted more recognition, more credit for what he had done. He wanted to be seen as the man who had made the revolution rather than leaving it as it was – very much a 50–50 share with Joe.

'The hardest thing in seeing Mal slide down the years was that you just couldn't forget all his shining gifts, all that he had brought into our lives. You couldn't help thinking, "Oh, Mal, you could have owned the world." When it all came to a head Joe wasn't so well, and maybe the directors fed that into the equation when it all broke up. When you look back at it you have to think that when Malcolm started to dig his heels in it wasn't really a fair fight.'

Cheetham agrees, saying, 'Mal got all his friends around him, including a takeover group, and there was frail Joe.'

The academy players have done their training now and they are coming in out of the sunshine into the big canteen and, as they rag each other in the timeless way of this old game of playing and fighting and larking, they barely glance at the table where old memories and theories, impregnated with both joy and sadness, are still jealously guarded.

There is just time in the rising clamour for Fred Eyre, who pursued this life for so long, and supported his friends Neil Young and Mike Doyle so faithfully in those hard days which came after their glory, to reach out for something that might just represent a bottom line. He says, 'No City fan I ever knew held back credit to Malcolm for what he had done. But then, of course, it wasn't his name on the office door.'

Unfortunately, the great coach never seemed to grasp that it had been painted vividly enough in the football sky.

Chapter 8

Looking back, rarely is anything more wrenching than identifying the time when a great, life-changing relationship begins to founder. Barbra Streisand sang sorrowfully of the absence of flowers. In the case of Joe Mercer and Malcolm Allison the problem in the end was the classic one of a missing element of trust. It was also the dwindling of a vital understanding of quite how good they were for each other. And, also, how important it is to remember that sometimes it is necessary to take the best of someone and live with the rest.

There lay the fatal flaw, along with the deadly intrusion of angst and fear – the angst of Allison over the denial of the unconditional recognition he believed was his due and the fear of Mercer that he could no longer hold on to the best, most exhilarating of his days since he ceased to be one of the great players, and characters, out on the fields of English football.

It was a breakdown of respect and regard that between the climactic glory of early 1970 and the final, bitter denouement of 1972 you could trace as easily as the change in the seasons. There was the spring, the high summer and then, without any mellow buffer of autumn, the bleakest winter.

A terrible rawness came to a relationship which had once been so warm and mutually enhancing. For a marriage counsellor the diagnosis would have been quite routine. One partner, Allison, had convinced himself he had become undervalued, taken for granted. He was desperate to exert his independence. The other one was threatened, reluctant to accept that relationships sometimes have to change if they are to survive. And suddenly there was flying crockery in the happy home.

Most dismaying, for the players caught in the middle and those who had simply marvelled at their ability to recognise and profit from each other's strength and experience and natural instincts, was the speed of the deterioration. For five years they were the model of football management – they had checks and balances and a crucial regard for each other. For an understanding of this you had only to look at the salient points in their charge to success. Both could claim vital roles in the shaping of progress that at one point had seemed to be inexorable.

Mercer, whose health had been so reduced in years of trial at Aston Villa where he suffered something worryingly close to a nervous breakdown, was soon enough a reborn figure. He made the first keynote signing of Mike Summerbee in 1965, the founder member of the great triumvirate he formed with Bell and Lee, and towards the end of that first season which brought the second division title Allison was also superbly vindicated when he pushed so hard for the signing of Bell.

So it went, through the first division consolidation of 1966–67, the soaring arc that reached to the championship of England a year later, the FA Cup win at Wembley over Leicester City, and then a double statement of elite status with the League Cup and the European Cup-Winners' Cup in the spring of 1970. By then Mercer no longer needed telling the value of his coach's instinct in the matter of player recruitment. In 1966 he relented when Allison insisted that the ageing Tony Book was vital to the team's progress, and then he cajoled from the board the £60,000 required for the signing of Lee. There, it was done, the show was not only on the road it was winning rave notices. Mercer was superbly ambassadorial.

If Busby was unique in his statesmanship, Shankly a passionate preacher and prophet, and Revie a superb if almost furtive team-builder,

Mercer seemed like a man who had embraced, for all its buffetings, the warmest aspects of life. He knew its cruelty but also he knew, and was clearly rediscovering, its joys.

Invariably, when I saw him he asked, 'How's your Mum?' He had never met my mother but once he had charmed my mother-in-law when she introduced herself at a social occasion. No matter how many times I corrected him, his enquiry never changed. He shared with the late Bobby Robson a largely indiscriminate, if sometimes imprecise, affection for the rest of humanity. Both had a tendency to mislay the names of all whom they encountered, however familiar they were. (Once, Robson cheerily said to Bryan Robson in the England team hotel, 'Morning, Bobby, how are you?' and his captain replied, 'No, boss, me Bryan, you Bobby.') 'The thing about Joe, though,' said one of his players, 'was that he was always spot on with your name on a Monday morning when you'd had a bad game on the Saturday.'

However, they knew what was what in football, and ultimately, who was who. At Maine Road the partnership was still vibrantly intact when I joined Mercer and Allison on a spying mission to Portugal in the late winter of 1970. They were running their eyes over Académica de Coimbra, quarter-final opponents in the European Cup-Winners' Cup which a few months later would be seized in the rainstorm of Vienna. They had also reached the final of the League Cup, which they would duly claim at the expense of West Bromwich. The City juggernaut was rolling on, crackling with life and superior football. We flew to Lisbon and then took a train up country. It was a champagne-fuelled journey, launched in Lisbon on the terrace of the fashionable Café Martinho da Arcada in the old square of Terreiro do Paço, and pursued with still more exuberance in the bar of the train.

In Coimbra, a university town of narrow, shadowy streets and ancient nooks, there was dinner and then more champagne in a nightclub which Allison, like a hedonistic hound, sniffed out down a back alley and besieged with typical vigour. Mercer was at his most amiable, grinning crookedly as he travelled to and fro between memories of his past and the excitement of his present, and it was only later, up in his hotel room, that he showed any sign of fatigue. Before we left him, tieless but otherwise fully dressed on his bed, he complained that the room was spinning before his eyes. 'That's no problem, Joe,' said Allison, 'just put one foot on the floor.' It was, as later events would maybe suggest, an instruction from an unlikely source, but Mercer complied – and announced success. 'Mal,' he said, 'did I ever tell you you're a genius?'

That was not quite his sentiment in another year or so when a dispute over team affairs turned heads in a bar in Sliema, Malta, where the team were due to play a friendly during a sunshine break. When the exchanges were over, and Allison had swept out of the bar, Mercer declared to the circle that had formed around him, 'I don't think I've ever known a man with a crueller tongue.' A little later, when the break-up was increasingly out in the open and would soon provoke his retreat to Coventry City, he asked, mournfully, 'How is it possible for a football club to be hijacked in full flight?'

It was a question which would never permit the easiest of answers – and certainly not when I pursued them a couple of years later with Allison when I went each day to his flat in Cromwell Road in Kensington from where, often pained and distracted, he would travel to south London in his desperate attempt to return some momentum to his career at Crystal Palace. We were working on his autobiography, *Colours of My Life*, and always it was easier to discuss that time which had gone right rather than the one that had gone wrong.

Indeed there was maybe a hint of defeat in the concluding words of a work which, just two or three years earlier, would surely have been shot through with the exhilaration of a lifetime's fulfilment. He said, 'If I still need anything from the game at large and the people I have known it is perhaps only the acknowledgement that there have been times when I have gone in and fought for things I considered important. Maybe I have left things unsaid and no doubt some of the achievements I seek will never be fulfilled but if I go tomorrow, I hope it can be said that I did a few things and I loved a few people.' In this at least he would not have been disappointed by the near-unanimous recollection of the young players he touched so deeply in the most affecting days of his life.

Indeed there is almost perfect symbolism in the tribute of Mike Summerbee, Mercer's choice as the first signing of the new City but also someone who embraced so rapidly, and so completely, the thinking and the passion of his new coach Malcolm Allison.

'A memory I will take to my dying day,' says Summerbee, 'is of walking through the gates of Manchester City after driving up from the West Country. I knew how big the old stadium was but I was not prepared for the stature and the impact of Malcolm Allison. He was a big man, extremely handsome and with a great physique, and he was shouting and screaming on the Friday morning before the opening game of the season at Middlesbrough.

'When I walked on the field, he just said to me, "Go and get changed, you're doing a session." I had done my pre-season training at Swindon and I thought I was pretty fit. I wasn't fit. At least certainly not when compared with what my new coach considered proper fitness in a professional footballer. I was Joe Mercer's boy, he had tried to sign me when he was at Villa, but I'd never met Malcolm. I'd read about him, seen him from afar, heard him shouting, but this was the first personal contact. The effect he had, not just on me but the entire training session, was quite remarkable.

'I liked him, instinctively. I'd played at West Ham when I was with Swindon and had become close to Bobby Moore, and he had told me what a great coach and mentor Mal had been. But I didn't know the history of his career, how it had been cut short by TB and losing a part of his lung. Bobby couldn't have given him a higher rating as both a football professional and an inspiring man. To be perfectly honest with you, when I met him on that first Friday it was the beginning of a love affair. I didn't realise it at the time, but I did soon enough, and if you ask any of the other players I suspect they would tell you something of the same. He was the first man in football who used such powerful psychology.

'I know he did it with me because he was sure from the start that he would get a response – and I believe it was the same with the others. Yes, we knew soon enough he had his weaknesses, but in the early days they were not what you noticed. That first morning I knew I had signed on to something great.'

In the Kensington flat Allison often found it hard to shake the bleak mood which deepened with each slide in his reputation. He joked about the comment of the Palace owner Raymond Bloye, a supermarket mogul, when Allison's promise of a swift return to the first division was ridiculed by Notts County in an opening 4–1 defeat at the start of his first full season in South London. 'Raymond put his arm around me,' Allison reported, 'and said, "Don't worry, Malcolm, I know how much hard work went into the defeat." Allison smiled but his eyes were cold. He wore a long Arabian robe, puffed a cigar and walked to the big window and stared down into the busy Cromwell Road. It might have been the artery of another planet.

Yet, still, he brightened when he spoke of the days which Summerbee would recall so warmly in the years after he was gone.

They were indeed exhilarating days – and all the more remarkable when you remember that just six months before his arrival at Maine Road City had drawn their lowest ever crowd – just over 8,000 fans – to see their team labour against Summerbee's Swindon Town. There was riot in the air and after the game a mob gathered outside the main stand. Stones were thrown. Many years later Francis Lee would joke, 'It's amazing how many people tell me they were there that night. At a rough count I would say it had to be around 20,000.' Yet there was nothing illusory about the despair felt for the future of a once great football club that cold winter night.

For Allison, the London boy who claimed an affinity with a City that won the first division title in his youth, it was always a crusade and the battlements he craved to storm were those of Manchester United. He remembered his flash of anger and then a flush of pride when he heard his second son, Mark, was involved in a fight on his first day in a new school. Mark reported that an older boy had taunted him, saying, 'Hey, Allison, four eyes, I want to see you after school. Your dad works for that useless team City.' Allison's son didn't wait for the end of class.

Nor did his father linger over any niceties when, a few days after arriving in town, he found himself at Manchester United's first division championship celebration. United's manager Sir Matt Busby, ever urbane, diplomatic, turned in the direction of his newest challenger and said, 'I believe there is room for two first division clubs in Manchester,' and Allison narrowed his eyes and muttered, 'Yes, baby, and you're going to get another team in town – and a real one.' Later in the evening he became more voluble, striking a soon-to-be-collected bet with United's skilled and passionate midfielder Pat Crerand, who had claimed he would never get a crowd of more than 30,000 into Maine Road, and telling Busby's son, Sandy, 'Your father has got a 20-year start but I'll pass him in three.'

In Kensington he reflected, 'Maybe that was a bad thing to say but it was a very good thing to think.'

It certainly represented his growing sense that he had something special in his grasp of what it took to lift a football team and carry it to a new understanding of what could be achieved if it did its work and began to believe in itself. He had had his lost years, rebuilt himself from the horror of being sent away from West Ham United – where he was not only a senior player but also a growing tactical influence over teammates like Noel Cantwell, Frank O'Farrell, Dave Sexton and John Bond – to a sanatorium deep in the countryside.

He had been a professional gambler in the company of his close friend, the former Arsenal wing-half Arthur Shaw, and had run a drinking club in Tin Pan Alley, where the young Jimmy Greaves had sat sipping beer and waiting nervously for news of his sensational transfer from Chelsea to A.C. Milan.

That move did not work out for the homesick east Londoner but it was a failure that carried an extraordinary qualification. He scored nine goals in just 12 games for the Italian giants in the world game's most rigorous and technically proficient defensive culture and, more than a decade later, when Allison was in the final stages of his brilliant work at City, he sought an extra flourish with an attempt to persuade Greaves to sign at the end of his amazingly fecund reign at Spurs. Greaves chose to stay nearer home in West Ham but he thanked his old friend for his faith and his interest, and for Allison then it was no more than a passing sigh. Heavier regrets were, after all, already beginning to take shape.

They could not have seemed further away, though, when Allison reported to Maine Road. He may have just been fired by Plymouth Argyle but no one believed that had anything to do with the arresting work he had done at Home Park after successfully coaching the undergraduates of Cambridge University and then Bath City. He had warred with the board over team policy and had been indiscreet enough to have an affair with a director's wife. It was, he agreed, the behaviour of a man who believed he had won the right to make his own rules.

He wrote in his autobiography, 'I suppose when I went to Maine Road for my interview my attitude to life was unusual. I was dressed casually – a fawn suit with an open-necked blue shirt – and I had been talking with the directors, who seemed a very elderly set of men, only a few minutes when I said, "Look, gentlemen, you don't know me and I don't know you, so I'll work for you until Christmas for £30 a week. Then we will have another talk."'

But if Allison was buoyant about his successes in Cambridge and Bath and Plymouth, if he felt he had unlocked the secrets of recasting and inspiring football teams, he was quickly aware of the scale of his new challenge. 'There was,' he recalled, 'clearly a mountain of work to do. Each time I moved, from Cambridge to Bath, from Bath to Plymouth, I felt I was leaving a much better team. And again I felt it in Manchester. I sat with Joe Mercer and watched our first game, a friendly with Dundee at Maine Road. We lost 2–1 and we were both very shocked. I turned to Joe and groaned, "What a terrible team."

'The atmosphere at the place was appalling. People who did not cheat were hiding, their confidence shattered. Alan Oakes, who would emerge as one of the best midfield and defensive players in the league, and came very close to winning an England cap, would break out in a sweat before a game. No one had got through to him and told him how well he could play. I could understand how it was that angry fans had stormed the ground the previous season. Joe and I had walked into a mausoleum. There was a friendly game at Tranmere, which gave us no more comfort. Catching Manchester United was going to be a marathon run. But we tinkered. We tried to patch up our deficiencies.

'It was crucial to get something out of our first league match at Middlesbrough. I had noticed in training the good running ability and toughness of a boy called David Connor. I thought right away he had the potential to be a valuable defensive player, a man to perhaps shut out the opposing playmaker. At Middlesbrough that was Ian Gibson, a very good and subtle player.

'Connor, who was also full of stamina, achieved the shut-out. Gibson never really got going and we came away with a draw. It was a good, solid start and very important in building early confidence. We went eight games without defeat, were nicking a few results but it all helped.'

Most helpful of all was the swift understanding of the players that behind the swagger, the frequently vainglorious demeanour, there was a man who knew what he was doing, who saw things others didn't, and nothing captured this more than the cultivation of the previously unheralded young Mancunian Connor.

He would never be a headliner, never create the excitement of a Neil Young, but where others had seen a good-hearted, up-and-down-the-field kid, Allison saw a sharply knowing destroyer of the creative strivings of even the most distinguished opponent. This talent reached its apotheosis when he played Everton's World Cup winner Alan Ball – one of the great midfielders of English football history – off the field in a Cup tie at Goodison Park. In all, Connor played 141 games for City, including 13 in the 1968 first division title charge. In a way, he was Allison's calling card, the first hard evidence that he had the nous and the communicative skill not just to improve players, concentrate their minds on their best attributes, but also make them champions.

Connor was the first encouraging example of the coach's ability to put in some of the foundations of a solid future. He looked at the boy with fresh eyes, and it was not the singular act of someone intent only on building his own aura. It was a general invitation. Everybody could do it. They could look at themselves and, with a little encouragement, discover new strengths. This, essentially, was the story of Manchester City, 1967–70. It was one of adventure, but only after the most careful taking of everyone's stock.

Allison's first big concern was a porous defence. An old centre-half, he shuddered at the space granted opposing forwards and he recommended that Mercer go back to his first club and sign George Heslop, an unspectacular but extremely polished and proficient understudy to the more elegant England player Brian Labone.

'Joe Mercer had made two signings, one brilliant, one somewhat less so,' Allison recalled. 'Mike Summerbee instantly began to pay off his transfer fee of £35,000. He came to us a rather defensive winger but I refused to let him play in his own half. I made him more aggressive and the result was devastating. Joe also signed Ralph Brand, a sensation in Scotland with Rangers, but it was a move which worked out badly.

He had lots of skill but he didn't have the power to put it together consistently enough for us. It was a sad thing to lose his skill but we had to discard him.'

Allison wrote down a shopping list which contained just two names – Colin Bell and Wyn Davies. But first, with money spent on Summerbee and Heslop, he recognised a clear priority. It was to galvanise the troops he already had.

Summerbee still feels an old burning in his lungs when he returns to those first days of previously unimaginable effort. 'Never before had I come across such a person – and never would I again. He gave us a fitness that made us so strong we felt unique. But before that there was quite a bit of resentment when we ran so hard at Wythenshawe Park. He brought in great athletes: Derek Ibbotson, who had broken the world mile record; Joe Lancaster, a world road racing record holder; and the leading sprinter, Danny Herman. The beautiful Olympic gold medallist Mary Rand also appeared, and in those first days this did make the lads more enthusiastic as they jockeyed for places to run behind her.

'The transformation of our feelings was quite quick, when I think about it. One minute we were saying, "We're bloody footballers not athletes," the next we're thinking, "This is doing us some good and we had better swap our pumps for some track shoes on these cinders." Very quickly we had grasped that the coach was the first person to bring English players to this level of fitness. We moaned like hell – and then suddenly we realised someone had unlocked a door for us and pointed us to places we would never forget. Whatever his critics say, I will always believe Malcolm was the greatest pure football coach there has ever been. You can have José Mourinho, whose father was a goal-keeper when Malcolm was winning a Portuguese league title, and of course the Special One has been brilliant. But Mal was the best.

'Joe Mercer was a good manager, a steadying influence on Mal – and the rest of us – but it was always Malcolm who would get the best out of us, get to the heart of what we were supposed to be doing. He knew how to handle me – and the whole team. He could have a go at me at half-time in front of all the players but be confident that he was going to get 25 per cent more out of me. Whatever he said, he knew he was not going to see me put my head down. He would be shouting on the touchline but I knew he was doing everything he could to make me a better player. And, of course, soon enough I was an England player.'

So, too, would be Colin Bell, Allison's pick when he was told by Mercer that he had to choose between the tall, natural-born athlete whose talents were glinting rather than radiating down the road at Bury, and the wonderfully combative front man Davies of Bolton Wanderers and then Newcastle United.

The latter literally stood out in any penalty-area crowd, but at that point in his career Bell's qualities were not overwhelming the scouts and managers who gathered in the old main stand of Bury's Gigg Lane. Interesting them, certainly, but none of them felt a thunderbolt of conviction when they transferred him in their minds' eyes into a well-organised leading team. But Allison surely did.

He said, 'I was pleased the jury seemed to be out on Belly, especially when Mercer told me the directors were clucking about the difficulty of raising Bury's asking price, which was £42,000. I was telling people in the game that Bell certainly had his appeal – great physical strength and stamina – but that I didn't think he could really play, not with the intuition and spark that marked out the really exceptional players – and all the time hoping desperately that the directors could get the money together in time.'

They did – but only hours before the end of the old March transfer deadline. The *Daily Express* sent me down to Bury to stake out the ground, along with a small group of fellow young leg men. It was not a huge story. There was nothing like the furore which greeted Allison's ill-starred move for Rodney Marsh a few years later, when a great media cavalcade followed him to Manchester airport – or when the new Manchester United manager Tommy Docherty smuggled his import from Celtic, the diminutive Lou Macari, through throngs of reporters and television crews blocking the entrance to Old Trafford. ('How did you sneak him in, Doc?' someone cried. 'I hid him in the glove compartment,' snapped Docherty.)

There was no such scene at Bury, though Ron Suart, the manager of first division Blackpool, an experienced football man and far too savvy to be fooled by Allison's smokescreen, arrived in the dusk and made one last entreaty. But the night and, he believed, the future belonged to Allison. When Bell signed for City, the double-talk promptly ended. 'You will see soon enough,' Allison declared, 'that this is one of the most significant signings in the history of Manchester City. We are on the move.'

Not, though, without some of the frustration which would build critically down the next few years. Allison recalled when he reviewed those days during one of our Kensington sessions, 'Bell's signing more or less guaranteed us the second division championship. It was in pure football terms a major achievement, unthinkable at the start of the season. But in a town which had become used to United sweeping to titles, it seemed to have little impact.

'That was a bit dispiriting but I had always known it was going to be a long, tough haul. More discouraging was the reaction of the board. The chairman, Albert Alexander, came to me and said, "Walter Griffiths is getting a bonus of £400, so are you, and Joe Mercer is getting £600. I was a bit stunned. Then I felt disgust. I felt I had been badly insulted. I couldn't stop myself saying, "Yes, I thought the secretary did very well. He booked us into some very nice hotels."

'I had worked up to Christmas on £30 a week as agreed. Then we had some talks and I got a £10 rise. But really it was chickenfeed. I didn't have a club car or any other perks. I knew the club wasn't rolling in money but this did seem very cheap. Eventually they agreed to pay off my overdraft, which stood at £600. I couldn't say I was bowled over by their generosity.'

However, the work continued to go well and City did manage to get their hands on the £16,000 needed to sign Allison's protégé Tony Book despite the misgivings of Mercer. Allison recalled, 'We had that issue of Bookie's age, which I got by when I mentioned Joe's own age when he left Everton for Arsenal for some extremely productive years – and I also told him that I had watched eight other right-backs, all of them younger, and not one of them had come close to Book in speed, control and class. Joe was still a bit uptight but the deal went through, and just how well we had spent our money didn't really become fully apparent until we experienced our first real crisis in the new season in the top division.

'We started that season briskly enough and again the confidence of the players was growing. We drew at Southampton, always a tricky assignment, in the first game and Bookie played particularly well. We came home to beat Liverpool and Sunderland. Two wins and a draw, it could hardly have been better for a team returning to the first division. Then the roof fell in. We lost at Anfield, went to Villa and lost 3–0. West Ham murdered us 4–1. We had crumpled. The defence had simply caved in. But it was now that the true value of Tony Book became apparent at Maine Road.

'I changed our system. Tony Book switched to the sweeping role, still a rarity in England, and the rest of the defence marked man for man. The improvement was immediate. We came out of our dive towards the foot of the table and in the sixth round of the FA Cup we nearly caused a sensation at Leeds. We lost 1–0 but we did outplay them. Colin Bell missed three chances, incredibly, and in every phase of the game we had an edge.

'The point was that we nearly caught Leeds with a sucker punch. I knew how thorough Leeds were, how Don Revie had his right-hand man Syd Owen and other members of his staff analysing every aspect of an opponent's game. So I suggested we completely change our system. We went to 4–4–2 and it nearly worked. Leeds had worked on undermining our sweeper system and then they went out on the field and found it had disappeared in a puff of blue smoke. We finished the season comfortably in fifteenth place, and Harry Godwin, our chief scout, came to me and said, "In the 13 years I've been at City we've only finished above the bottom six in the first division four times. You have put in some very good foundations."

Allison knew that well enough, but he was pleased to hear it from a man universally respected in and out of Maine Road. A wryly witty north Mancunian, Godwin had a problem with overstatement – and a worldly wise concern that the coach's extravagant ways would bring, however many years down the road, a less than triumphant ending.

From time to time I would drive the scout on some of his night-time assignments, and so often the conversation would settle on the impact and the potential of Allison's work. One night he said, 'I love what Malcolm represents in football, I love his boldness and his intelligence, but, you know, I cannot help worrying for him. I have this terrible picture of Big Mal in his old age. All the back-slappers have disappeared and he can no longer take over a nightclub and order the champagne and pull the birds, and I fear that he will feel terribly alone and disillusioned. I hope so much that I am wrong, but I'm afraid the picture will just not go away.'

This would prove to be among the most prescient of Harry Godwin's confidences, but then when you were young and there seemed so much time to correct all of your own follies it seemed too sombre a prophecy. Old age could wait, and if not for Big Mal who else in a football world through which he was cutting such a thrilling path?

He was still further emboldened by that tantalising near miss at Elland Road when the brilliant midfield combination of John Giles and Billy Bremner were not only shaken out of their normally dominant rhythm but were carried so close to a crushing defeat.

'That performance at Leeds,' Allison told me in Kensington, 'had given me the first inkling that we could go on and reach for the big prizes. On the face of it we were merely consolidating our promotion, our march away from the idea that City was once a great club destined for the margins of the game, but working with the players each day convinced me that a lot more was happening. The great disappointment of the season was our failure to beat Manchester United – and especially our performance at Old Trafford. All the doubts and frailties came flooding back once we arrived in that place which had so overshadowed Maine Road for so long. We put on a terribly limp performance and I remained disgusted for days. Once more we had been cuffed aside by a team which loomed so large in the minds of our players.'

What Allison needed most vitally now were players who could most easily shed such inhibitions, players like Summerbee, young Doyle, the policeman's son, and the old head Tony Book. And he would take such self-belief, as long as it was accompanied by a significant level of intrinsic talent, wherever he could find it and afford it. This led him, in the face of Mercer's acute scepticism, to the knockdown, £12,000 purchase of Tony Coleman from Doncaster Rovers. Allison was hardly unaware of the risks, saying, 'I had to agree with Joe that Coleman's record seemed like the nightmare of a delirious football probation officer. Nobody needed to tell me I was proposing a gamble.'

At the very least, it seemed that some resolute demons lurked behind the cherubic smile of the young Merseysider. A brilliant natural talent, he had been thrown out of Stoke City and Preston North End as 'unmanageable'. You couldn't get odds against the likelihood that he was on a one-way journey when he signed for non-league Bangor City in North Wales.

The verdict of Godwin was that Coleman's ability was there for anyone to see, it was strong and vital, but he worried that so much evidence said that it was also ungovernable. That conclusion was swiftly vindicated when, after City passed on the opportunity of picking him up from Bangor for a mere £3,000, he returned to the league with Doncaster. He promptly punched a referee in the face.

When he came back from suspension he played with a renewed strength and purpose and Allison was still haunted by his possibilities. Coleman was strong, quick and brave and he would provide City with some much needed width and bite along the left wing.

It was also true, as he made the case for Coleman, that the coach could already point to the dramatic development of City players who seemed to be acquiring a little more poise and gravitas in each new game: Summerbee, Book, Pardoe, Oakes, Young, who had moved so effectively in from his original role on the wing, and Doyle were all pushing back their own and the team's horizons. Allison said that he believed he could add the problematic Coleman to their number. 'I came away from one game believing that Coleman was still being offered cheaply,' said the coach. 'He dominated the match, was full of powerful running and he crossed the ball beautifully. In the end Mercer put on a resigned expression and said, "Go on then, give it a go."

'Ultimately I failed with Tony Coleman, but for a couple of years the club drew huge benefit from having him in the team. At our best, the forward line was perfectly balanced and he played an integral part in that. Even so, and though I got those two superb years from him, I could never deal fully with his wild, strange streak. There was simply something in him that nobody could get to. I remember a training session before the 1969 Cup final. I said to him, "Come on, Tony, you can give it more than that," but he just sneered and said, "What's the point?" I wanted to smack his choirboy face – and eventually I did.

'I placed a midnight curfew on him. Generally, he did behave himself and his face often broke into a boyish smile when I praised his work in training. He had tremendous natural strength, and this made it difficult to know if he had been out on the tiles. You only have to glance at most players to know how much sleep they have had. But that was impossible with him. One night I got a tip that he was out after midnight in a Manchester nightclub. He was with Ken Mulhearn, another Liverpool boy I had bought from Stockport County who had nice, clean hands and was nearly a very good goalkeeper for us.

'I drove straight to the Cabaret Club and there was Coleman, smiling and laughing and propping up the bar. I slapped him across the face. It wasn't a punch but it did express my anger and disappointment that, after putting so much faith in the kid, changing his career around, he was now letting me down. He had been given a chance he had had no right to expect, and here he was wanting to make a full-scale fight of it. I got him out of the nightclub, but as I did so I realised he had to go. The team was moving so well, the players displaying so much trust in each other, I just couldn't afford to let anyone get away with it.'

That, though, was a problem much further down a yellow brick road. When Coleman arrived at Maine Road his first months saw his seamless absorption into a team clearly moving on to new levels of confidence and accomplishment.

If 1966–67 was the campaign of digging in, of developing new resilience, new muscles, the season that followed resembled more a cavalry charge of panache and, ultimately, irresistible momentum. Wherever Allison and Mercer looked they felt a quickening of their pulse and their hope. They purred into the autumn and it is easy, nearly half a century on, to haul back a sunny September afternoon when an extremely impressive Nottingham Forest team were systematically dismantled. I drove away from Maine Road with the inescapable suspicion that we may have seen new champions, and not only winners but flag-carriers for a new and intoxicating phase of the national game.

Against Forest the unlikely star was a young, clever little winger named Paul Hince, who would make a successful career in sports journalism. Yet so many players would take much longer journeys through the game without ever finding an afternoon of such extraordinary fulfilment. Hince ran and jinked the big Forest full-back John Winfield to the point of distraction, and when the defender's tackles became heavier, and wild, Allison roared from the touchline, 'Get that man off the field, ref.' Hince may have been a passing performer in the big show but he held the grand stage now and called to his coach, 'Don't get him sent off, Mal, I may not beat the next man they put on me so easily.'

On the greatest afternoon of his football life Hince emerged from obscurity to express the ethos of a team that, it was suddenly hard not to believe, was brushing against a thrilling destiny. It was one of insistent opportunism, of a growing sense that it had the nerve, and the ability, to take its chance.

The new season was not yet a triumphant march, though. Some setbacks had come right at the start. There was a disappointing, goalless draw at home with Liverpool and defeats at Southampton and Stoke. But the Forest victory certainly provided an exciting glimpse of the future, and soon enough it would be augmented by the Ballet on Ice extravaganza against Spurs, and as the possibility of a serious title challenge strengthened, a watershed spring-time victory at Manchester United.

With Mercer's backing, Allison had built the foundations of a champion team. He had flair and discipline and remarkable fitness – and a coterie of young and gifted players who were seizing their opportunities in a way that was exceeding his most optimistic projections.

His old friend Arthur Shaw, who had guided him around the racetracks of England and France, came to him and said that watching his side had reanimated his old love of the game. He had, this old Arsenal man, become a Manchester City fan not out of association with their coach but because of the brave and exciting football they played.

Peter Doherty, his boyhood hero and one of the great figures in the history of City, told Allison he was bringing great credit not only to his old club but to all of English football.

What more did he need? He thought about it hard and long before answering the question that would shape his last crucial decision and submission to Joe Mercer in the making of the team that was already causing such a stir. He needed, more than anyone, Francis Lee.

Chapter 9

Francis Lee's move from Bolton Wanderers to Manchester City in October 1967 at the age of 23 was rather more than just another high-profile football transfer. It was the consequence of something that in those feudal days could only be seen as an extraordinary act of will.

Apart from being a fighting cock of a player, dynamic and pugnacious and never afflicted by a sliver of doubt about his own ability from the moment he made his Bolton debut as a 16-year-old, Lee was also in one other way the rarest of professionals. He believed he owned his own destiny in a game that was, essentially, run by fools.

When I see him now in his Cheshire mansion – with the attached stables from where he operated as a successful racing trainer when his playing days were over and his fortune assured – he is about to leave for his annual Christmas pilgrimage to Sandy Lane, Barbados. Touching 70, he still exudes all the breezy confidence, which can tip into belligerence, of a thoroughly self-made man.

If he has regrets for some of the misadventure of his four-year stint as chairman and chief shareholder of City, which he ended somewhat bloodied in 1998 – and not least the rupture that came to his relationship with his great colleague Colin Bell – they have long been absorbed by a broader view. His understanding is that few men, let alone leading professional footballers of a generation which now seems (from the perspective of these days of unbridled wealth) tragically ill-served, have more reason to be more satisfied by the course of their lives.

He also argues with typical conviction that if results on the field declined during his stewardship – through the managerial regimes of his friend and former England teammate Alan Ball, and then Frank Clark – he was at least able to reverse the catastrophic business practices, increase the annual turnover by 600 per cent (from £4 million to £32 million), and make the deal with Manchester City Council which took the club to the new City of Manchester stadium on the other side of the city.

Lee was a millionaire before he was 30, and uniquely in those days he said that although he loved to play football at the highest possible level it was always going to be on his own terms. And so it was. But first he had to make his stand.

When his wife Gill brings in cappuccino to a beautiful, beamed drawing room, his re-creation of his past is in full, frothing flow.

'By the time I joined City,' Lee says, 'it was clear that Joe Mercer and Malcolm Allison had created an instant chemistry and that was so vital to a club attempting to turn around a terrible decline. They had won promotion back to the top division at their first attempt while at Bolton we had gone the other way. Joe and Mal had got rid of some older players, and when City started indifferently in the first division in the 1966–67 season they realised they were still a couple of players short. I was signed early the next season, following Mike Summerbee, Colin Bell and Tony Book into the squad. When I joined City they had just been beaten by Manchester United and were on the fringe of the relegation zone. In the meantime, I had fallen out with Bolton Wanderers. I was playing without a contract. After being relegated, Bolton tried to sign me at various times but I said, "No, I'll play week by week." What brought the pressure on them was the fact that I was the leading scorer, having scored 12 goals before the end of September. One of them helped knock Liverpool out of the League Cup, and after that Bill

Shankly always said to me, "I should have signed you after you scored that goal at the Kop End. I shouldn't have listened to anyone, I should just have gone ahead and signed you."

'Around that time Bolton made their biggest effort to re-sign me, no doubt because there was a lot of speculation that some of the big clubs were about to come in and offer something in the region of £100,000. I was called to a board meeting at Burnden Park and told that they had a new offer for me. But I insisted I wanted to go. I was on £35 a week, which was the most I ever earned at Bolton despite the fact that I had been their top scorer over the last six years. I certainly wasn't the best-paid player. Eddie Hopkinson, the goalkeeper who had played for England, Freddie Hill, a very skilful player, and Wyn Davies were all ahead of me. I had always argued that I should be on the same money as Davies because he was supposed to be the centre-forward striker and I always scored more goals than him. The manager, Bill Ridding, said I couldn't be on the same wages as Wyn because I was too young. I told him, "Well, I'm old enough now, I'm certainly old enough to score more goals than anyone else around here." But he just wouldn't have it and that was how my contract came to expire. The directors saw a problem arising in that they knew I had started a business and though they didn't know exactly what I was doing they had probably heard that it was OK and no doubt they thought, "He could walk away and then we would be out £100,000."'

Lee unfurls the relish of a born fighter as he outlines the build-up to the kind of battle the likes of Colin Bell and Sir Bobby Charlton, rooted in their times and the existing mores of the game, could not have imagined, never mind contemplated. For them it would have been an outrage against the natural order; for Lee, player, ambitious businessman and zealous guardian of his rights, it was more a rite of passage.

'Now they told me in the boardroom, "If you sign now we'll give you £150 a week." I said, "Look, you've been paying me £35 a week and I've been arguing over my wages for three years. It's very good of you, thank you very much, but I'm not going to sign for you." This was too much for one of the directors, who cried out, "What are you saying? The chief executive of my company only gets a third of what we're offering you. Are you really turning down £150 a week?" I said, "I'm sorry but you've been underpaying me for so long I just don't want to play for you. I want to get away from this club and see how far I can get in this game. If I stay here on £150 a week nobody in the team is going to give me a bloody pass. If somebody does, it's going to be one of those that either sends you to the hospital or says, "OK, let's see how good you really are?"

'I could see all the dangers. They couldn't because they knew bugger all about the game. Finally, I told them, "Let me relieve you of the problem. You give me my National Insurance cards and I'll carry on working in my business and if you ever fancy selling me, sell me – but until then don't bother me again."

'So that's how I finished with Bolton. They gave me my insurance cards and I got on with my life, without football if necessary.'

His exile lasted just three weeks and, typically, he had made sure that it would be at no cost to any chance of a swift return to the game: 'I got the athlete Peter Keeling to help me with my fitness. I would leave the office each day and run around the track with him. Eventually City came in, but before that Bolton tried to sell me to Wolves for £60,000 plus their player Terry Wharton. I told Bolton I wasn't interested in the move. My business was flourishing and I didn't want the extra travelling down to the Black Country. Naturally, Bolton were more peeved than ever and soon after I left they signed Wharton, which, I calculated, gave him a value of around £120,000. For me it was another example of the anomalies that cropped up so frequently in the football of those days.'

The circumstances of his move to City could hardly have been more bizarre: 'I got a call from Bill Ridding to say that I should drive down to Burnden Park and meet him in the car park. "Bring your insurance cards," he said, "because I've got a club for you." When I asked him which club it was, he replied, "You'll find out soon enough," and when he said that it took quite a lot of restraint not to tell him to piss off. But the truth was I was wanting to get back to football and I looked forward to playing for one of the big clubs because I was confident I could do well wherever I went.

'Later, Matt Busby told me he should have bought me for United. He had signed John Connelly and Willie Morgan from Burnley but, as he noted, he could have got two for the price of one with my ability to play either wide or inside.

'It saddened me that the people in Bolton attempted to blacken my name. They said I was trouble, and I suppose in one sense I was – I wasn't ready to be pushed around, touching my forelock to the directors and generally being treated like a chattel. I was certainly determined to see just how far I could get in football – and on the best possible terms. I had seen, for example, Freddie Hill, an extremely talented player, ruined by staying at Bolton too long. He was a class player but he found himself dropping down the divisions to Halifax before City, so late in his career, came along to rescue him with a £10,000 bid.'

When Lee drove out of the Burnden Park car park behind Ridding he still didn't know his fate. He re-conjures a delicious tension as he recounts his journey into the unknown: 'Ridding told me, "Get back in your car and follow me." So I followed his Austin Cambridge, and when we got to the new bridge over the Manchester Ship Canal on the M62 I saw my petrol gauge showed empty. I was driving a second-hand Austin Westminster, which I had bought to convince everyone I was truly hitting the big time, and when I noticed the needle was on zero I thought, "Fucking hell, he's told everyone in football I'm trouble and he's going to arrive wherever we are supposed to be going and he's going to say, 'Look, I told you he's a funny bugger and now he hasn't even turned up.'"

'I thought I could be going to one of three places – Old Trafford, Maine Road or Stoke City, where their manager Tony Waddington had made it known he was very keen to sign me. We did a few more miles and went past the Old Trafford turn-off, so now I knew it was going to be either City or Stoke. Then, with the petrol still holding, we were going down Wilbraham Road in south Manchester on the way to Maine Road and I was quite pleased.

'A few weeks earlier Malcolm and I had our famous meeting in the social club at Bolton, when he told me he was going to make me a great player and I said, "Well, thank you very much, but I think I'm pretty good right now." The truth was that, right from the start, we got on like houses on fire.'

First though, there were some minor but in those days potentially costly complications. The Football League demanded to study the City deal before clearing Lee's registration, which meant that he wasn't able to travel with his new team to Sunderland.

'In my opinion I should have got five per cent of the £60,000 transfer fee but the league's first ruling was that I should not receive anything. They said there were too many anomalies surrounding the transfer. The main problem, they added, was that I was out of contract with Bolton and never before had a deal been made in such a situation.

'Eventually, the league secretary, Alan Hardaker, wrote to me saying that it had been decided that I could receive half of the five per cent in view of the unprecedented circumstances. I wrote back to Hardaker thanking him very much for allowing me £1,500 but also wondering if he could possibly explain how it was that I had been only 50 per cent right. He wrote back saying he had acted under a certain rule and that was that. So I got on with my new life at City.'

Lee's career was soon going riotously well. City had proffered their title credentials and they had not been found wanting. For both the coach and an increasing number of battered opponents, the arrival of

Lee was the confirmation that City had the means to reach the end of the road in triumph.

Three dates, three places, in 1968 leap from the itinerary of the march to glory: Old Trafford, 27 March, White Hart Lane, 4 May, and St James' Park, 11 May. These, when all is said, were the occasions when the Forever Boys achieved their immortality. These were the marks of perfection which meant that, for all the disappointments and grievances which would come so quickly, the work of Malcolm Allison and the old-man-of-the-world guidance he received from Joe Mercer, would always shine in the memory, separate and free of any reproach or any sorrow.

In the Kensington flat Allison recalled each one of the landmarks – and a state of exhilaration which at times touched on delirium. 'When we went to Old Trafford and beat United 3–1 I knew it in my bones that we could go all the way,' he said. 'It was one of the great nights of my life in some ways – given all that had gone before and all the pressure on us to perform, maybe the greatest. Bell was staggering and Lee and Summerbee responded brilliantly to the need to put pressure on United.

'Yet it started badly. United scored in the first minute and my plan for Book to mark Best was in tatters. Best was over-running Book, a formidable feat. So I immediately told Book to play his normal game and wait for Best. It worked. Best lost some of his menace and Bell, Lee and Summerbee began to stretch United at the seams. We were the much better-conditioned team and our skill factor rose dramatically.

'We set up the title, and it was as though we had just walked out of the wilderness. The win gave us the nerve and the momentum to stretch out to win the championship. But it was still a close, hard run along the rails. We entered the final phase with a night match against Everton and, with the tension building as the title came into focus, I believed that if we were to stay in the battle we needed both points from the game at Maine Road.

'Tony Book broke the tension when he raced into the penalty box and snaffled a goal off the toes of Everton. Almost as he scored, the news came in that United were losing at West Bromwich. The atmosphere was electric. It meant that if we won our last two matches we would be champions. In three years we would have travelled from nowhere to the peak of English football. It was a dramatic prospect.'

By now Lee had utterly vindicated the coach's belief in what he had seen from his first glimpse of the poised, even strutting young contender at Burnden Park. 'I loved the way he approached the game,' said Allison. 'He expected to win, and when it didn't happen he wasn't so much disappointed as astounded. It was an offence against his nature.'

For his part, Lee felt that his mystery drive of a few months earlier could not have had a more satisfactory conclusion. 'The training was very hard – and very enjoyable,' he says. 'Malcolm was an excellent coach and he made it very clear what he could see in me. Equally apparent was that he could get from me everything I had to offer. I had never experienced anything like it. At Bolton, even when I was 16, the coaches just told me to play on the right wing and when the other team got the ball chase back. When I was in their half I had to clop it into the middle at the first opportunity.

'At a lot of clubs in those days the coaches didn't do individual work with the players. There would be some general discussion and then you had to get on with it yourself. Ken Barnes, a good, highly intelligent coach and a fine player for City in his time, said that I played so well as a kid at Bolton somebody must have been coaching me, maybe a schoolteacher. But I said, "No, I didn't get any advice from anyone who knew anything about the game." He shook his head and said, "It's amazing that as a 16-year-old you helped beat City 3–1 and no one had helped to bring you on."'

But if there was a shortfall in Lee's early football education, one he had soared beyond with native gifts and a ferocious ambition to win – he could also have been a professional cricketer – there was spectacular compensation as he came to an early peak of confidence and accomplishment as City's momentum was magnificently restored in the run-in to the title.

'If we had been racehorses,' says the old trainer, 'Mal would surely have been trainer of the year. We had classic speed – and we proved we could stay the distance. We were in danger of tailing off at Christmas but then we came back so strongly through the field – and then pushed hard for the finish. Beating United at Old Trafford was key, it was a real psychological breakthrough, and everything came down to beating Spurs and Newcastle on their own grounds. The win at Newcastle was one of the best games I ever played in. It seemed that every time we scored they were likely to come back at us and score – and they were all great goals. Throughout the game we had to keep digging down deeper and deeper and then, when we thought we were home with a 4–2 lead, they scored again and won two corners at the end of the game. Anything could have happened. We didn't know that United, our only rivals now, were struggling at home to Sunderland. Then we had the title and the relief was fantastic. But when we got back to the dressing room it was as though most of the team didn't really realise what had been achieved. They didn't seem to understand what had happened, and this was because none of them had won anything in their lives before. They hadn't won a fucking thing. They were all singing in the coach and they stopped to get some crates of beer and they tried so hard to make it a celebration, but it was difficult because they were in unknown country.'

For the coach they were the best of his days. Nothing that followed would ever match that rush of the blood, that certainty that he had enough players to meet any demand. His great rival Busby once explained how it was to have players like Best, Charlton and Law. 'It meant,' he reported, 'that I never went to a game with any fear. I was always sure about my players. I never had to indulge in Dutch courage, pour myself a wee dram before the kick-off, as some managers did.'

Nor did Allison need any such fortification as City reached for their prize. If Busby had his great trio, Allison had Bell, Summerbee and Lee. It had been a superb riposte. He recalled, in a pleasant Kensington reverie, 'Though I say it myself, the victory at Tottenham was a brilliant tactical success. We had the men to hit Spurs at their weakest point, which was the slowing of Dave Mackay, and all our planning was geared to that. Frannie was required to draw Cyril Knowles out to the right touchline. The Spurs man had to counter those mazy, incredibly powerful little runs. Summerbee, possibly the most aggressive forward in the football league, would strike out to the left, pulling Tottenham's powerful, excellent centre-half Mike England with him. The running and pressure of Lee and Summerbee were designed to set up our big play. This was to give Colin Bell a clear run at the vulnerable Mackay.

'It worked beautifully. Summerbee and Lee at times had Knowles and England stretched 40 yards apart. Bell simply overwhelmed Mackay and we won 3–1. Bell was freakish. He was slowly grasping how much talent and strength he had inside him.

'Later I talked to the great Dave Mackay, who had been such a dominant player at Tottenham for so long, and he told me, "I knew what was happening but I just couldn't do anything about it." It was then that he revealed how he had gone to his manager Bill Nicholson the following Monday morning and told him it was probably time for him to move on.

'We laid siege to Newcastle. About 20,000 of our fans made the journey, and before the game Newcastle's manager Joe Harvey said to me, "This is the first time I've been beaten at home before the kick-off." We knew a point might not be of use so we had to put on a show of tremendous confidence. I was very happy about Lee, Summerbee and Bell. They were still full of their triumph at Tottenham. But then no one could have anticipated the defence would play so badly, so nervously. George Heslop, for a time, froze completely. He panicked every time the ball came near to him and this was alarming. Fortunately, the forwards were performing brilliantly again and we were two up in 20 minutes.

'Our defence, though, was determined to make a game of it. They let in two goals but our attacking rhythm was not affected and we went back to a 4–2 lead, with Frannie having a superb goal disallowed. Newcastle did score again, but despite a lot of anxiety all around me, I felt it was irrelevant, I knew we were home.

'I felt drained in the dressing room afterwards. Lee and Summerbee were jumping in and out of the bath, champagne corks were popping, but I couldn't quite catch the mood. The title had come on a flood tide and I think that deep down I was a little bit stunned.

'It was only back in Manchester at a big party at the Cabaret Club that the scale of the achievement began to dawn on me. We had carried off the league playing football which brimmed with skill and aggression. We had done it with a game that was quite out of the pattern which had been laid down by England's World Cup success. We had proved you could still win something significant with five brilliant forwards. Lee, Summerbee, Bell, Young and Coleman had exploded as though out of a more colourful past.'

Allison took just an hour's sleep before striding into Maine Road the following morning to announce to a crowd of reporters, 'There's no limit on what this team can achieve. We will win the European Cup. We will terrify Europe.'

They didn't, of course; within a few months they faltered against Fenerbahçe of Istanbul in the first round of the great tournament. It was a horror beyond the coach's worst imaginings. Well, perhaps not quite, as he later reflected, 'Only one thing could have spoiled that morning of triumph for me. That would have been the knowledge that within a month, Manchester United, the red cloud over Maine Road, would be crowned European champions for the first time.'

Istanbul was a nightmare for all of City after the impasse of a draw at Maine Road; the crowd was hostile, the opponents variously opportunistic, ruthlessly cynical, and passionate. Defeat, the crushing humiliation of it, would leave a permanent scar on the coach's psyche, cost goalkeeper Ken Mulhearn his brief career at the top of the game, and for Lee represented one of those offences against nature. It also briefly dislocated his belief that he belonged to a team capable of meeting any challenge.

He remembers, 'Istanbul was such a shock to our system because we all believed we had gone past the possibility of such a breakdown in performance. We had played without any inhibition in that push to the title, and we were very, very fit. You see players today who go down with cramps. You never saw a player in that City team go down, however heavy the pitch or whether or not there had been extra-time. We had just trained so hard. We had world-record breakers setting the pace in our training runs – and then we did weightlifting.

'At Salford University they devised a way of training world-class athletes. It was born there and we helped to bring it to life. We were wired up to running machines, and when we were absolutely knackered they used to slit our ears with razor blades and take a blood sample to see how much oxygen depletion there had been. It was all very scientific and we found we were getting an increasingly large audience whenever we trained, and this was especially so when we were on tour in places like Scandinavia.

'Of course, Malcolm loved it. For him it was the stage he had had to leave when he stopped playing. Unfortunately, for us, some mornings it was a case of the bigger the crowd the more he wanted to work us. He would have us running around a Swedish track at 6 a.m., and as we came out for the session you would hear the lads saying things like, "Fucking hell, the TV camera's here and we all know what that means." One year he had us running with big backpacks and with heart-timers fitted. We would curse him often enough but then we knew he was always going to try everything that came into his mind, and we never doubted that he was a marvellous coach.'

The ambush in Istanbul was all the more shocking because it countered the widespread impression that City had, in the most exciting way, separated themselves from the rest of the pack. United, as their triumph over Benfica in the European Cup final confirmed, were still a most formidable team – Best had achieved a remarkable level of performance – and under Brian Clough Derby County were about to join the elite, which still included Leeds United and Liverpool. But City were maybe different, fresher, more inclined to produce something unexpected.

West Bromwich were eviscerated 6–1 in the curtain-raising Charity Shield going into the 1968–69 season and Lee recalls, 'Most people thought we were going to steamroller our way to another title. However, a big problem came to the surface very quickly. Everyone had become a bit frightened of us and so they set up their defences against our style. It checked our momentum quite a bit, though it did not prevent us winning the FA Cup and then going on win the League Cup and the European Cup-Winners' Cup the following season. We were also a bit unlucky not to make that a treble with another FA Cup win.

'However, when we look back there will always be one big question: how good were we, and why wasn't it that we won more? Certainly the four or five extra trophies which would not, I believe, have exaggerated the all-round quality and extraordinary fitness of the team.

'One thing is certain, we were playing superbly going into the spring of 1972 and we should certainly have won our second first division title. I'm sure we would have done if Mal had not signed Rodney Marsh. Hell, we were on fire before he did that. The combination of Wyn Davies playing up front and me playing off him was very strong.

'Basically, I started off as a winger but then we won the championship with Mike Summerbee playing centre-forward, and it was only when we made an indifferent start to the new season I moved back into the middle. Then we were playing pretty much as Mal wanted us to play all the time, with the ball coming to my feet and him saying, "Look, don't give the ball away, because if you get it and hold it we can all join in. If you give it away, well, we're fucked." And that's how we played our way to the League Cup and Cup-Winners' Cup wins.

'When Wyn Davies came he was the target man and I dropped in beside him. I could do it well because I'd had a season with him at Bolton. Most people thought of him as a battering ram but we told him, "Go wherever you want to go and get the ball back to us – we'll play with you, not just try to feed off you." So I got 45 goals that season. Mind you, there were a few penalties and that's when I was christened Lee Won Pen. Then Malcolm bought Rodney, and we couldn't believe it.

'I never gave Rodney stick behind his back. In fact, I tried to settle him down. I took him fishing on the Ribble on a Sunday morning. The problem was that he had come with the image of being the big star from London, and he wasn't. He wasn't as good as three other players in the team.'

Colin Bell was not the least of the dressing-room sceptics, despite admiring Marsh's extravagant skills. He says, 'When I started working in my restaurant on a Saturday night I always tried to slip away and watch *Match of the Day*, and often the highlights featured Rodney at Queen's Park Rangers. I quickly reached the conclusion that he was an entertainer, an extremely good one, but he wasn't a City player, and I believe he always knew that.

'When we signed him we were entering the home straight for a second first division title in four years, which would have entrenched our place in the elite of English football. It would have underpinned that great burst of success in 1968–70 and it would have shown that the work of Mal and Joe had been laid on very firm foundations. Unfortunately Mal's belief that Rodney would add a final flourish, and a touch of glamour to compare with that of George Best at United, rocked everything.

'While watching Rodney produce his tricks on *Match of the Day* you might have thought that his going anywhere would be great, but the more you considered it, the more you speculated on his place in our team, the more you had to doubt it. Mal had developed us brilliantly as a one-touch team – quick, fast and with skills applied in the most ruthless way. This meant that Rodney, for all his touch, was quickly revealed to be a square peg in a round hole. Whenever the issue is resurrected, and I suppose it always will be as long as there are people still around who remember those days, I cannot but help recall a passage of play soon after he joined us: he took the ball to the left hand byline and I nearly burst a blood vessel getting into the box for the cross. But Rodney checked back, went over the old ground he had already won, and so I retreated from the penalty area to await the next outcome. He made the same run and got into the same position and I made my second charge into the penalty area. Again he checked back but then, suddenly, he put in the cross and now the question was, "Where is Colin Bell?"

'The point was that the entire team, with one exception, was still playing one-touch football, with two touches almost invariably the absolute maximum. I must say that as a man I regard Rodney very highly. I always found him a very nice person, very likeable, and he was also an entertainer of great ability. I was never surprised that fans, including the new ones he encountered at Maine Road, loved him. But then I also have to say I never thought QPR were ever going to win much with Rodney playing his tricks.'

Here, at least, Bell and Lee retain a high level of agreement.

Lee recalls, 'Rodney must have weighed 15 stones when he arrived at Maine Road. He vomited when he came training. I like Rodney, I like him a lot; he came to stay with us in Barbados last year, but he does admit he cost us the title. He was Mal's big mistake, and it was such a bewildering one because it went against some of his most fundamental football values; it betrayed so much of his most brilliant work.

'Even with the complication of Rodney's signing – and another problem was that it cost us the services of Tony Towers, a kid who was beginning to play out of his skin – we were still two points clear at Easter, but then we had two very bad results, dropping a point at Coventry and then losing at Ipswich. Ipswich knocked lumps out of us, even though they had nothing to play for, in our penultimate game of the season. There was a rumour that one of our rivals had provided them with a big incentive and that was maybe inevitable because of the physical battering we took. Wyn Davies required 25 stitches in his face. We hit the bar and we couldn't get a penalty when Mick Mills punched one over. We couldn't believe it. It was as though everything had turned against us. I always say that when luck turns against you in football it doesn't matter what you do, or however hard you try, you cannot get it back.

'It happened to Manchester United a few years ago when City won the title for the first time since we did it in 1968. Watching City score a couple of lucky goals, I turned to my son and said, "This is the kind of good fortune that wins titles." United's Patrice Evra headed the ball against the post and then Everton go down the field and, bingo, they score. And that's what happened to us in 1972 – and the rest is history.'

But then if, to use the term employed by Lee as he sighed and drained his cappuccino, the spell was broken it was hardly surprising that before the end of his playing career he would, like some rumbustious Merlin, manage to create a few more of his own.

Chapter 10

No one celebrated so fiercely, or was more central, to the sunburst of City's success between 1968 and 1970 than Francis Lee, and no one understood better the dynamic of it. Thus, inevitably, he was among the first to see that both on and off the field the old certainties were dwindling.

He was not only shocked by the Marsh deal – seeing it as the expression of a fatal vanity in the coach he admired so much – but also by the inescapable evidence that in all likelihood something vital had been broken beyond repair. This was the drag on the spirit of the dressing room. When the title of '72 slipped away, when first Joe Mercer, then Malcolm Allison left Maine Road, it was as though a wonderfully secure and happy home was being abandoned. Suddenly, you could hear a rattle at the windows, a creak in the door hinge, and the requirement was not the kind of maintenance that Harry Dowd, the goalkeeper-plumber, could provide. Nor, it was quickly evident to Lee and most of his teammates, could the new manager Ron Saunders.

It probably needs to be said right away that Saunders was rather more than some passing football adventurer who came blundering into a scene, and a culture, which he could not begin to effectively influence – though that would be the overwhelming verdict on his aggressively pitched but ever-dwindling command of less than a year. He was a hard, free-scoring pro from Merseyside who scored more than 200 goals in the lower divisions, most notably with Portsmouth and Charlton Athletic, and when City summoned him to replace Johnny Hart, who retired through ill health after a few months in charge following Allison's resignation in the spring of 1973, Saunders brought some impressive credentials from his work with Norwich City.

And then, after so quickly crashing at Maine Road, albeit with the brief encouragement of a place in the 1974 League Cup final against Wolves, Saunders proceeded to build a strong and enduring reputation in the Midlands, where he shaped and drove forward a first division title team at Aston Villa and then moved on, uniquely, to also manage that club's ferocious city rivals Birmingham City and West Bromwich Albion.

It was almost as though Saunders's failure at Maine Road, given his accomplishments either side of the experience, underlined the extraordinary nature of the chemistry that had created so much success for Mercer and Allison. As their relationship deteriorated ever more bleakly in the year before the new man arrived, and as Mercer retreated, bruised and disillusioned and not quite believing that it should all be ending in such a raw fashion, there was the terrible sense of a squandered dream.

Mercer left for Coventry as general manager in the summer of 1972. Allison, buffeted by a run of poor results, including a 5–1 defeat by Wolves and an excruciating home defeat at the hands of Mercer's Coventry, moved to Crystal Palace the following March. Allison was coaching in Cape Town when Mercer announced his departure – tersely and with no attempt to disguise a bitter sadness – and he said he was relieved to be thousands of miles away from the scene of the break-up.

A peculiar, precious magic had simply trailed away. The Saunders regime was marked by more than a hint of the barrack square. His voice had a sergeant major's tone. He was on his players and he wanted them to know he was the boss. There was no champagne irrigation, no whimsy, and certainly no riotous changes of pace and mood. This helped him to a much respected place in the roll call of Villa managers, and certainly carried him beyond the record there of an embattled Joe Mercer. But his problem at City was, paradoxically enough, that he wasn't Mercer. Still less was he Malcolm Allison.

Lee is very precise about the time he first sensed, overwhelmingly, that his football Camelot was being divested of so much of the old spirit. 'I saw the decline coming with the arrival of a new chairman, Peter Swales,' he says. 'Swales came in initially as a mediator between two factions, one supporting Joe and the other Malcolm, and then after Saunders had come in and we lost the League Cup final to Wolves, he and another director, Ian Niven, got all the players into City's hospitality lounge and started to grill them. Some of the players complained about the training regime of Saunders, but when they started talking to the younger ones I said, "Hang on, I'm not getting on with this manager but I'm not criticising him behind his back. If you want me to say something about him bring him in here." Swales said, "It's not like that." And I said, "It sounds like it to me and I'm off."'

Lee marched out of the lounge with the sniff of conspiracy in his nostrils and went straight to the coaches' room to speak to a manager who, if he could not embrace, he certainly wanted to see treated as a professional of good standing. Lee said to Saunders, 'The news from up there is not good for you. They're all having a go at you and you're going to find out what they're trying to orchestrate.'

Lee drove home more than ever convinced that he was seeing the end of something that he would always deem precious in the uncertain world of football. The psychological paraphernalia of success, of bone-deep confidence in the certainty of future achievement, was being dismantled before his eyes. He recalls, 'Now I was thinking, "If this guy

Swales was going to be a proper chairman he wouldn't be doing this, he wouldn't be asking 30 players, 'What about the manager? What about the training? What about this, what about that?'"

The Swales regime would never be free of boardroom in-fighting. It is true that there were times, after the appointment of Tony Book as manager and an accumulation of notable signings like Dave Watson, England's commanding centre-half (and such superior and proven forwards as Brian Kidd, Dennis Tueart and Mick Channon), when City reappeared among the elite of English football. They had serious title pretensions for a while, but missing, irretrievably, was that old glorious rush of the spirit and the blood. Lee's first suspicions could never be quite banished.

When Allison made his ill-fated second coming to Maine Road in 1979, Book stayed loyal to his mentor despite his misgivings that the old aura, and momentum, could never be recreated. The reality was that only the ghosts of Lee and Mike Summerbee remained, and the fitness of Colin Bell, it was increasingly evident, had gone beyond anything approaching adequate repair. Allison was a lost, dislocated figure. He spoke of the great days as though they could be revived by the sheer force of his will, but it was clear to even his warmest admirers that he had begun to inhabit a time warp.

Because he was Francis Lee, because his self-belief still had some years to run, he had been able to trace the enactment of his bleak prophecies from still another citadel of success at Derby County. But that didn't make it any easier to absorb.

'At the end of that season, with Saunders gone,' he remembers, 'we went on a tour of Greece. We had three games and won them all. We beat Panathinaikos 6–0, which cost the great Hungarian Ferenc Puskás his job. After the third match, which we also won handsomely, we had a bit of a party for the players and we invited the chairman, who had flown out for the final game. It was all very convivial and the wine was passed around, but despite this I formed the distinct impression that Swales had decided Summerbee and me were strong characters he wanted out of the club.

'When we got back to England Bookie was appointed manager and I was told they wanted to sell me. As soon as I heard this, I thought, "OK, this is because of what I said to the old manager."

'Derby came to sign me during pre-season training. Just before I signed City tried to work the fee up from £100,000 to £120,000 and I told them that these were "barrow boy" tactics. I went straight to Swales and said, "Excuse me, but Dave Mackay, the manager of Derby, is one of my oldest friends in the game and he tells me that you asked £100,000 for me and he has come up here to pay you that amount. Now you're telling him it's £120,000."

'Swales said, "Well, we didn't expect a top club like Derby to come in for you. Maybe a second division team, something like that.' And I said, "A second division team, are you serious? Listen, I'm not playing in the second division and I'll tell you what to do. You better make your mind up because it's either you accepting £100,000 as per the agreement, or me packing up."'

It was the old Bolton routine, the take-it-or-leave-it option guaranteed to concentrate the mind of a football director. Swales tried to engage Lee in a little extended conversation, pleading, 'Hang on a minute . . .' But as far as Lee was concerned there was nothing to talk about. 'I just walked out of the office,' he reports, 'and said to Dave Mackay, "It's all right. It will be £100,000."'

Mackay didn't need telling he was getting value for money. One of his Derby predecessors was the legendary football character Harry Storer Jr, and there was no doubt he would have thoroughly approved of the business. Storer was remembered fondly at the Baseball Ground for his knowing management and his periodic assaults on the language (which included such excruciating examples as 'our success has to be put down to the harmonium in the dressing room' and 'the lad played so well today, I'm going to take him out for a steak with all the tarnishing'). More relevant to Mackay's move for Lee, though, was the occasion when Storer was counting his players as they boarded the team bus before a tough away game. All the players had boarded when it was pointed out to the manager that his tally had reached just four and a half. 'I'm not counting heads,' he explained. 'I'm counting hearts.'

In the cause of both City and Bolton Lee's heart had always beat in the most exemplary fashion, and no matter to what degree he was out of sympathy with the club administrators. His passion for City, and what they had represented at their best, was now given one last and highly emotional expression. 'After speaking to Swales and then Mackay I went straight to the training ground,' Lee says. 'As I did so I couldn't help registering that it was eight seasons since the start of the Mercer–Allison regime and that the training ground was still a borrowed school field.

'I shook hands with the players, the guys I had grown so close to over the years, and then, just as I was leaving, I turned round to them and said, "I'll tell you what, lads, I've got some bad news for you. We've been here all these years, and won the things that we have and made all of that money for the club, and we're still training in a school ground. That shows you the kind of twats who are running this football club. You can guarantee, as long as it is run like this it will go nowhere."'

Mackay explained to Lee the main motivation for his signing. 'I want you to make us play away from home – we've got a nice team with lots of potential but we've got to get stuck in when we go on the road. This is the main reason I've signed you.' And soon enough it would prove a masterstroke. At 30 Lee calculated he had two more big seasons left, and by the spring he had another first division title medal. Looking back, he is convinced that if he had stayed at City that summer, and Summerbee had not been exiled to Burnley a little later, it would have been City rather than Derby winning and then contending for English football's top domestic honour.

'I had a nice start at Derby,' he says. 'They had skilled, quick players and a culture developed by Brian Clough was being maintained by one of the greatest players the game had ever seen. We beat City at Maine Road, and I scored a goal in our 2–1 win. Nowadays when a player scores a goal against his old club the fans don't appreciate it at all, but when the ball went in and I ran around the field all I could think about was Swales, and the thought came into my head, "Right, stick that right up your fucking jumper." It was amazing how all the fans stood up and applauded. You would have thought I'd scored for City.'

If the personal victory was sweet, though, it did not proof him against a little more seepage of the old sadness. 'On the journey home,' he recalls, 'I found myself once again looking back at my City years. I had to conclude that Mal had got carried away. His mistake was the one that José Mourinho is in danger of making today, even as he builds a brilliant career profile. Mal finished up trying to win games on his own, telling the press, "I'll do this or that [or the other]." And, of course, the truth is that no coach, however much a genius, can do this. It is the guys who cross the white line who win the game for you. The coach can never decide everything that happens in a game. Anything can happen. He can set you up brilliantly, as Malcolm so often did and Mourinho so obviously can, but he has to let you play, he has to have faith in you and give you a certain respect and freedom.

'Mourinho is a brilliant coach, as Malcolm was, when he is just working with and getting involved in the team. Now he is doing things like running behind the dugout and giving his son a hug. If Chelsea lose he says he has picked the wrong team, as though everything depends on his each and every decision. There is a lot of Malcolm in Mourinho, and though he has had such a great career you sometimes have to wonder if he might not finish up going down the same path. He thinks he can win games on his own and he simply can't. The point is that once you start believing in your own propaganda you are setting yourself up for a fall.'

In the spring of 1972, when City failed to integrate the new man Marsh and that second title in four years was swept away, Lee and his teammates had the growing dread of witnesses to an inevitable car crash. Lee recalls, 'Mal was going out with Serena Williams of the Playboy Club at that time and their affair was in the papers all the time. Johnny Hart or Dave Ewing would frequently take training, and one morning we were working away at Cheadle under the flight path of Manchester airport when a British Airways plane came over. Alan Oakes looked up and said, "That will be Mal on his way back from London."

'Half an hour or so later Malcolm would be at the training ground, asking how things were going and then saying to Dave or Johnny, "Give them a five-a-side," and everybody was thinking, "He's jumped ship, he's not really interested any more. He's with us but he's not with us." I think it was the same when he moved to Crystal Palace, and then for a little while when he came back to City. He worked on the young players, trying to reproduce the old bite and excitement, but he realised quickly that he faced an impossible task from where he was coming from.

'Later he told me he used to think of how it was in the good days when he played forwards against defenders in 20-minute sessions and the forwards would knock in three or four goals. And how, second time round, the goals wouldn't come any more. He told me, "It was then that I really got to thinking about what players I had first time around."

'I always thought he read too many books about Churchill and Stalin; he read about so many people, and then when things started to go so well, he was no longer happy to be just a coach. Then he wanted to be manager, chairman and, in Portugal, when he won the title with Sporting, he wanted to be president. But then that was Malcolm, and for a few unbelievable years he did seem to know all the answers.'

Apart from his other achievements, the coach created a huge appetite not only for supreme success but that heightened state of mind and fitness from which it is most likely to spring. It meant that even though Mercer and Allison had gone, even though it was no longer such an excitement to go out to the training field, Lee still felt a heaviness on his spirit when he answered the call from Derby.

'When they sold me to Derby I didn't really want to go there, not deep down,' he says. 'For one thing I had heard Manchester United, who were coming back after relegation, wanted me, and that would have been a lot more convenient with their training ground only seven miles from my factory. But then there was no doubt that Derby were a good club, and I helped a very good side win the title in that first season. We might have done even better the following season when I got sent off before the second leg of a European Cup tie with Real Madrid, in which we'd won the first leg 4–1. I missed the second leg at the Bernabeu, which we lost 5–1.

'Yet part of me couldn't get over the disappointment of having to leave City at the age of 30. When you are 28, 29, 30, when you play up front against the best in the world, you know it all if you are ever going to, and it would, I reckoned, be at my disposal, all that knowledge and instinct, to give me two last, good years at City. I do believe they would have done better if I'd stayed those extra years, but a policy decision had been made and the chairman had decided I had to go. They wanted to sign Asa Hartford, the Scottish midfielder from West Bromwich, so they took my transfer fee and used it as a deposit for Hartford, and that was the way the club was going to be run for many years. Players came on hire-purchase deals.'

Lee played his last game for Derby at Ipswich, at the end of that second season, and he discovered that he was wrong about being around the game at its highest level long enough to know all of it, the highs and the lows, the wonderful surges, the unforeseen traps. 'Yes, it's true, I was wrong to think there was nothing new for me under the football sun. I learned something in the last minute of my last game, which we won 6–2. It was that it was possible to score two goals in a minute. However, it did not persuade me that I should go on. I'd travelled too far.'

When Derby made an indifferent start to the new season, Mackay was back on the phone. He wanted a little bit more of Lee's fighting persona. He wanted to get him back in the ring. 'I was on the beach at Newquay when he got a message to me to call him,' recalls Lee. 'When I spoke to him he said, "Do you fancy one more season?" and I told him I didn't really know at that moment, I would think about it. Then I went to Derby to play a testimonial for their old player Alan Hinton. It was against United and I scored two and I said to myself, "Well, nothing's changed." But of course it had. In all the years of playing football and running a business I had always been able to walk down the tunnel, take a deep breath and say, "I'm the best player on this team and only at twenty to five will I know different." But in my last few games for Derby, including the one at Ipswich, I'd tried the same thing and it didn't work. I had to say, "No, you're not the best player any more, and when the bad players are able to get the tackles in and do some hurting the good ones find it very difficult. I suppose it is nature's warning.'

After one last spate of agonising, Francis Lee heeded the warning, and not least influential was the vividness of his memory of how it had once been when playing football that came so naturally. 'The great thing was that you got so much pleasure from it, you were well paid for keeping fit, travelling the world, playing against the best players, and most enjoyable of all was the fact that it was so easy. You didn't worry before a game. You didn't ask, "Am I going to play well today?" The worst case scenario was that you would play pretty well, not pass the ball to the opposition, and make a very good contribution to your team's effort – and you always went out with the expectation that there would be some flash of ingenuity, and then, bingo, the game is stood on its head, and it's all down to you. Often you didn't know quite how you had done it, it had just happened.

'You can get a bit blasé. I remember in that season when we signed Marshy, and I was scoring goals for fun, and the physiotherapist

Peter Blakey announced that everybody had to weigh in on Monday morning. The new routine was that you got weighed on Friday morning, as usual, and then again on the Monday to see what you had done to yourself after the game on Saturday. I saw straight away it was a bit of psychology aimed at Marshy, who was considerably overweight by the standards demanded by Malcolm. (He'd made a similar move in relation to Tony Coleman, who was notorious for staying out late on Wednesday and Thursday nights. A notice went on the board saying, "Any player who is not in his place of abode at midnight on Thursday will be fined two weeks' wages." TC's reaction was to show up the next Friday morning in evening dress. He explained that they had been the first clothes he had laid his hands on.) On the weight issue, I reacted quite strongly. When on the first Monday morning Blakey asked me to get on the scales I gave him a curt reply. I told him to fuck off. When he asked me what the matter was, I said, "Look, I'm playing brilliantly, I'm scoring goals, I don't want to know the reasons, and I'll only get on the scales when I stop playing well. So I'll see you then." When Mal spoke to me, I repeated my speech, more or less, and he just shrugged and said, "OK, I can see where you're coming from." He conceded that the move was only relevant to about 10 per cent of the squad.'

So there, in microcosm, was the playing career of Francis Lee: dynamic, almost seamless in its bestowal of well-being, utterly secure in a cocoon of self-belief. He knew what he could do and, almost unfailingly, he did it. None of it was a mystery to him and he was bewildered, for example, by his impression that Colin Bell did not seem to quite understand how good he was, and how easy it might have been for him to dominate any game he played.

Lee carried that conviction, that self-belief into a new world of horse race training and had considerable success before retiring in 2001, a decision he now considers one of the most prudent of his life. 'I never won a classic but I had some good horses and I was always pleased by my strike rate – for six years I averaged 25 wins a season, which was pretty good when you remember I never had more than 30 to 32 in my string. But some aspects did begin to fray my nerves. It wasn't always easy getting the money in from the owners. It was fine when some of them were winning but it could get difficult when there were injuries and vets' bills and all the hassles that can come in that business. There was also the problem of the lifestyle and finally I decided that if I kept on I would probably hit 18 stone and just keel over.'

It was, though, ultimately a clean severance, with none of the angst that came with his attempt to reshape the football club which, in an earlier life, he did so much to animate out on the field and make his most comfortable, and stimulating, habitat.

His four-year chairmanship of City, from 1994 to 1998, is not quite a closed book because the animosity of Colin Bell still, from time to time, riffles the old pages. There was also a period of friction with Tony Book, another on-field comrade he had come to revere at the height of their success.

He plays out his version of these breakdowns in a familiarly brisk style. If he felt reasons to apologise, if he carried a burden of self-reproach for a failure to bring back days of 'champagne and happiness' to Maine Road – his promise on taking office as chairman after buying up £3m worth of shares – he insists he would find no hardship in the atonement. 'You do your best in life and if you fail you have to take it on the chin,' he says. 'But I can put my hand on my heart and say that I don't feel any such need.

'The dispute with Belly is unfortunate. I wish it hadn't happened because through all of it we still share great days together, but I have to tell you that it's not a pain to me because I can still look in the mirror and say that I know I was a 100 per cent right in what I tried to do when I was chairman of City.

'Colin was sacked along with Neil McNab and the rest of the youth set-up because it had been proved to be inefficient to the point where we couldn't attract young players any more. Scouts were on at me all the time when it was raised at board meetings, and don't forget this is in the minutes. Because of Colin's involvement, when the matter was discussed I handed the chair over to the vice-chairman Dave Bernstein. I made the point that I had a great affinity with a man who was an ex-teammate and a friend.

'The issue had been instigated by then manager Frank Clark and his assistant Alan Hill, who sent in a report saying that our youth system just wasn't working. There were no new Neil Youngs or Mike Doyles or Glyn Pardoes in the pipeline. When Bernstein said in the boardroom, "That's it, we have to do something," I said, "There's one thing you have to do. You have to find a place somewhere for Colin Bell. He's a man who means so much to the club. He only works part-time, after all, and some other role has to be created."

'At that time I was due to take my wife Gill and the kids to Jersey, where I was also going to meet the local supporters' club. I was putting in seven days a week. Before I left, I said to the board and the staff, "Now, make sure you leave it to me to deal with Colin Bell. I'll have a think about the best way to handle this because I certainly don't want to see him blemished.

'I'd been in Jersey two days when the *Manchester Evening News* called me and asked, "Why have you fired Colin Bell?" It turned out that Alan Hill had got all the youth staff in and sacked them on the spot. Belly had immediately gone to the newspaper rather than coming to me and asking, "What's this all about?"

'My first decision was to have them all, including Colin, paid up. I said I didn't want this to go to an industrial tribunal, I didn't want to even think about Belly in that situation. The club lawyer came to me and said, "It's an expensive decision but you have made the right one because I think Colin needs a bit of protection."

'Earlier, Colin had come to my home to say he was angry with a member of the staff who had threatened to punch him. I said to him, "Colin, what do you want me to do? I can't come down to the club getting grown men by the scruff of their necks. I can't punch him for you. Sort it out among yourselves, take him to the dressing room, lock the door and say, "Now, what do you have to say?"

'At the club AGM I was unhappy with the manager when the questions concerning Belly came raining in. Frank Clark had raised the issue, made a manager's decision, but at the meeting he didn't say a word. He should have said, "Look, I'm the manager and I decided on this, which is part of my job." I turned to him and said, "Frank, why don't you say something?" but he refused to say a word. So Colin thought it was my work to get rid of him. If Bernstein hadn't told Hill to get rid of them all while I was away I think the worst of the fallout could have been avoided.'

Lee felt similarly compromised, and ill served, when Tony Book's long relationship with the club was brusquely shattered at the time of Clark's appointment in 1996. Again, Lee pleads innocent of any charge that he treated a hugely honoured colleague with less than due respect. Again, he says, circumstances conspired against him.

He was in Barbados when the axe fell on the man who is now enshrined in the honorary presidency of City. Before leaving, though, Lee met the man who would take over from the fallen manager Alan Ball, and during the conversation he had with Clark, in the company of Bernstein, the prospective boss made a point not unfamiliar in football transitions. He said that he would prefer it if Book, a man of great standing at Maine Road, was no longer around when he took office.

Clark wanted to operate away from the shadow of a man who, apart from his unforgettable captaincy of the great City side, had managed the club for six years in the seventies and had already served two caretaker stints in the manager's office. Clark wanted a clean sheet untouched by the past, and Lee was a little startled and disconcerted when he heard Bernstein say, 'Frank, there are no sacred cows at Maine Road.'

When Bernstein called Lee in Barbados to report Clark's acceptance of the job, Lee – as he did in the Bell situation – said he would cover a situation hugely important to the image of the club. 'I'll deal with Tony Book,' he said.

It was another good intention which Lee swears was taken out of his hands. He says, 'When Clark arrived and addressed the staff for the first time, at one point he stopped and asked, "Where's Tony Book?" Someone said, "Well, he was told not to attend this meeting." And when I heard this, I thought, "Well, this is another stick of dynamite that's been handed to me."'

Lee, for all his success in business, and all the hauteur of his personality on the field, admits to less of a feel for the politics of life, and the implication here is that the ambitious Bernstein, who would eventually ascend to the high office of Football Association chairman after succeeding Lee at City, was considerably more adept.

'I was upset when Tony Book gave a very hostile interview to a Sunday paper,' says Lee. 'Naturally, I reviewed my relationship with a man who I liked and respected enormously. He had said to me some time earlier, "If you want to get rid of me, just make sure my contract is paid off and my pension is sorted out." I said to him, "Tony, don't worry about that, I'll always look after you." And I did.'

However, Book was deeply wounded by the nature of his dismissal from Maine Road and, as the weeks and months passed by, Lee felt increasingly besieged by the impression that he had callously disregarded the meaning, to both himself and the football club, of two of City's greatest, and best-loved, players.

He did, however, achieve a peace with Book that Bell has always steadfastly rejected. 'I happened to be sitting next to him at a dinner of the former city players' association, of which I was chairman at the time,' Lee recalls. 'I turned to Bookie and said, "Tony, let me tell you something, and you know I don't tell lies." I went back through the whole affair, chapter and verse, and concluded, "Now, Bookie, you can believe anyone else you talk to, or you can believe me – but if you believe me you are believing the true story." He thought for a moment, then said, "All right – and held out his hand."'

He would give much for a similar conclusion to the Bell row, and the possibility occasionally returns to him when he sits next to Bell's son Jon, a leading Manchester surgeon and, according to Lee, 'a great, top-notch lad' at the Etihad stadium while watching City's home games. 'It does hurt me because his dad and me shared all those great days, and it encourages me that Jon is always affable and never gives me the impression that he believes I did his father a terrible wrong. Yet I know Colin, I know how stubborn he is, how firmly he dwells in his own world. When we were players I sometimes said to him, "For God's sake, Belly, come out of yourself, you're a great player and you could have the world at your feet." I said this to him when he came on for the last 10 minutes of the World Cup quarter-final against Germany in Mexico in 1970 after Alf Ramsey had pulled off Bobby Charlton in order to rest him up for the semi-final. I said, "Belly, we had this bloody game won and now we're struggling. Take it by the teeth, you can outrun anyone on this field. But it seemed to me that Belly had, to a degree, again stayed in his own zone. Of course, this isn't to say he wasn't a magnificent player, one of the very best I ever played with or against.'

The break with Bell assails one of Lee's most important beliefs about himself. As he said to Book at the old players' dinner, 'You know if any member of our team was ever in trouble, in a bar or anywhere, I would sort it out. I wouldn't flinch from anything, and now do you really think I would do anything so bloody sneaky behind your back?'

He is less troubled by the idea that he failed as City chairman. There will always be sadness that, after promising managerial beginnings at Southampton, his friend and great England teammate, the late Alan Ball, lost his way at Maine Road, and that took away momentum so early in the regime. 'Bally would discuss things with me, and I would say, "That's fine," and then he would go away and do something else. He was every emotional, and because he was such an honest player himself he couldn't deal with what he considered a failure to put in a proper effort. I told him, "Alan, you have to remember the golden rule of employing people is to never criticise them until they're gone. Then you can say whatever the hell you want."'

Lee failed to achieve any kind of rapport with Ball's successor, Clark. 'His assistant Hill would come to dinner here every so often to keep me up to speed with dressing-room affairs, but though Frank lived just a few hundred yards away from here he never came along. He rarely spoke to me then, and he doesn't at all now. One rare exchange, though, was very discouraging.'

It came early in Clark's unsuccessful reign and it concerned Georgi Kinkladze, the mercurial little Georgian from Tbilisi, 'the City of Fire', whose popularity among the City fans was achieved, at times quite stunningly, despite a team decline that would leave them, after two relegations, in the third tier of the English game. 'Frank said he wanted to see me, which was extremely surprising because that often suggests a manager is looking for a rise, but I still couldn't have been more staggered by what he had to say.

'He told me that he and his coach Richard Young were at a loss to know Georgi's best position. They just couldn't work it out. I said, "What! Don't you know he hasn't got a position, he's a brilliant player, and with him you don't play 4–4–2 but 4–4–1 plus Kinkladze and then let him just follow his instincts, because that way he can win you a game at any moment. Give him a fixed position and he's that much easier to mark. You can't tell someone like this where to play. He's a one-off." It was a worry to me that Frank didn't seem to grasp that this was someone who could change his mind three times in a second and still come up with something utterly brilliant. This was because he was a hugely creative player.'

The denouement of Lee's chairmanship was always going to be hard on his spirit, and when Bernstein was appointed in his place and an early move was to bring the former, highly popular player Dennis Tueart on to the board, he had the sinking feeling that his four years of effort were being airbrushed from the history of the club. It was especially difficult for a man who had always heard cheers in his ears, who had won so many of his battles in football, racing and business – and had also been, almost incidentally, a hero of his local cricket club – and it left him with a rare need for a certain consolation.

He could, he told himself, at least say that he'd made a fight of it, tried all he could to help a club he had come to love and with whom he would always be associated. He had also done certain basic things without which Manchester City may never have been so attractive to the Middle Eastern investment that today makes the club potentially one of the powerhouses of the world game.

'Things did not go as I wanted, a lot of my work was frustrated,' he says, 'but I do know something that can never be questioned. When I came in as chairman everything I said so angrily when I left as a player had come true. The club's first public accounts when I arrived showed a turnover of £4 million, and they had bought two players, from Wimbledon, for £6 million. Furthermore, they had bought them on hire purchase, £3 million for Keith Curle, £3 million for Terry Phelan. You didn't have to be Columbo to see that things were not right.

'A million and a half had also been committed to the signing of Alan Kernaghan, who spent a lot of his time at City out on loan, and then soon after I arrived another half a million had to be paid to Wimbledon when Phelan completed 80 appearances.

'When I left in 1998 the turnover had risen to £32 million and we had also put £16 million into the new Kippax Street stand. The club was on a proper business footing, and I have to say that what I inherited was something that had been turned into a personal empire by the previous chairman Peter Swales. He ran the show completely, and I have to say his business instincts were not mine. I found inflated player contracts and no earthly chance of beginning to balance the books. I also negotiated with Manchester City Council for the move to the present stadium and that, too, proved a vital factor in making the club more appealing to investors who had the means to move City to another level. Obviously, I don't claim to have solved all the problems, there was still plenty of work to do, but I can say I had the best of intentions and I left the club better equipped to survive into the future.'

It is, by Franny Lee's bracing standards, the least triumphant of statements. But when I leave him at the door of his Wilmslow mansion his stance is as buoyant as ever. As always, he is saying, 'This is me and I did my best.' One thing is certain. He will never ask himself if, from the moment he drove over the motorway bridge and found himself at Manchester City, he might have tried to do more.

Chapter 11

Someone had to go first, step down from the juggernaut which hurtled Manchester City to the 1968 title. It was not just this old reality, however, that left goalkeeper Ken Mulhearn more sad than bitter when he felt the hand on his shoulder. If he wanted to shout out his anger and his pain he was less sure about to where he should direct his tumbling emotions. He had to admit that he also felt a degree of resignation, a mood that was fuelled by an understanding that he had contributed to his own downfall. This was largely, he concedes now – 46 years after he sat clammy with sweat and regret in the Istanbul dressing room – because at the most vital and encouraging point of his professional life he had done what Malcolm Allison did rather than what he said. He bought, extravagantly, into the style rather than what he should have seen was for him the most relevant content of the great coach.

I meet Mulhearn, a big and notably amiable man, again on a moist early summer morning in the impressive new stadium of Shrewsbury on the outskirts of the prosperous, mellow Shropshire town where he is still fêted for his heroic, accomplished years at the old Gay Meadow ground.

He tells me he had two choices when he paid the price for letting the ball slip out of his hands and into the path of a Fenerbahçe marauder who promptly ruined the coach's boast that City, the new champions of England, would terrify Europe. He could rail against some arbitrary injustice. Or he could take a cold, long look at himself.

When Shrewsbury, managed by the fine old Irish goalkeeper and hero of Manchester United's Munich air tragedy, Harry Gregg, noted that Mulhearn's status at Maine Road had slipped to that of young Joe Corrigan's understudy in the wake of his Istanbul nightmare and made their bid, the goalkeeper was already deep into the latter course of action.

Now, before anything, and like every one of his old teammates, he wants to say quite how much his brief time at City still means to him. He may have set back his career there, he may have mislaid his professional priorities, he may just have been too young and too daft, but he did not commit any wilful sabotage of an experience which, however ultimately flawed, he always knew he would carry to the last of his days.

'It was a different world when I was at City, and my strongest memory is being part of a team,' he says. 'We thought of ourselves in that way before anything else. Harry Dowd and I had a remarkable relationship when you think we were both fighting for the first-team place. Harry, as everyone who ever encountered him knows, was an unassuming guy who thought of himself more as a plumber than a football star. He would say to me, "Who are we playing on Saturday, Mullers?" And I would say "Tottenham" or "United" but it might have been Cheadle Hulme.

'All the players are getting on now, of course, pushing into their seventies, but you can ask any one of them and they would all say those days are deeply etched into their memories – indeed they are still very much part of us. Those were days Malcolm Allison did so much to create – and Joe Mercer, of course. I had just one season in the sun, when we won the title, but it was my fault I didn't play longer there. I ended up playing 10 years for Shrewsbury and I went five years without missing a game.

'No one needs to tell me what went wrong for me at City. It's a terrible thing to have to admit to but I allowed myself to get caught up in the champagne era of Malcolm Allison. It was detrimental to me and it took coming down here to Shrewsbury for me to realise finally that it had to stop. I was caught up in that champagne life and I got lost in it. I thought I'd done everything at City, then soon enough I realised I had come full circle.'

At his first club Stockport County, after years of trial at Everton, the young and, as he says himself, brash Merseysider had been nurtured by another superb goalkeeper, the City legend Bert Trautmann, and now he is quick to acknowledge that his life was shaped by two magnificent practitioners of his trade. It just happened that the counselling of Gregg only arrived after his days in the big time had come and gone. Ironically, his last game for Stockport was at Shrewsbury, where he achieved a clean sheet under the gaze of one of Harry Godwin's City scouts.

'On the following Monday,' Mulhearn remembers, 'I was on the television news signing for City. Stockport got £36,000 and the goalkeeper Alan Ogley. That week Harry Dowd was injured and I went straight into the first team. At the end of the season I'd won a first division winners' medal – and lost my head. I was only young but that's no excuse.

'Instead of working hard, fighting like hell for what I'd got, I took it too easy. It took me 10 years here in Shrewsbury, very enjoyable ones I have to say, to fully grasp the scale of the mistake I had made. I don't blame anyone but myself but, of course, Malcolm was the kiddie, always at the centre of things, and that's how I thought it should be, that's how I should live. The trouble was I was too young, too green to understand that Mal was a one-off – a fantastic coach with his own style, and a big star – and my mistake was to think that I could live like that too, before I had achieved everything within my potential. I just wish someone had got their hands around my neck and said, "Hey, pull your horns in, you've still got a lot to prove, a lot of matches to play, before you can begin to put your feet up."

'I really owed that to myself and the talent I had been given. It was a talent good enough for two world-class goalkeepers to believe I was worth investing in. In my time at Shrewsbury there were a couple of chances to get back into the big time. West Ham told Harry they were interested in me but by that time I was married, my kids were in private school here in Shrewsbury and I was enjoying my life. I was also probably playing the best football of my career.

'I've talked about a side of me that damaged my future, that made me too eager to believe that I had already arrived, but there was a good one and I think I proved that when I played all those years without missing a game. I showed that I could get my head down and concentrate on the business that had given me a good living and so much enjoyment.

'I couldn't imagine all the experiences I would have when I was growing up in Liverpool. Now I think I can look back with some professional satisfaction. I won a few medals in the first, third and fourth divisions, so I tell myself sometimes that in the end I did find the best of myself.'

Mulhearn is plainly a man who has learned the value of living in the real world – one which, good and bad, he has shaped for himself. So he takes the best, and discards the rest, as he fights with a resilient cheerfulness the first effects of Parkinson's disease: 'I grew up in Liverpool with three brothers who are no longer with us – and I certainly had some discouraging moments. Professionally, though, the big nightmare came in Istanbul, where we lost 2–1 in the first round of the European Cup after winning the English title so brilliantly and hearing Malcolm say that we were on our way to the football equivalent of Mars. I played so badly, according to Joe Mercer, that I was responsible for all "three" goals. I laughed about it later but at the time I didn't have the heart to ask him what I had done right when we scored our goal. Talking to lads like Tommy Booth after the disaster, they were very kind. They said that the real problem was that we hadn't scored at Maine Road. Unfortunately I did have, in club football's most important tournament, the kind of game you want to forget – and certainly Joe and Malcolm were quite unforgiving.

'As a young lad I had, quite stupidly when I look back, modelled myself on Malcolm, but then I was a young boy from Liverpool with a bit of a gob so maybe Malcolm resented my swagger a little. Maybe he decided I was racing ahead of myself, trying to invade some of the ground he had mapped out for himself. I probably fancied myself back when my hair wasn't blond like it is today, and possibly he took a little umbrage. So at the end of the day I guess our personalities rubbed against each other. Certainly things were going downhill before Istanbul. Whenever they did press and TV sessions at Maine Road they asked for the big goalkeeper to get in the picture and I was always happy to be involved. This I think brought a little resentment in Malcolm. I may be wrong but I'm sure a few of the other lads would back this up.'

It was possible, you had to think while driving away through the leafy lanes, that down the years Ken Mulhearn may have been a little hard on himself. He had, after all, been catapulted from one football world to another at a breathtaking pace. 'One Saturday I played for Stockport against Shrewsbury, the next I was running out for City against Manchester United at Maine Road. For a little while I suppose I didn't really know what the hell was going on. My main memory of the game, which we lost 2–1, is of Bobby Charlton knocking two in from a distance – and the presence of Denis Law.

'Denis was immense, a huge figure in football and the life of Manchester, and I was a Scouse kid of 22 who had been playing for Stockport. I caught a high ball and there was this figure in front of me. It was the great Lawman and he said to me, "Go left, son, go to my left." And the next time it happened he said, "Go to my right." In those days you could only take four steps and you couldn't bounce the ball.

I took my stepson and his father to a City match not so long ago and Denis was there. He came over and said, "Hello, Mullers, you know I wished you'd kept playing in the first division because I could have scored another 40 goals." And I said, "You're probably right." But that too was how it was, 60,000 people in the stadium going crazy and out of the corner of his mouth one of the great men of football is giving me a little help. In those days everybody mixed together and that included the likes of Law and George Best. Alex Stepney, who made that fantastic save from Eusebio for United in the European Cup final, finished up at Stockport, and we would often talk about those amazing days. There was a wonderful atmosphere in Manchester football.

'My first days as part of it were a blur. Before that first game against United I arrived hours before the kick-off and they had to put me in the Maine Road medical room and calm me down. I'd only had four days' training with them and Harry Dowd broke his finger the same day I signed. When I joined them they said they didn't think I was ready for the first division, I'd been signed for the future. Harry was first choice and I would continue to learn my trade in the Central League.'

It was different in Shrewsbury, so much more measured, of course, but it was a place where a man could take stock of himself and build the rhythm of a life which was still rewarding in a way that he couldn't have imagined, for its ease and status, in the tough streets of Liverpool.

'When West Ham showed interest in me, it made me think again about taking a second stab at becoming a top professional. I was having a purple patch here in Shrewsbury,' Mulhearn remembers. 'I was voted player of the year by the fans and everything was going well on and off the field. I was a local hero, everyone wanted a word with me when I walked down the street. You see, I had learned a lot from my mistakes. It means I'm a bit of a legend in this town – it's a small town but it's a very beautiful one. We've been happy here and the kids have had a good upbringing. I've been involved with the cricket club, and now my grandson is starting off a professional career with Shrewsbury. His

Waiting to strike. The champions-elect prepare for their classic Ballet on Ice victory over Tottenham in December 1967, the nationally televised performance that announced the arrival of a great team. *Left to right:* Tony Book, Tony Coleman, Mike Doyle, Colin Bell, George Heslop, Francis Lee, David Connor, Glyn Pardoe, Ken Mulhearn, Neil Young, Alan Oakes, Mike Summerbee.

Here I come… Malcolm Allison, just one game away from the title, exults at White Hart Lane in May 1968.

Alan Oakes and Mike Summerbee lead the title celebrations at Newcastle, May 1968.

The Newcastle stands are dated
and rickety but the joy is timeless.
Welcome to the promised land.

Home, sweet home. Two north-
easterners, George Heslop and Colin
Bell, savour the title win at Newcastle.

Ringing the bell for the title win. City fans welcome home their champions.

Men on a most serious mission. Alan Oakes, Mike Doyle, Colin Bell, Neil Young and Tony Coleman about to board to train to London for the 1969 FA Cup final against Leicester City.

Joe Mercer waves happily to fans as the train carrying his team to the FA Cup final pulls out of Manchester's Piccadilly station.

Tony Book, on top of the world and the shoulders of Mike Doyle, brandishes the FA Cup.

It's our property… Members of City's first-team squad celebrate the FA Cup win back in the Maine Road tunnel. Glyn Pardoe and Tony Book hold the trophy; *second row (left to right):* Colin Bell, Francis Lee, Mike Summerbee, Derek Jeffries; *back row:* Tommy Booth, Ken Mulhearn, Mike Doyle, Alan Oakes, Ian Bowyer and George Heslop.

Poise, aggression and killing vision: Mike Summerbee on the move.

Some said Allison made Joe Corrigan. *Below*, the England goalkeeper displays all of his own work, at Elland Road in the 1969 Charity Shield game against Leeds United.

© OFFSIDE SPORTS PHOTOGRAPHY

When Francis was on the charge even Bobby Moore was obliged to bend his knee. *Above*, in December 1969, Lee leads City to a 4-0 win at Upton Park.

Tony Book once feared a gold watch from non-league Bath City would be the legacy of his football days. Here he shares the Footballer of the Year award with the great Dave Mackay in 1969. Sir Alf Ramsey is there with a seal of approval.

© OFFSIDE SPORTS PHOTOGRAPHY

Driving on. Allison, flanked by world-record breaking athletes Joe Lancaster *(left)* and Derek Ibbotson, leads one of the training sessions that made City uniquely fit. Colin 'Nijinsky' Bell is a few yards behind Ibbotson's shoulder but, as always, is cruising.

Still the best of times for the partnership that shook the English game with its force and its brilliance. Two more trophies came in 1970 – and hardly a glimpse of a dark cloud.

One more for the road. Allison raises the League Cup at Wembley in 1970 after the defeat of West Bromwich Albion.

Allison with the author at Leeds United in 1976. Third-division Crystal Palace scored a stunning FA Cup upset but the great coach's days of glory in English football were drawing to a close.

name is Harry Lewis. He's my daughter's son and I really think he has a future, especially if he avoids some of his grandfather's mistakes, the biggest of which was to forget my place in the big-time could only be guaranteed by the hardest work. I was keener on the celebration than the work. Harry's just signed pro and he has the same agent as the England goalkeeper Joe Hart. I don't get involved in coaching him, I'm just his granddad, but generally I do touch on a few things which might just nudge him in the right direction.

'I certainly don't begrudge today's players the money that is flying about in the game, but I do think quite a lot of them could put a bit more back into a sport that is rewarding them so well financially. Joe Hart is very good in this respect, in fact I would say he is exceptional. He played for Shrewsbury, starting off, and we both played local cricket to a good standard – and we both played for Shrewsbury at Lord's. He comes back to town quite often but he's such a celebrity with City and England it's quite hard to have any kind of serious conversation with him. Wherever he appears everyone reaches for their mobile phones to take photographs and then they want his autograph. Sometimes I look at his situation and it reminds me quite what a different world I inhabited with that great City team.'

The debt to Harry Gregg, his role in remaking Mulhearn's life and the reordering of priorities, will always be huge. Gregg was the angel of Munich, dragging casualties from the burning wreckage, imposing a powerful demand for survival, but his compassion came from a deeply competitive, and sometimes ornery, nature.

'I realised where I had gone wrong at City and I also understood that if I wanted to play on, and I did, I had to buckle down, and having a great old goalkeeper like Harry in charge of my career made it so much easier. He was very hard but he was fair, and he said, "You wasted your time at City, you should have played a lot more, done a lot more." I could only say, "I will not waste my time or yours here, I know I have a lot more to offer."

'Inevitably, I suppose, I still think a lot about the City days, even though the worst memories – when, for example, I broke curfew with Tony Coleman and was dressed down in public by the coach – have been softened by what happened here. In one way they were for me wasted, even silly years, but there was also an excitement you could never forget. We had taken over from United, we had a manager in Joe Mercer who was a good lad, a real character and, of course, in Malcolm we had a most brilliant coach.

'Many years later I was playing golf at Hoylake with a friend who had come up with me from Shrewsbury, and later I was sitting with him in the clubhouse when the steward came along and said, "Hello, lads, where are you from?" And my friend said, "This is Ken Mulhearn, he played for Shrewsbury Town and Manchester City." That was all that was said, but about an hour later I heard someone coming into the room saying, "It was the worst £36,000 I ever spent in my life." It was Joe Mercer, who lived just off the eighteenth green at Hoylake. I asked him if he wanted a drink, but he said, "No, you're coming back to my house – bring your friend." Joe's wife brewed some tea and Joe showed my friend around his house, pointing out his medals and his caps. But that was what he shouted all over the clubhouse – "the worst £36,000 I ever spent" – and that too was how it was.'

The truth, like a little piece of grit in the corner of his eye, is that for all his confessions of culpability something still rankles deep inside Ken Mulhearn. 'I suppose I did in the end feel that I was harshly treated,' he says. 'I know it wasn't only the younger lads like Tommy Booth who tried to soften the pain. The big lads, Summerbee, Lee and Bell, also came to me and said, "You know you got the blame, it all fell on you, and no one ever came out and said we would have scored four or five goals at Maine Road if we had been doing our jobs." I had one of those games that all goalkeepers have from time to time, but my misfortune – my career disaster – was that it came in the European Cup. That was why I felt for Joe Hart when he experienced a rough time recently. He is undoubtedly one of the great goalkeepers of his generation, but he made a few mistakes in big games and he was pilloried. But then in the end you have to accept it goes with the job; it's the pressure you always have to live with.

'There's no doubt the goals in Istanbul were down to me – at least the ones we conceded and, to be honest, I will always feel responsible. I got a real slating after the game. Malcolm came into the dressing room and went off on one – and so did Joe. It was head-down time. The thing is, you know well enough when you have played badly. When I thought about it I had to agree: it was the European Cup and the last thing you want in such a tournament is for the goalkeeper to play badly. I can understand the reaction now, I couldn't then – well, not completely.

'I thought the pressure on me had been enormous – and that now they were picking on me. The crowd was all around me and it always seemed on the point of spilling over. They were practically in my net. It was not an excuse, and I'll never offer excuses, but it was a hard experience. The Turkish fans had been going around the hotel all night, blaring their horns, and I was sharing a room with Tony Coleman, which was a bit of a double whammy. We had met years earlier when he was selling ice cream on Southport beach, and I was a lifeguard. He was a hell of a character but you never knew what he was going to do next. However, even at the worst of times you had to admit he was a very good left winger, and he and Neil Young did so much damage along that side of the pitch.'

When the curtain fell beside the Bosphorus, when the minarets of the old city became the haunting landmarks of his passing as a top-flight footballer, Mulhearn consoled himself with the knowledge that if closure came with a jarring suddenness it was not before he had accumulated the most durable of memories: 'Even today, I can return to those days as if they were only yesterday. Just a couple of months before we went to Istanbul we had toured America as first division champions and I just wouldn't have believed that my time with the team was rushing to a close. So many of the incidents have entered the folklore of the game. Most vividly I remember arranging to meet Youngy in a certain bar in New York but when I arrived there it was surrounded by the yellow tape of a crime scene. Someone had come in and shot one of the customers, and Neil was very shaken as we walked back to the hotel. "This place is rougher than Liverpool," he muttered.'

It is the part of his life which he knows well enough he has to filter carefully for points of relevance to the future of his grandson Harry. 'I try to explain to the boy,' he says, 'that the most important thing in life, whatever you are doing, is to be able to say that you made the best of what you had. In the end I could say that – and I even had the chance to go back to the big league. But then I believed that with Harry Gregg's help I had built something sound and real after making such a mess of my life in the big time, and that now I had a duty to maintain the happiness of a life I made not just for myself but everybody I cared about. I could finally, and with a clear conscience, settle for my lot.

'I could also tell myself that even in that time which went wrong all those years ago I still helped in the winning of the English title, and this is something that so many of the old pros I meet say they would give anything to be able to claim. I got that medal and I played 60 games for City at one of the greatest points in their history. I got in 60 games – and a thousand memories.'

They spill from him through the Shropshire morning. Old conversations spurt back to life. One came back to him the other day when, while moving house, he discovered old City payslips tied in an elastic band. He had been sitting in the Maine Road dressing room with Tony Coleman at the end of the championship season when they were handed their new contracts. Eagerly, he tore open the envelope and discovered that he had been given a rise of £8 a week. 'When I told TC,' he reports, 'he just said, "Well, I got 12 quid." I said, "Hang on a minute, I'm not having this, you little Scouse sod." But I was also wondering what the big three, Lee, Summerbee and Bell had received. So I went to the trainer, Johnny Hart, who sent me to Joe Mercer. I asked the boss, "How is that I get only £8 and Tony Coleman gets £12?" He got up from his seat and said, "Follow me." We walked out on to the pitch and stood on the touchline. He said to me, "Picture this, Mullers. This pitch is a big well filled with money. I've had some off the top because I'm the manager of the team that's just won the title. Mal's had some because he is the best coach in the game. Colin Bell, Francis Lee and Mike Summerbee play for England so they had to have some too." He went on like this for some time, running through the virtues of different players, pointing out how important they were to the club. And then he said, "Look, there, right at the bottom, eight quid is left. That's yours, now fuck off."

'I said, "OK, thank you, boss." I was showing young Harry the payslips the other day and pointing out to him, gently, how different his world is to the one I occupied. It is underlined by so many comparisons between today and my time, and not least maybe the fact that I understand somebody of Joe Hart's status is paid around £17,000 a week for wearing a certain kind of goalkeeper glove.

'We used to get more in crowd bonus when we played United than in our basic pay, which in my case was £40 a week. We would get £60 or £70 from those games, and then there were the other bonuses for wins and league position. Harry is starting his professional career as a 17-year-old with a top professional agent. He's a sensible lad and I think he will handle things well. He's in the England Under-16 team, he's 6 foot 3 inches, and he is bombarded with all kinds of free kit, boots and gloves, and sponsorship.

'They treat me very well here at Shrewsbury, make me feel part of the place, and when Harry is training I come to see how he is getting along. Of course I'm very proud of the lad – but I'm also very careful to step back. We can talk about specific things like setting up defensive walls but I'll never get involved in coaching him. That's not my job and, anyway, I'm too close to him.'

Mulhearn feels least constrained when advising his grandson on the brevity of any footballer's prime and that vital need to seize every opportunity that is presented. 'It's true,' he says, 'that footballers, like soldiers, live most dramatically at an early age and then run the danger of spending the rest of their lives in anticlimax and maybe regret. My father, Stanley, served in the Navy on the Russian convoys during the war, and then afterwards he worked on the docks. When I first started in football he thought £20 a week was extortionate. When he told me to be in at 9 p.m. five past nine just wasn't good enough. He would say, "You weren't listening, I said 9 p.m." He was torpedoed on the convoys but he never talked about it much. What he did say, though, was, "When I was in the Navy I had to follow orders, and it is the same for you as long as you live under my roof." It was the same when I started training with Everton. He was a stickler for discipline and I never wanted him to think I was a slacker. He also told me that I had to show respect for people around me. I fall out with kids now when they push in front of an old lady approaching a door. I say, "No, you don't do that. You open the door and step back."

'I was always telling kids off for poor manners at the golf club, which I went to a lot before I started to struggle with Parkinson's. Not so long ago I had an argument there when a kid barged in front of me at a doorway. I said, "No, son, you got that wrong. You open the door for me. I think you need to get your mother and father to teach you some manners." My father would have knocked my head off my shoulders if I had behaved like that at home.

'He watched my brother Peter and me play for Everton (as kids) with great attention. Peter was a good, natural player, but he started smoking and drinking, which I never did as a boy. When Peter fell by the wayside, my dad was very upset.'

When Peter failed, his brother fought his own temptations the first time they came around. Ken started as a 15-year-old groundstaff boy at Goodison Park, helping to touch up the paintwork of the beautiful old blue and white stadium where Joe Mercer and his teammates helped to preserve the aura of the legendary Dixie Dean, and where now the hard-headed old player Harry Catterick was beginning to reclaim much of the old glory with the help of some performers of the highest quality, who would eventually include the brilliant midfield axis of Alan Ball, Howard Kendall and Colin Harvey.

'Before I was moved on to Stockport,' says Mulhearn, 'I spent a lot of time looking up to the established stars, like goalkeepers Albert Dunlop and Gordon West, and playing in the reserves with such great players as Bobby Collins and Roy Vernon. Also there was Alex Young, small, blond and, you might have thought, as delicate as a piece of china, and he was christened "the Golden Vision". Our father was a fervent Liverpool fan and Peter and I joked that we only went to Everton to spite him, but I knew that behind all the hard talk he was desperate for both of us to succeed – even if we were playing in the wrong colours.'

Leaving Goodison was as hard on Mulhearn's spirit as his subsequent misadventures in the celebrity zone of the Allison culture at Maine Road. 'The more I think about it,' he says, 'the more I see how I was drawn into the shadow of Mal. He used to come into the dressing room and say, "Put ten bob on this [or that] horse," and then you got a big payout and thought, "How easy was that?" He was big fry and I was very impressionable and so a lot of Malcolm's stuff rubbed off on me. There was a picture in the paper of me wearing a cravat. I did look a dick but you think you are something.

'Neil Young became my chauffeur at City. He lived in Wilmslow, and picked me up and dropped me off at my house in Cheadle Hulme, which was next to the Cross Keys pub. The pub had a bowling green which had a big hedge around it, and soon after I moved in there was a big hole in the hedge because I didn't fancy taking a roundabout route to the bar. Youngy and me were in there one night when the landlord, a City fan, said, "Mullers, are you due home?" I asked him why he said that, and he said, "Look over your shoulder." Our bedroom light was flicking on and off and the landlord asked me what I was going to do. "I'll tell you what I'm going to do," I said. "I'm going to close the bloody curtain."'

Regularly he trawls back through the good days, the good spirit. 'The thing about them,' he says, 'was that though City were a big team, with the "big three" of Bell, Lee and Summerbee, there was no envy, no animosity. I've spent all my life in football and I have to say I've never seen a better player than Belly. He had everything, just everything: power, skill, control. Physically, he was amazing, an absolute freak. I'd catch the ball one second and the next he was gone, running into a brilliant position to receive the ball. He just devastated defences, and never more so than when we beat Spurs in that last but one game before we took the title.

'Bell's speed and power summed up the big difference you saw in the top league after coming up from the lower divisions. Bell was exceptional, and so were Lee and Summerbee. They had so much presence, confidence. Mike could wind up anybody. I remember when Tommy Smith took a kick at him and Mike jumped over his leg and Tommy said, "My, you're a good jumper." Mike snapped back, "Not as good as your Mrs." Tommy chased him all over Anfield but he didn't catch him.

'These are the kind of things which stick in your mind. In one game against Villa, George Heslop had a battle with Andy Lochhead, a raw-boned striker if you ever saw one. They were banging heads for 90 minutes, and then when I walked into the players' lounge George was handing Andy a pint. I don't think it works quite like that today. You knocked lumps out of someone and then you asked him, "What are you having?" I was just a young kid, but I loved this aspect of the game, the spirit of it.

'The only problem I have now is this bit of trouble with Parkinson's. I'm struggling with it at the moment, as they try to get my medication right. One problem is that you get quite forgetful, but I try to remember there are lots of people in a worse position. For some time after I left Shrewsbury I worked as a porter in a mental hospital. I used to say I was never quite sure whether I was a porter or an inmate after all those years of diving at people's feet.

'They were certainly quite rugged days if you were a goalkeeper. It was fantastic the way someone like Wyn Davies could hang up in the air. And somebody like Lochhead would be quite open about the fact that he was going to make you feel the pain.'

Of all the players at Maine Road who still run through Ken Mulhearn's memory, with all their skills, and their foibles – the established stars and the kids trying to push through – perhaps no one is more haunting, or engaging, than Derek Jeffries.

He played 73 league games for City between 1968 and 1973 before Allison, a huge admirer of his skill, took him to Crystal Palace, for whom he appeared 107 times before drifting down the tables with Peterborough, Millwall, Chester and, finally, non-league Telford. Maybe it is that Mulhearn sees in Jeffries some of his own story – and at least some aspects of his own nature.

'Derek was a brilliantly gifted young player and a very funny character,' he says. 'I don't think Malcolm did him any favours taking him to Palace. Eventually he came back to play for Chester, and I must say it saddened me to think what he might have achieved in other circumstances. He had a lovely touch, a natural understanding of the game. He was also a bit crackers, though very endearingly so.

'When I had a pub in Shrewsbury he came to see me and we had some good nights, going over the old days. I went up to Chester to see him play, and there it was again, the overwhelming feeling that this was a kid who might have gone all the way to great and lasting acclaim. I often chuckle when I look back on some of his sayings and his antics.

'At City the young players were sent for driving lessons, and I remember an instructor coming into the ground in a very agitated state. He had just given Derek his first lesson and he said he had to see the boss urgently. He was taken to Joe Mercer's office, where he

announced, "I have to tell you I have just slapped one of your players."
Joe said, "Oh, really, who was that?" and when he heard he said, "Well,
I'm not surprised."

'In the first game against Fenerbahçe at Maine Road we were under
a bit of pressure, conceding a few corners, and Derek came up to me
after I'd just tipped one over the bar. I thought he was going to say
something like, "Watch that guy trying to sneak in behind you," but
instead he said, "Mullers, look at the top of the Kippax, there's a lovely
white pigeon there."

'Once, he was in the dressing room and Joe Mercer asked him what
he was doing. "I'm here for the team meeting, boss," Derek told him –
and Joe said, "Derek, son, do me a favour, fuck off home, you'll only
confuse the issue." But, of course, he was very much part of the team –
and what a team spirit it was.'

Mulhearn says he could eat up a day providing examples but instead
he returns to the old Wythenshawe running track on a Monday morning, when the post-match indulgences had to be run off and the coach
was in an especially unforgiving mood. 'He told us,' Mulhearn remembers, 'that anyone who didn't get round the course to his satisfaction
would have to do it again, and that filled me with dread because I was
a goalie, I didn't really run.

'Colin Bell, who was by far the best athlete at the club, made sure
I got round. He pushed me along. He ran the course quite effortlessly
every time he was asked but on this occasion he also carried me around.
He didn't want me to get into trouble.

'Belly and the cousins, Oaksie and Glyn Pardoe, were the quiet types
but they were never separate from the team. Nor was Mike Summerbee,
even though he would sometimes go off for a night with George Best.
If someone mentioned there was a fans' night in the City director Ian
Niven's pub in Denton six or seven players would automatically show
up. Then when you went out on the pitch and there was the same unity.
Bookie was a magnificent captain. He set the tone. He could hardly

believe that at the end of a long career he had finished up such a celebrated player so secure at the top of the tree.'

And then, for Mulhearn, there was the supreme experience of being part of a team which had so beautifully seized its moment and swept to the title that day in Newcastle.

Afterwards, getting on the coach home with all the blue banners waving and all the cheers ringing in his ears he said to himself, 'This will stick in my mind for ever.' Now he squints in the summer sunshine, stares briefly into the distance and then turns back to the moment and says, 'Nearly 50 years later I can at least say I got that right.'

Chapter 12

There is one easy way to insult Joe Corrigan, not passingly but at a depth that is integral to how he has always seen himself, and I am reminded of this in our first meeting in nearly 30 years.

I had last seen him in Vancouver in 1983 at the home of former Arsenal and England full-back Bob McNab, where he came on a warm summer's day with another Arsenal star of the 1971 Double team, goal-keeper Bob Wilson. They had driven up from Seattle, where Corrigan was concluding a brief stint with the Sounders, and as McNab, in an old Gunners' shirt showing number three, barbecued the crab he had brought in on his dingy from the inlet beyond the great evergreens at the foot of his garden, the football of the sixties and the seventies crackled back into a sun-lit focus.

Now, on this spring morning in Cheshire, Corrigan again exudes the warmth of a familiar and comforting presence as he eases into a booth in the bar of his local golf centre and we order the first pot of coffee. It seems that he has barely aged in all the intervening years. He is, at 6 feet 5 inches, as imposing as ever.

Clearly, he is physically well kept, and the range and the sharpness and the intensity of his memory is also impressively preserved. He is not, I am reassured at once, a man who has been cowed by the years that came after his superbly created career at Manchester City. There is a flicker of angst, it is true, when he discusses his rough dismissal after 10 good years as a goalkeeping coach at Liverpool, a termination administered without grace by the new manager, Rafa Benítez, but he clears it away as briskly as he once did a cluttered penalty area.

Yet, soon enough, there is that sense of a place in an otherwise perfectly grounded psyche where it is necessary to tread . . . well, just a little warily.

The big man inherited a world that had slipped away from Ken Mulhearn and Harry Dowd before the great City resurgence had run, and what hits on the raw for him is a suggestion that still occasionally surfaces so long after he elected himself to the great tradition of English goalkeeping. It says that, for all his dedication, his relentless growth of nerve and courage, physical and moral, and increasingly sound judgement, he would always be a manufactured goalkeeper. It hints, at the very least, that Malcolm Allison was not so much his coach, his motivator, but his Dr Frankenstein.

Corrigan won nine caps for England, aside from the honours that came to him in City's burst of golden years, and he did it in the company of superb rivals like Peter Shilton and Ray Clemence. He was a link in a chain of goalkeepers which was the envy of the world game, one that included such titans as Frank Swift, Bert Williams and, supremely, Gordon Banks. Corrigan is fiercely proud and protective of his place in such a pantheon but he is also, I am reminded quickly, the most agreeably modest of men. He makes clear, straight away, that he would never for one moment dismiss the huge role played by the coach in such a potentially dizzying graduation. And if his predecessor Mulhearn speaks candidly about the damaging effects of fame, of believing too early that his place at the top of football had been safely secured, Corrigan is quick to say that he too might have been unhinged by a rush of success. The temptation was there, all right, and there was a time when an accumulation of weight, and yes, some complacency, might have brought him down. But then time after time he also asserts, as though he is again beating away waves of attack, what he believes to be an immutable truth.

It is that you cannot make a goalkeeper, you cannot reassemble his genes; you cannot turn him into something that deep down he never was. He says it with a passion that resonates through every reflection he brings to the story of his rise to the highest peaks of his most challenging trade.

'I always wanted to be a goalkeeper, from the earliest records of my life,' he says. 'I think anyone could check it out and find that was it. Nothing else. An obsession, really, and it filled my boyhood. I went to St Joseph's Roman Catholic primary school in Sale and I was desperately knocked back when the sports teacher said, "You're not going to play in goal. John Birch is going to play there. You're going to play centre-forward." I suppose he decided on that because I was a big lad, and maybe I might knock in a few goals. But I was still gutted. I wanted to be a goalkeeper more than anything. Goalkeepers were my people, my heroes, they were big and strong and they all had courage, and I wanted to be like them.

'Men like Ray Wood and Harry Gregg of Manchester United, and Bert Trautmann at City, seemed to be larger than life, gutsy and full of character. There was no place for sissies between the sticks. They seemed to be saying that every time they went out on the field and, of course, Greggy proved his courage and nerve at the Munich tragedy when he dragged some of his teammates, including Bobby Charlton, away from the burning wreckage.'

He is also extremely proud of what, when set against the tribal passions of Manchester football, has to be described as a remarkably liberal education. 'My family were Reds,' he says, 'but it never influenced me too much. My uncles Thomas and Brian took me to Old Trafford, where I saw the great Duncan Edwards and the rest of the Busby Babes. They seemed more than anything an advert for football rather than one club. They showed you the game's wonderful possibilities.

'I got a lot of open-mindedness from my father. He was an army man and a boxer. He took me aside one day and said, "Son, there are two teams in Manchester, so if you love football, love it without tunnel vision – take the best of it wherever you find it." So when I wasn't playing football (and then later rugby) for my school, I went to watch United, and then the following week I'd make my way to Maine Road. My father wasn't so intensely interested in football, he didn't get caught up in it like so many of the people, and I think I understood what he was saying about not just seeing one team when two were available. Perhaps if I hadn't heeded his advice, I might not have been dazzled by seeing Bert Trautmann keep goal for City.'

There was a limit, however, to the Corrigan family's willingness to embrace new, broader football horizons. 'One thing I never managed to do was convert all the Reds in my family,' he says, with a shrug. 'And this was even when City were winning everything and I had won my first-team place. It was a time when the leading players were still very much part of the community and the attachment to the teams they played for was nothing less than tribal.'

Given that old ambience, which was so beautifully captured by L. S. Lowry's painting of the river of cloth-capped humanity pouring towards the local stadium on a Saturday afternoon, *Going to the Match*, it was a considerable shock to the young Corrigan to discover one disastrous consequence of passing the eleven-plus exam. His reward, he was aghast to discover, had carried him to a small island of English prejudice, the refusal of the grammar school system to acknowledge the round ball of the world's most popular game.

'The only football you could play at Sale Grammar was snatched in the school breaks. It meant that I had to play rugby for the school team on Saturday mornings and then football for a local team in the afternoon. There was only one bonus. In those days there was no lifting in the line-out, so as a second rower I had to jump high to get hold of the ball. Later on, I felt the benefit of this when cutting out big crosses while being challenged by men like Wyn Davies and Andy Lochhead.

'I left school to go to work as an electrical engineering apprentice at Trafford Park, which was one of the biggest industrial complexes in Europe. I was going through the training school. Everyone got a job then. It was automatic. I played for the training school in inter-factory games but still I wasn't in goal. At half-time and after the game I went between the sticks when lads would be shooting in, messing about, and I was throwing myself all over the place.

'One day a guy came to me and said, "Would you like a trial?" and I said, a bit sarcastically, "Oh yeah, United or City?" But he said he would write away on my behalf. I didn't know who he was going to write to, or for what position he might recommend me, which was a bit strange. All he had seen of me as a goalkeeper was in those little games at half-time and after the match. I don't know if anything came of it but, finally, at the age of 16 I got a place in goal in the Sale and Altrincham Open League, and after I'd played there for a month or so another guy came up to me following a game and handed me a card. It said that I was invited to a trial with Manchester City on a Thursday night in October. It was signed by Harry Godwin, City's chief scout.'

For the teenaged Corrigan it was more than a late invitation to a football recruitment process which until then had completely passed him by. Except, that was, for the unlikely overture from the stranger who had for some time seemed only to emphasise the huge gap between his dreams and any chance he might have of investing them with a touch of reality. The card from Harry Godwin, which quickly became dog-eared, was both thrilling and haunting. Yes, it might, against all odds, open a door. But then it might also confirm the wildness of his dreaming.

'My auntie Beadie had come over from Canada for the funeral of my Nanna and I went to see her the day before she flew home, which was also the time of my trial. I confided to her that I wasn't sure I was going to go. I had a great fear of failing and I told her I had been tempted to toss away the card. I said I would be going among lads who had so much more experience, who had become part of a very demanding selection process. I was an innocent and I couldn't get that out of my head. Beadie insisted I went to the trial, she said it with great force. She said I would never forgive myself if I didn't give it a go. I had nothing to lose, apart from, maybe, an illusion or two, which all of us had to shed from time to time. Her words struck home and I still have them in my head. "Don't let fear of failure get to you, it ruins so many lives," she said.'

So when Aunt Beadie was flying home across the prairies to Alberta, her giant nephew was clocking off at Trafford Park and taking the two-bus journey via the city-centre Piccadilly depot to Maine Road. As he recalls the autumn night, it is evident enough that he has retraced a thousand times the bus route that carried him to his change of life.

'When I got off the bus I walked down Lloyd Street to the ground. The thing that hadn't hit me before when I was going to watch a game was how big the ground was. When you go as a spectator, with a big crowd around you, it is as though the stadium is being scaled down. You don't grasp the immensity of the buildings, you don't take it all in when you're just part of the crowd, but then I felt very much alone as I looked around before getting on the bus which was taking me and the other lads down to the Cheadle training ground where the trial was being held.'

As Corrigan gives the detail and the emotion of almost certainly the most pivotal night of his young life, he is for me fulfilling the purpose of this itinerary of nostalgia that has engaged me for some months now. Like all of his old teammates, he is recreating all the impulses of a distant youth, he is reliving the days of both trepidation and the old exhilaration which had come to us all so tangibly that day of the great coach's funeral. When Joe Corrigan remembers the dark bulk of Maine Road, I am back in Withy Grove, a few miles towards the east of the city, and nervously announcing myself to the reception desk in the biggest newspaper plant in Europe.

The emotions bursting out of Joe Corrigan's account might be claimed by so many of us operating this side of the certainties of a Francis Lee. 'The sight of Maine Road that night, in my state of mind, was simply awe-inspiring. I said to myself, "Oh my God, this is something I want so badly, something I've always wanted more than anything." And I got on the bus carrying all those hopes and fears and thinking, "Could this possibly happen? Could I make it happen tonight?"

'A lot of the boys in the trial were in the City youth team and had signed on amateur forms, lads like Tommy Booth, Ray Hatton (the father of the fighter Ricky), Tony Jackson and Dave Cunliffe. Naturally enough, I felt like an outsider with everything to prove. As it happened, I didn't have too much to do in the game, but I did it well enough, I thought. When we were in the showers back in Maine Road, Harry Godwin came in and said he would like to see me in his office. So I dressed in a hurry, went up the stairs, turned right and went down to the bottom of the corridor. When I knocked on the door he said, "Come in," and I went in there with my heart jumping in my mouth. After a brief pause, he said, "Joe, you have got something about you." I could hardly speak but I do remember managing to say, "Thank you very much." He then told me City wanted to sign me on amateur forms. I said that was fine, though I didn't have a clue how anything worked. Compared to lads like Tommy Booth and Ray Hatton, I was completely green. I thought of my feelings being forced to play rugby while yearning to play in goal, and then my first Mickey Mouse steps as a goalkeeper, and I could hardly believe I was now being asked to sign for Manchester City.

'There was a guy called Dick Johnson in Harry's office. He was one of the youth coaches, and when Harry asked me how I was getting home Dick said, "Oh, we can give him a lift to Piccadilly." So I got in the car, which might as well have been a magic carpet as we went down

Lloyd Street and into town. As I got out of the car in Piccadilly I left my hand trailing in the open front door and Harry suddenly slammed it shut. He was very relieved when I told him that nothing appeared to be broken, [he was] laughing, a little uneasily I think, and saying that he might have contributed to one of the shortest careers in the history of professional football.'

In fact, it was a career that stretched, as player and coach, 44 years. Corrigan played 592 times for City, a mark bettered only by Alan Oakes, and his England career, which started against Italy in 1976 and took him into the 1982 World Cup squad in Spain, would, in other days, have stretched way beyond the nine appearances won under the shadow of the phenomenal Peter Shilton, the nation's most capped player, and his brilliant understudy Ray Clemence. His consolation, beyond being three times voted City's player of the year and winning the Man of the Match award in the two 1981 Cup final games against Spurs, was a widely accepted place alongside the City legends Swift and Trautmann.

'I would have settled for a fraction of that as I rubbed my hand on the bus ride home to Sale,' says Corrigan. 'I had some conflicts to deal with back at the factory training school. My night-school obligations clashed with training at City and my father said to me, "Joe, you are going to have to resolve this. If you give up on the engineering and the football doesn't turn out as you hope, you're going to have a very big problem."

'Unknown to me at the time was that on the Monday after my trial, Harry gave a report to Joe Mercer and Malcolm Allison. He said he was intrigued by the prospects of a big, raw young goalkeeper, adding, "He is either a clown or someone who one day might wear a crown." Down the years Harry and I used to laugh about this [but] back in those days I was no doubt more of a clown than a jewel in anyone's crown.

'If I did wear some kind of crown in the end, Malcolm was the man who did so much to fashion it. He was the key to my progress. He said he was going to work me as hard as I could take it because he believed I was going to make it. More than that, he swore he would make me an international. Now, when I look around the current game and see how kids are processed from a very early age, I know such a thing could never happen again. You just couldn't have a kid without any background coming into a club as late as 16 and then going all the way.

'We have a huge problem in coaching in this country, and that is why so many foreign football men are coming into our game. It is an area of huge neglect, rooted in the past and getting worse. You don't like knocking the Football Association all day and all night but somebody has to face up to the fact that we are paying for what happened in the past or, to be more precise, what didn't.'

Prodded by Allison, supported by his father, Corrigan accepted professional terms of £10 a week and walked away from the factory – after being told by a training school teacher, 'Joe, you're making a huge mistake, football is such a precarious business and here you have a job for life.'

His agony of decision was brief enough. He thought of what Aunt Beadie had said, and then his father made a speech that has always been a guiding light: 'Dad said to me, "Think about it hard, Joe, maybe it is the most difficult decision you'll ever have to make, but be sure I'll back you whichever way you go. Remember, too, that you have only one life and you have to make the best of it. I'll be with you every step of the way."'

In a year, he was in the first team. Again, he is able to unfurl every detail of his rite of passage: 'It was a League Cup tie against Blackpool. City had bought Ken Mulhearn from Stockport, but when Harry Dowd was injured it gave me my chance because Ken was Cup-tied and I had had a run in the reserves with Harry out of the picture. So one morning I walked out of the dressing room and Dave Ewing, the trainer, said, "Just stay there, don't move," and when Big Dave said to do something you tended to do it.

'I stood outside the dressing room at the bottom of the stairs for about 15 minutes. When Dave returned he barked out, "Be back here no later than 4.45, you're in the first team tonight." It didn't really sink in and when I got home I told my Mum that I had to go to bed. When she asked why, I said, "Well, I've been told to do so, and I've been told to do this, do that, and to make sure I don't eat anything heavy. I'm playing in the first team tonight." I kept running the fact through my head.

'When I got back to Maine Road, Mal took me to one side and said to me, "Don't worry about it, circumstances have given you this chance and you just have to go out and do your best. If you do that you will be fine. This is a great day in your life, enjoy it, be natural." I got changed quite deliberately, did my warm-ups and then went out on the pitch. Before this night the biggest crowd I'd played in front of was 15,000 at a Youth Cup tie against United. In those days the fans used to come out for the youth teams because they wanted to be informed in their anticipation of the future. It was a good subject to chew over at the workbench.

'Fifteen thousand is a big enough crowd to play in front of but there were nearly 30,000 for the game against a Blackpool team that was still very decent. They still had the veteran England full-back Jimmy Armfield, and Tony Green, a little Scot, was a top-notch attacking player. It suddenly struck me that 30,000 is really quite a lot of people. For all of Mal's calming talk, it hardly helped that many of them would have read his pre-match comment that, "I'll make Joe better than Frank Swift." That, I thought quite ruefully, is a nice little millstone around my neck. Big Swiftie, who'd died nearly 10 years earlier in the Munich air tragedy while working as a sportswriter, was still revered by the City following. He had long been a Maine Road legend. Those who had seen him never tired of telling a new generation how great he was, and it was the supreme achievement of Bert Trautmann to be quickly embraced by the crowd after the big man put down his gloves.

'But then if I thought the comparison with such a great player was a terrible burden when I went out on to the field it was nothing to how I felt when I touched the ball for the first time just before it ran through my legs. As I picked the ball out of the net and booted it downfield I could just hear all those thousands in the main stand and the Kippax saying, "Better than Swift? Allison must be joking."

'Before the game Mike Summerbee had said to me, "If there are 15 minutes left and we need a goal just start kicking it long." The tactic worked and we finished up with a 1–1 draw. We got so much on top of the game I just wanted to find the biggest spade ever made and dig the biggest hole in which to throw myself. Mal's Swift statement had heaped up the embarrassment level, and had it happened away from home it would have been completely horrendous. As it was, some of our fans were quite supportive.

'With Ken Mulhearn free to play in Saturday's League match, I was back with the reserves. There, I was told that despite my calamity I would be playing in the second game at Blackpool if Harry Dowd didn't pass fit. When I got to the hotel in Blackpool, Dave Ewing said that it looked as if I would be playing so I should get a quick meal and plenty of sleep. That was so much easier said than done at that delicate point of my career. However, I played well, making two particularly good saves from the always dangerous Green. It meant that when I got on the coach for the ride home I could feel happy that I had come through my first major crisis as a professional footballer.'

That was his first exposure to the Big Show, the touching point between fantasy and real life. If Corrigan had to return to the margins of a dramatically emerging championship side for the best part of two years, with Mulhearn claiming his title medal and then, a year later, Dowd enjoying his Cup final glory at Wembley against Leicester City, he had an increasing sense of the rewards, and the excitement, now within touching distance.

'It was a time when I had to work so hard under the tutelage of Malcolm, accept all of his demands, and understand that this was so vital if I was to convince myself I might indeed be a permanent part of this new world. We were knocked out of the League Cup in the next round against Fulham, but I was taken down to London as cover for Harry and though I didn't get to play I had the clearest idea of how it would be rubbing shoulders with men like Frannie Lee and Mike Summerbee. I knew I had to be patient, but in London I said to myself, "So this is what it is like being on the big stage." After the game my roommate Tommy Booth and I went out on the town, and I remember the awe I felt when we went into a nightclub which seemed to be part of another planet, where a hostess showed us to the table by torchlight. I also remember venturing to the toilet, groping through the dark, parting curtains and feeling that I was indeed entering another world. In the subdued lighting of that opulent toilet, though, I did see something that was rather less thrilling. It was a discarded syringe.'

What the young Corrigan didn't know was that all of his hopes might have foundered, or at least been seriously set back, by one of those examples of football's precarious plot lines against which he had been warned about back in the factory. The advance of the precocious Shilton at Leicester had endangered the place of the great Gordon Banks and his club let it be known – three years before he made his save of the ages against Pelé in the 1970 World Cup – that he was available for transfer. The fee, which seems so quaint now, was at the time considered exorbitant for a goalkeeper: £50,000. Allison argued strongly to Mercer that City should make the move, and it was an opinion shared by Francis Lee, who says now, 'I certainly believe that if Mal had got his way, we would, speaking quite conservatively, have at least doubled our haul of four major trophies. Any man of football will tell you that the most important player in the team is the bloody goalkeeper. He lifts everybody, and the fact was that Banks, for all the promise of Shilton, was still the best in the world. Stoke's Tony Waddington, who had made a career of drawing the last of the best of great players, didn't need telling twice, and when he pushed through the deal he had an expression on his face of someone for whom all his Christmas Days had come at once.

'However, none of this detracts from the fact that Joe became a fine, ultimately magnificent goalkeeper,' continues Lee. 'It was just that he was at a very early stage of his development when Banksie became available. After making very good progress, Joe hit the crossroads. He was over 15 stone but to his great credit he understood what was required and made a supreme, career-shaping effort. He honed down to less than 14 stone, which for such a big man was very lean indeed. Technically, also, his improvement was immense.'

Crucially, the big young goalkeeper never lost sight of the rewards he had at his fingertips. Not the least contribution to this understanding was the day he travelled with the rest of the City reserves up to Newcastle for the title decider. 'We went on the bus that was going to bring the first team home from the game,' he recalls. 'The plan was for the reserves to take the train back to Manchester. During the match Ray Hatton and me were standing behind the City dugout and completely immersed in a brilliant game. When the final whistle came and City had the title Ray and I went over the wall with the rest of the crowd.

'Before that it had been incredibly exciting and a lot of that had to do with the fact that George Heslop, who had been such a brilliant contributor during the campaign, seemed to lose the ball whenever he went on his up-field travels – and Newcastle scored. You could hear Mal bellowing to George, "Get back, get back." But then everyone was up when we survived for the 4–3 win. John Hart, the great old City player who was now first-team trainer, got hold of Ray and me and told us to stand in the corner of the dugout and then to come to the dressing room once the field had cleared. When we got to the dressing room the champagne was flowing and we were wide-eyed. We also forgot about the need to get to Newcastle station for the train. After running down the sloping street outside the ground, we realised it was hopeless and so we had to return, very sheepishly, to the dressing room. Ray said to me, "I suppose we ought to try to get back on the first team bus." And I said, "Ray, you must be joking, they've just won the fucking title." When we explained our plight to Dave Ewing, he spoke to Joe Mercer at the door of the bus. The boss said to us, "Right, get to the back of the bus, stay there and shut up." So there we were, Ray and me, the kid reserve players gatecrashing one of the greatest nights in the history of our club. When we stopped somewhere in Yorkshire for dinner we agreed we were the luckiest lads in the world.'

There it is again, something I have encountered throughout this journey back to the heart and the joy of an old football team. And this is so even as they are asked to contemplate the ever-spiralling riches of the men who play the game in which they rose so high, and for financial rewards which would bring a sneer of disbelief to the lips of the agents of today. It is the lifelong gratitude that comes with the sense that, for once in your life, you were in the right place at the right moment and that the experience, whatever came in its wake, would bring an enduring brightness to all your days.

Corrigan re-conjures a hundred moments which down the years serve to strengthen that conclusion. Quite a number concern, ironically, the teammate who had most difficulty in absorbing the team ethos which Mercer and Allison saw as so central to all their work, the resolute loner and frequently troubled Tony Coleman. 'TC was a hell of a character,' says Corrigan. 'I remember very well one of my early games for the reserves. We were travelling to Sheffield United. Tony had been dropped from the first team for disciplinary reasons, and he sat across the aisle from me as we rode over the Pennines. He stared out of the window with a very miserable expression on his face. Dave Ewing came down the bus with a big wad of 10-shilling notes in his hand, and one was handed to each of us. Usually we would spend it on fish and chips on the way home. When TC received his 10-bob note he scowled and said, "I don't want your money, give it to him," pointing at me. We got a 1–1 draw at Bramall Lane and I played well. So I was very happy going home with a good feeling about that – and also having an extra 10 bob in my pocket.

'We don't have a lot of contact with TC these days. A few years ago he amazed everyone by turning up at an old players' gathering, but he did happen to be wearing, of all things, a red jacket. At the end he just seemed to fade away at City, after two extremely good years. He played a big part in winning the title but he was disappointed with his performance in the Wembley Cup final, and though it was sad it wasn't surprising when he suddenly signed for Sheffield Wednesday before drifting off to South Africa and then spending some time in Australia. The last I heard he was in Thailand.

'Mal had to fight hard to sign him – Joe was aghast at his disciplinary record – but his reward was two very productive years. It seemed something went out of him when he disappointed himself in the final, which started so brightly when he brought a big smile to the face of Princess Anne by saying, "Give my regards to your mum and dad."

'It was sad the way it turned out for him because my overwhelming memory of those years is how we grew up as a team, how we fed on each other's growing confidence, and there was so much humour. For a while TC made a good, and often hilarious contribution, but there was something he carried inside him which prevented him from going the distance.'

For Corrigan the Coleman story has special poignancy in that it was so out of sync with the flow of that dressing-room experience. 'The rest of us seemed to grow up in the team because it seemed so clear that we had found a perfect football scenario,' he says. 'Joe Mercer was a brilliant father figure, he understood the ways of the directors, the media, the world, and he gave us a discipline and an understanding of the need for restraint in those days when Malcolm, for all his brilliant inventions, could go sailing over the top, both on and off the field.

'Malcolm was simply the most fantastic coach and if sometimes I respond angrily to the idea that I was manufactured – some kind of robot goalkeeper with someone else flicking the switches – I have to hold up my hands and say that he brought all his knowledge and his passion to the challenge of improving my game. He could be so fresh, so inspiring, that sometimes I walked away from the training ground shaking my head and saying, "This guy is just phenomenal."

'Early on under his regime I did think, "Why am I running into the furthest corners of Wythenshawe Park when the longest distance I ever have to cover on any occasion during a match is 18 yards?" But he straightened me out briskly enough, saying, "If you can't run around this park you won't be able to turn the 18 yards quickly enough. First you need your basic fitness, then you have to work on speed."

'I put weight on in my first season in the team but I was reluctant to face up to it. I pointed out that if I was 15 stone I was also an extremely tall lad. I also argued that I was sharp, but there it was, I was dropped just after we had beaten Manchester United in the League Cup semi-final, and I thought, "Hold on, we're in Europe, we've got a League Cup final coming, and he's left me out of the team." I was hurting quite a bit at that time, which was an unusually important one for me because I had decided to get married after the club announced a summer tour in Australia. In the end I concluded that Joe had made the decision to drop me and Malcolm had gone along with it – and then told me that he was going to work as hard as he had ever done at anything to get me back into the team. Mal said to me, "You're a big kid who has made a huge amount of progress but you've still got a lot of work to do, and at the moment you're in danger of letting yourself go." I listened and I battled on, and in the process I learned that being a goalkeeper fighting to restore his self-belief can be a very lonely existence. I was dropped in the December and brought back at the end of January, so I had a month or so to think about things. It was not an easy period, especially with my decision to take on the responsibilities of marriage, but I knew

I couldn't dodge the big issue. You could boil it down easily enough. How hard was I going to fight to keep my career on course?

'It turned out that I had fought hard enough. Joe told me I was back for a game against Wolves, and that as we approached a series of massive games neither he nor Mal, despite the decision to drop me, had doubted that in the end I would be the man for the job.'

This was indeed the blossoming spring-time of his professional life. When the team bus arrived at Wembley for the League Cup final against West Bromwich Albion, the coach put his arm around Corrigan's shoulder and said, 'Go up the tunnel now.' As the rest of the team settled into the dressing room, and began their usual pre-game rituals, the big goalkeeper walked up the tunnel alone.

'It was a little bit like walking through a waterfall – or maybe parting an invisible curtain. It was an experience that you knew you were experiencing very deeply but one which you probably would never be able to explain properly. As I walked up the tunnel the noise level out in the stadium grew a little higher with every step. Mal had also laid down that I walk to the middle of the pitch.

'So I stood there at the centre of one of the world's most famous football fields quite alone. So many thoughts flashed through my head. We had just come back from Coimbra in Portugal where we had taken another stride towards the European Cup-Winners' Cup final in Vienna. The Wembley pitch was like a ploughed field after the Horse of the Year Show but it didn't take anything away from the fact that this was the ground I had always dreamed of occupying.

'It was only later that I would see clearly the value of Malcolm's instructions. He wanted me to absorb all of the atmosphere, all the distractions and awe that most people in my situation would experience, and then focus entirely on what I had to do when the match started.'

If we needed a microcosm of the growth of the football team's ethos Joe Corrigan's account of the final would serve well enough. 'Albion got their noses in front,' he recalls, 'when George Heslop backed off Jeff Astle and stood on my toe. This meant I couldn't get up for a cross and Astle nodded it home. I'm not blaming George, it was one of those things that can happen in a game, and I have to say I was confident the character of the team would carry us through. The captain, Tony Book, came up to me and said, "Now's your test, don't do anything silly, this is what you've been working for all this time." At half-time he gave me more encouragement. It went to extra-time after Mike Doyle equalised, and then Glyn Pardoe got the winner. It was what we had come to believe would happen, and Bookie's words and my experience before the game were so important to my state of mind. The support of my captain was brilliant after we conceded the goal and if there were some flashpoints of anger when it happened all my teammates helped to restore my confidence. He goes from name to name in a familiar litany but maybe it is only when he goes beyond the days of Mercer and Allison, when Book the captain-turned-manager was attempting to make a second phase of the extraordinary rebirth of a great football club, that he gives you the full weight of his regrets when the first glory had passed. It is provoked by his recall of the fate of Colin Bell: 'Belly, as everyone knows, had a quiet character, but his influence was in his example and it helped so much that he was such an incredible athlete. He slaughtered everyone in training, and on the field he could do every-thing: he could score goals in every way, he could defend, he could run all day and demolish any opposition. When Bookie was attempting to build a second great period, and [throughout] the coming and going of Ron Saunders, the loss of Belly through injury was just devastating. It stopped us. It took away our deepest strength, it took away our heart. It took away belief in the second stage of our progression. We never replaced him because he was irreplaceable.'

He covers the bleak terrain of the team's lost horizon with the same kind of sadness that you encounter in all of his old teammates. It is the regret of misadventure that cried out to be corrected, though there is a particularly raw edge when he discusses the Rodney Marsh episode: 'It was a tragedy when the Marsh business exploded around us in the spring of 1972, when it seemed we had the race for our second title in four years won. When Rodney said that the reason we lost the title was that I was in goal I had to make the point that we were clear when he entered the scenario. Nobody had a problem with Marshy joining the club, no one could question his talent, but the trouble was that he was rushed in after suffering an injury and getting unfit at QPR. It didn't help that Tony Towers, who we christened "the Growler" lost his place despite being in magnificent nick and getting more confident with each game.

'Everyone in the dressing room knew that the decision to play Marsh, not to buy him, was wrong – and we all had to suffer the consequences. I like Rodney. I don't get on with him, as I do, say, Tommy Booth, but I have a laugh with him easily enough and I'm the first to acknowledge that he had fabulous skills. Yet I just don't think there is any question that it was at the time of his arrival in Manchester when things started to go seriously, and irreparably, wrong. Soon, Frannie had left for Derby and another title, and Marshy stayed; Mal and Joe went their separate ways, and the new chairman Peter Swales wanted City to be another Manchester United.

'I got on with Swales well enough. I was prepared to believe he had his heart in the club, but the problem was the way he went about things. He didn't seem to understand the basic demands of a successful football club, which have so much to do with a mutual respect between the directors and the professionals who have to go out and do the job.

'When Ron Saunders was appointed manager I'd just had my jaw broken and then wired up. I was out six weeks and could only take in liquids. In that time I lost about a stone. One day the manager asked me how I was doing and I told him I was feeling better, I was on my way back. He said, "That's good because I see you as my first-team goalkeeper." When I got back into the team we lost to Sheffield United and

Manchester United at home and I made a couple of mistakes. I heard stories that he wasn't happy with me, he had made a mistake in picking me. And then he left me out of the team. One day he took me into the gym and said, "I'm going to smash some balls at you and I want you to dive out of the way," and I said, "For fuck's sake, Ron, I've had enough trouble diving into the way of the ball."

'But that was the way he was and he did have the problem of dealing with strong characters like Lee and Summerbee, Doyle and Marsh, who made it clear that they didn't like the new methods he had brought in after Malcolm. The reality, though, was that he was the new manager and you could do one of two things: go against his style of management, or conform. Most of the players didn't want to conform because of the way it had been with Malcolm and Joe. It seemed to the players that it had been too easily forgotten that all the success in such a short time had come from some brilliant players responding to a manager and a coach they had come to love. Adapting to Ron, it has to be said, seemed just a little too much to ask.'

There would be other adaptations to attempt, with varying degrees of success and satisfaction, down the ensuing decades of his football experience, but as still more coffee arrives, and the sun begins to dip towards the Cheshire tree-line, Joe Corrigan makes it clear he has a few more things to say about those few years which he will always believe formed the time, the great buttress, of his life.

Chapter 13

The compulsion to linger in the company of a man like Joe Corrigan is triggered not by any hurtling pursuit of mythic Good Old Days. No, the promise is in his account of how day by day, year by year, his experiences have conditioned his reaction to each passing football age – and each new set of values that has been imposed at dismaying, often wrenching pace.

It is not *The Footballer's Tale* of a pilgrimage but a journey of discovery, of himself and those of his companions down an extremely long road. He moves from narrative to reflection as quickly as he was once required to shift the ball out of Manchester City's penalty area to the feet of a Bell or a Lee or a Summerbee, and then he goes back again. It is not so hard to be drawn into the rhythm of it. One flaring, passionate example is when he recalls the career-wrecking injury of his beloved teammate Glyn Pardoe.

'It was a tragedy when Glyn broke his leg at Old Trafford in a naughty tackle by George Best,' he says. As he does so he is not only back in that wretched moment but also re-engaging a fierce proprietorial pride in who he was and the company he was keeping. 'The bone was sticking out through his sock and we found out later that the artery in the lower part of his leg was wrapped around the broken joint. It was only the skill of the surgeon that saved his leg. George had left his foot up and that was the damage done. We were in shock, really. Doyley stood over him and said, "What's the matter with you, you've got another leg, haven't you?" It was a sort of defensive reaction, you know, "Thank God, it's not me," and at the same time you are trying to make light of it. It was, I suppose, a knee-jerk reaction to the tragedy of one of ours, a guy who is the same today as he was then – an utterly reliable, decent guy.'

The flashpoint of memory, as it does so often in our conversation, provokes a broader sweep of recall. 'Do I think back to those days? All the time. I suppose most people build up the greatest days of their lives, but in our cases they all came so very quickly, very brilliantly, and when it was over it didn't take you any time at all to realise that you would never be able to replace the feelings you had in a dressing room like that.

'The field was where you did your job, the dressing room was where you learned to deal with the pressures which came with it. Your life was centred on the dressing room, it was where you got your strength, your understanding of who you were and what you had to do. That was the achievement of our dressing room; that was where we became the people we were, people who had learned how to win. We were working-class lads who had come to understand how important it was to respect each other. We respected our elders, coaches, manager and senior players. If a senior player told you to jump, you jumped. You didn't query whether it was right or wrong. Of course, it was a different kind of society we had grown up in. When I was a boy you knew you could go to a game and be safe. You could sit by your dad or your mum or other members of the family without a care in the world. Then, later on, you knew that nobody was going to interfere with you when you had a pint.'

But then nothing is entirely straightforward and, for the young Corrigan, there were some complications in his idyll when he began to encounter the foothills of what in those days passed for celebrity:

'When I grew older people began to know who I was: I was a local boy making good, and I had an experience that jolted me – no, more than that – it hurt me.

'It happened after I bought a car, a Ford Cortina 1600E, which, I suppose, reflected my new status along with the fact that I had also bought a house near my mum and dad. I was driving home after visiting my parents when I saw my cousin, Thomas Finbar Corrigan, walking along the street. I stopped to ask him where he was going and when he said he was off to see some friends in Sale I told him I would give him a lift. After he got in the car, he said, "Joe, I don't feel right." I asked him what he meant, and he replied, "You're Joe Corrigan." I said, "Of course I'm Joe Corrigan, and you're Thomas Finbar Corrigan, what the fuck are you on about?" He said it just didn't feel right travelling along with me, it was as though I had become a different person, and I said, "Thomas, please never feel that way. I'm your cousin, I'm your blood, and this hasn't changed."'

It was an experience which still helps soften Corrigan's view of what today so often appears to be the hopeless disconnection of the modern plutocrat player from the rest of society.

'Certainly I thought of that strange meeting with my cousin when jeering fans gathered around Wayne Rooney's mansion in Prestbury after he had asked United for a transfer,' he says. 'There was a picture of him staring morosely out of his window, and it made me wonder how he was coping inside after moving so far away from his old background in the backstreets of Liverpool.

'People are probably right to think that a lot of today's players are detached from everybody else's reality, but then there are pressures along with the rewards. Now a kid signs for a club's academy at the age of eight and his parents see a Rooney earning £300,000 a week and buying a big pile in the stockbrokers' belt and they build up their hopes for a great life built around a little boy. Yet he can be told at the age of eight or nine that he is not good enough. Come on.

'I was 16 and more than six feet tall when I got down to the big challenge of my life, and now I look at a kid from Malaga, Brahim Abdelkader Diaz, signing for City with £300,000 paid up front and a total cost estimated at £2.4 million, and for all his precocious ability we don't even know if he is going to have the endurance and the character to make a top-flight footballer. One early estimate is that he will repay all the investment with a valuation of £40 million. How is the kid going to operate under that kind of pressure? Really, it is unbelievable that such situations come to exist. There are so many questions. How are his family and advisers going to react to every fluctuation of form and strength and commitment? Are they going to create a stable atmosphere around him? You have to worry about the odds. How many are going to go to the family home, which will be so far removed from their origins and all that is familiar and reassuring, and say that they are the people to give the best advice on how to handle his career and all the financial possibilities?'

He draws back, shakes his head – a man contemplating a series of nightmares, a sustained assault on anyone's ability to keep themselves anchored in something as blessedly simple and inspiring as hell-bent ambition. He says, 'When I came into the game it was just a matter of achieving something for myself, something I wanted more than anything else. I didn't think of a flashy car or a mansion in Cheshire. I thought of being a goalkeeper, going out to play. And I could go about that nurturing of my dreams without a legion of hangers-on pushing me in one direction or another. I had Malcolm Allison kicking my backside, or putting his arm round my shoulder, and I had Harry Godwin giving me a sweet from the packet he always kept in his pocket.

'You can't guarantee anything in football and, of course, the focus has changed so much since I stopped playing. In my time you thought you were part of a little world in which everyone was pursuing the same hopes, the same ambition, and it was not so much a case of grabbing personal advantage and the next contract. Now, there is so little contact

223

between players and the rest of the world, except in staged, commercially favourable circumstances.

'When I look back at my early days in the game I must say I do it with humility. People talk about legends but I'm not a great believer in that word. More than anything, I think some people are lucky to be in the right place at the right time and surrounded by the right people, and that what has separated them from the rest is that good fortune. I sometimes wonder how many kids would become "legends" if they had the right help and the right encouragement in the formative stages of their lives.

'The truth is that I don't think I would have made it in today's system of such early selection and huge contract scales. My humility comes from the fact that I believe I'm still the same Joe Corrigan who grew up in Sale Moor, and that whatever I did wrong – and they were the mistakes a kid makes when he doesn't really know what the world is – I was surrounded by good friends, good coaches, people who made sure I got the best out of myself. They made sure that everything came right – and this is the fact that colours all my thoughts.'

Corrigan was most conscious of the division between today's leading players and the rest of the world when his successor in a City and England shirt, Joe Hart, encountered his first career crisis. 'I would have loved to have called Joe when he had a rocky start to the 2013–14 season,' he reports. 'I wanted to help him work through his problems because I went through exactly the same kind of scenario. When Joe was making a few mistakes and a lot of people began to doubt him – and Manuel Pellegrini left him out of the team – my mind went back to the game against West Ham in 1970 when Jimmy Greaves made his debut for them. I kicked the ball out and Ronnie Boyce saw I was off my line and sent it straight back into the net. More than 30,000 people seemed to be saying, "Oh shit, here we go again," and I was thinking, "This really comes at a bad time with us playing in the European Cup-Winners' Cup final just a little way down the road."

'Now, talk about somebody being in the right place at the right time. Bert Trautmann was in the crowd. After the game the club commissionaire, Len Davies, knocked on the door and told our trainer, Johnny Hart, that Bert wanted a word with me when I was dressed. I thought, "I've let in a nightmare goal and now one of the greatest goalkeepers the world has ever known wants a word with me." So I got changed and, with a lot of apprehension, walked up to the boardroom. There was Bert standing among a group of admirers. He took me to one side, put his arm around my shoulder, and said, "I wanted to tell you that you shouldn't worry about that goal." I said, "Mr Trautmann, what do you mean, 'don't worry about it'? – it was a terrible goal." Then he uttered the words that at the time I felt might have saved my career. He said, "I say that because everybody's forgotten I let in a goal here every bit as bad just 16 seconds into a match. I came out for a ball that was rolling along the ground, then hit a divot, brushed against my shoulder and went into the net. That goal seems to have disappeared from everyone's memory except mine, and the one you let in today will go the same way if you go about things in the right manner." Being told this by a man I admired so much had a brilliant effect, and I'm just sorry I didn't get the chance to do something like that for Joe Hart.

'At a meeting of FA scouts I mentioned to the England manager Roy Hodgson that I would like to speak to Joe, and he said that would be fine with him. Then I met Joe briefly and told him that I had gone through the same kind of phase that he was now experiencing and I gave him my phone number and said, "Give me a call and we could go for a coffee and have a chat." He didn't call, which was fair enough, because maybe he wanted to keep his own counsel, but I was sorry I didn't get the opportunity to tell him there are times in every football career when you just have to go back to all the basics.'

Corrigan had plenty of opportunity to impart such fundamentals in the 25 years of coaching which followed his enforced retirement as a player in his late thirties. He left City for a summer stint in Seattle, then moved to Brighton and Hove Albion for a year, and 36 appearances, plus loan stints at Norwich City and Stoke, before a neck injury forced him to put down his gloves. He did his 10 years as goalkeeping coach at Liverpool, another five at West Bromwich and, after being recalled from retirement by Hull City, spent another six months there. That ended prematurely when he collided, more than figuratively, with the Yorkshire club's flamboyant, highly paid Jimmy Bullard. Partly as a result of the incident, Bullard had an expensive contract torn up. Corrigan elected to walk away and now doggedly declines to shed much light on the affair beyond a clear implication that Bullard's behaviour did not pass his idea of professionalism.

He says, 'I'm not going into the details of what happened between me and Jimmy Bullard except to say that when you come away from something like that you feel you have seen the epitome of the worst that today's football is about. People can read between the lines of that any way they like. I was certainly able to walk away from Hull clear in my mind that I hadn't done anything wrong. I left the club £5 million better off when they were able to cancel Bullard's contract – and I was able to sleep at night. Such a scenario would never have occurred in the days of Lee and Summerbee at Maine Road. The players would have sorted it out.'

The Bullard eruption is a rare point of rancour as Corrigan goes back down the years – that, and the end of a decade of extremely satisfying work at Liverpool.

Corrigan's charge against Liverpool is of a lack of courtesy. 'I felt this strongly when my years at Liverpool came to an end,' he says. 'It was a period in which I think I did my bit towards winning the FA cup twice, three League Cups and a UEFA Cup. After the last match of the season at Newcastle the manager, Gérard Houllier, told all the staff that, despite a disappointing season – when the club had just made Champions League qualification, but a long way behind the first three (led by the 'Invincible' Arsenal) – our jobs were safe. He had been told by the board.

'Then I went to Amsterdam for summer coaching, and while I was away I heard that Gérard had been sacked. Phil Thompson had also gone and Sammy Lee had joined the England set-up. That left me hanging around wondering about my fate. Eventually I got a call from the chief executive, Rick Parry, who told me I had to come in for a talk with the new manager, Rafa Benítez. I asked him if I was gone, and he said, "No, no."

'When I drove into the Melwood training ground I asked the guy on the gate if Benítez was in his office. He said no, he wasn't there, and when I told him I had a 10 o'clock appointment he just said, "You'll be lucky, he's gone on holiday." He had left word with Rick Parry that I was indeed fired.

'To tell you the truth, I thought that spoke volumes. I loved the Liverpool people, I enjoyed working there and I always enjoyed playing at Anfield. In fact, I was very interested when I heard that Liverpool had expressed interest in signing me in my playing days, but apparently the move was blocked by Peter Swales.

'It seemed hard to be sacked for no other reason than there had been a change of managers, but of course it happens all the time. However, that doesn't make it right. To be fair to Benítez he did win the Champions League on penalties in Istanbul the following year, though it was largely with Houllier's team. In the end Benítez spent more money than Houllier while chasing the Premier League title, and I must say I wasn't a great fan of his style.

'One day I watched him running a training session at Melwood and it really did look like a schoolteacher at work. He was moving players by inches if he thought they were out of position. If someone was a foot out by his calculation the game had to be stopped and that player had to move.

'There was also a certain irony in Liverpool's win in Turkey. If it had been 1–0 to Milan, rather than 3–0 at half-time, I doubt if Liverpool would have won. They would have had much greater difficulty in getting some steam up if Milan had been defending a smaller lead rather than believing the game was won. No one knows how to defend a one-goal lead quite like the Italians. But instead of that they were apparently celebrating at half-time.

'I moved to West Brom after Liverpool, and when we went to Anfield the coaches were invited into the Boot Room after the game. I was introduced to Benítez but, after shaking hands with me, he made no reference to the fact that I had spent 10 years there or that he was sorry the way it turned out. All right, he was the manager and I know he had to have people around him he knew he could trust, but then he never had any kind of relationship with arguably his greatest player, his compatriot Xabi Alonso, and it is also a fact that the day Benítez left was the day Steven Gerrard decided to stay at Anfield. Initially, Benítez wanted Alonso in the team but not Gerrard, and he didn't want either Michael Owen or Danny Murphy.

'I'd come back from Amsterdam early to help the injured reserve goalkeeper Chris Kirkland, and I worked with him for a couple of weeks but I didn't get any thanks for that either. Manners cost you nothing but they do show quite a bit about someone's character.'

It was, though, a small sadness when set against the pain he experienced so many years earlier when his mentor, Malcolm Allison, who used to give training sessions that would make some of the work of Benítez seem prissy, began to lose his imperious touch.

'I had a few little chuckles to myself when we were in the funeral chapel for Mal,' he says. 'I thought of all the laughs we had as we went about work that always brought us to an edge, always made us think about what we were doing. He was always striving to bring some improvement to the team, and I remembered one of his initiatives that came on a trip to Sweden, where they play a lot of handball.

'One day a top handball player introduced himself to Malcolm, and in conversation it came out that the top goal-minders in handball put a spray on their gloves. So Mal sent out for the spray, and before going to the stadium for a tournament match I put some of it on my gloves. Then, before going out to play, I sprayed on quite a bit more. The first time I touched the ball it dropped out of my hands. All the lads moaned, and then in the dressing room Mal bellowed at me, "Read the fucking label, Joe." When I did that I saw, in quite big letters, the words, "This product should be used sparingly."'

That was Allison, says Corrigan, always pushing, always looking, always trying to learn and transmit something new. As his emotions rose and fell in the chapel, Joe kept coming back to that supremely uplifting quality. 'I felt one overwhelming emotion,' he says. 'You heard people talking about coaches but I always knew I had the best. It made it all the harder when he came back that disastrous second time and you realised all over again that his great vocation was to coach footballers. He understood so well all the dynamics of a football team but he just didn't have the ability, or the nature, to step away from that, and there was no way anyone, not even Joe Mercer, could get through to him. It hurt in the funeral parlour when I thought of how he was derided as a manager after all his brilliant work as a coach, how he made everyone come alive, understand the value of making an extra stride.

'When I think of that, I have to return to the Football Association and ask why no one there saw the impact he could have had on the national game, how he could have revolutionised the way we brought on the kids at all the levels, building up to the national team. But, of course, they didn't do that. They played it safe. They just saw a play-boy, a headline grabber, not the football genius. They ignored Mal and Brian Clough; they just weren't FA men. They made a lot of noise but unfortunately it wasn't the right kind. They didn't doff their caps to the committee men, with the consequence that they would never be recognised as two of the most original thinkers to come into the game.

'It was amazing to contrast their style with that of Don Revie, who got the England job after all his success with Leeds United. In his own way, Don was a formidable football man, meticulous in every detail. Mal's attitude was more a case of, "Let them worry about us." Of course, Leeds were a great club filled with great players, but it was only in the team's last years that they were really let off the leash. They were never allowed the expression of our teams, and I think Johnny Giles, who was such a hard, shrewd and superb professional, recognised this when he admitted that even at their peak Leeds could never be sure about getting the better of City.'

Corrigan once again weighs such an assessment and shakes his head, his agreeable, open face clouded by an old shadow. He admits that if he smiled in the funeral chapel, he also felt another rush of the old regrets. The central one was that it was not as though Malcolm Allison edged towards decline, like so many who at some time in their lives race across the sky like meteors and then find themselves reaching a little too hard for the old momentum. No, what Corrigan saw in his mentor and his hero was a full-blown descent from the high ground he had once occupied as a most natural habitat.

'There were two fine City teams after the title win in the thirties, before the big money came in from the Middle East – and the one that slipped away without fulfilling its potential,' says Corrigan. 'The first one was of Don Revie – and the Revie Plan, of the withdrawn centre-forward – Ken Barnes, Bert Trautmann and Bobby Johnstone. The second was the team of 1967–70. Then there was the one that crumbled so badly despite the addition of such excellent players as Joe Royle, Brian Kidd, Mick Channon and David Watson. The really terrible thing was to see Malcolm floundering when he came back to his old hunting ground. As manager, Tony Book battled hard for success with that team after the coming and going of Ron Saunders. Bookie fought with everything he had to prevent the decline, and he got close to some very notable success, but what was shattering was that when Mal came back he seemed unable to do anything but accelerate the failure of our hopes of getting back to where we had been just a few years earlier.

'I remember doing a football camp in Florida with Bob Wilson, Lawrie McMenemy and Steve Coppell (who suffered a brief ordeal as City manager in the nineties) when a call came in for Lawrie while we were taking a break by the swimming pool. When he came back to the pool he said, "What the hell is your manager up to?" I just said, "What's Mal done now?" and Lawrie replied, "He's gone and signed Michael Robinson for £750,000 – and how many goals did he score last season? Twelve." And Bob Wilson just said, "Oh my God."

'Now Malcolm was creating terrible problems for City by making such a signing. After spending so much on an unproven player it means that the next time you go in for any player you're going be asked for a million. That was Mal the second time round, and it was very, very sad because you realised that everything had started to go wrong, from board level downwards, when he had made his first big push for increased power and status.

'I suppose he was saying to himself something he had said to me back when I was I kid, something to the effect that "if you don't give it a go you'll never know what's inside you". Still, there was a big difference because I wasn't a goalkeeper who wanted to be something else. Mal was a fantastic coach but he was never going to be a manager. That was the reality so many could see, right from the start, but unfortunately he couldn't. He didn't see Joe Mercer as a shield, a protector against his own worst behaviour but someone who was beginning to ruin his life, his ambitions.

'As time went on, some of Mal's behaviour was just mad. When we went on the 1970 tour of Australia the first thing he said to the reception desks at all the hotels where we stayed was, "Make sure there's a crate of pink champagne in my room every day and send two bottles to the rooms of all the players." He must have spent all the tour earnings on pink champagne.

'In Sweden, on a pre-season tour which was supposed to be alcohol free, the bar bill was so massive Mal asked for all of it to be listed as laundry charges.

'In his second regime his decisions were increasingly erratic. On our trips to London he would have us up at 6.30 a.m. and running around Hyde Park or Kensington Gardens when the tramps were still sleeping on the benches. Then he would send us back to bed for a nap before a 10 a.m. breakfast. We would say to each other, "What's this all about – what's happening to Big Mal?" That was the way he was, the way he had become. You just wanted to turn it back to how it was before, how everything was so simple, so clear cut, so filled with certainties about what was right and what was wrong in the winning of football matches.'

It is a prolonged sigh now as much as a statement, a calling for a past gone for ever. No one needs to tell Joe Corrigan this. As he points out, he has had so many years to deal with this particular reality. Nor does he need telling that when you try to recreate the past you are obliged to include all of it. His good luck is that when he comes to balance the good and the bad, it is not the pink champagne and the tramps on the park benches that he remembers most vividly. It was the time when a big, undamaged man offered him the world and then helped him to deliver it. It was when he felt stronger, more accomplished, with the arrival of each new season. When he could greet a man like Bert Trautmann, for so long such a fabled figure in his mind, and stand his full 6 feet 5 inches.

It is now, when he walks away knowing that, yes, he has for a little while recreated a past which will never vanish.

Chapter 14

Seeing again the old players of Manchester City leads invariably to marvelling again at the strength of the links which have bound them so closely, both geographically and emotionally. To encounter them, on every journey around the urban kraal they have made their own, is one supremely engaging phenomenon. To a man they seem to take more seriously the achievements they became part of, which for a few gilded years lifted them so high, than they do themselves. They give the impression of men returning so frequently to the past – not for self-aggrandisement, rather for a feeling for a world that may have been supplanted in so many different ways but for them can never be allowed to disappear.

The sense of this is overwhelming when I talk with Tommy Booth – sitting in a corner of the North Manchester Golf Club, the warm and noisy clatter of the bar lounge behind us – especially so when he smiles broadly and tells me, 'All my medals for the FA Cup, the League Cup, the European Cup-Winners', and nine England Under-21 caps are wrapped up in the loft at home. Now it just so happens that about 40 years ago my wife Carol came third in a netball competition and her bronze medal is on the mantelpiece.'

However, Booth is quick to say that she also won a gold in the matter of rearranging his life when, buttressed by prudent investment in his players' pension fund, he decided that his active involvement in football was over.

He was 40 at the time, disenchanted by his brief experience of management with Preston North End, who valuing his contribution as captain of the team, his easy humour and his feel for the needs of the people around him, had announced that he would succeed a man he liked and admired, the celebrated if sometimes abrasive Tommy Docherty.

'I have a good wife and two sons we are very proud of,' he says. 'The younger boy is a solicitor. The elder one went into football, briefly. Now he has a top job with the giant German firm Würth, which has a turnover in the billions. Both of them are in jobs I couldn't do.

'From my own point of view the best thing I did was take the advice of a bookmaker relative who knew someone at Leeds United and had heard about how the lads there were securing their futures through the players' pension plan. He told me that if I joined up I wouldn't have to worry about money for the rest of my life. While I was winning trophies I received some lump-sum bonuses and they all went straight into the pension. Basically, I've lived off that ever since.

'One thing that did change my attitude to life, and how I would spend the rest of it, came to me in this golf club when I was doing what I did most days – playing golf with the old boys. It suddenly struck me that the way things were I would be doing this day in, day out, and I thought, "Hold on a minute, I can't spend the rest of my life playing golf." One day I was talking to my wife about this and she said, "Why don't you come into television with me, come and work for Granada?" Granada TV Rentals that was. She worked for them in their office. "But doing what?" I asked her. She said, "Don't worry, just come into the office and they'll have a chat with you."

'I saw a lad there and he said they would train me up to fix televisions and satellites and videos. I said, "Look, mate, I'm not being funny but I can hardly replace a plug." He said they would sort me out and, sure enough, after a couple of weeks in the workshop I was ready to go out on the road. They wanted me to install new sets and fix broken ones. I liked the job and, in about two or three weeks, I was really quite a dab hand. Best of all, I was home around 1 p.m. every day.

'Soon enough it got around among City fans that I was doing the job and three or four times a day I was going to houses where the tellies were as right as rain and they just wanted me to talk about football and sign programmes and books. I did 10 years as a telly repairman-cum-football hero, and then retired at the age of 50, which I'd always reckoned would be a good time to do it.

'Another piece of good luck was that around about that time Granada TV Rentals were looking for some voluntary redundancies. I took the deal, got 15 grand and said, "That will do me." I haven't worked since, at least not at anything but hospitality work for City, which I enjoy very much. I work match days, taking people through the training complex, and the other night I did a question and answer session with the manager Manuel Pellegrini and Patrick Vieira, who is in charge of the young players.

'One of the saddest things in the days since I played is seeing lads of my time struggling, really hitting the rocks. When I was playing you never had the idea that you were set for life financially but nowadays, with all the money sloshing through the game, it's hard to see lads who were really great players – like Alan Hudson of Chelsea – who are obviously struggling. I suppose the big problem was that they had trouble accepting that the playing days, the glory days, were over for them. It was hard for them to accept that they were no longer at the centre of the football world, and now they had to get on with the business of living through the rest of their lives. I know I was lucky in the way I wasn't so bothered about staying in the game, that I saw some of the pitfalls of it, and that there might be other things to a life lived away from the spotlight.

'Of course, I would never give back a day of my time as a pro, all those feelings of satisfaction playing for a team like City, but I didn't feel any great need to hang on. Some lads are so desperate to stay in the game it makes you sad. You want to say to them, "Look, thank God for all the good times you have had, now make a life which will have other rewards." Football was great while it lasted, but it was over and I had to get on with the rest of my life.'

It was not, though, a door he closed without any significant regrets. Maybe the greatest of them is that in the loft where he keeps his football prizes there is no League title medal – nor a senior England cap. The pain is that he brushed so closely to both distinctions in a career which flowed so assuredly from the day Harry Godwin took Malcolm Allison to see the big, promising lad from north Manchester.

'I was born just a little way from this golf club where I have spent so many of my days,' says Booth. 'One Sunday I was playing for my local team, St Mary's Parish, when Harry came along with Mal. As they watched the game, Mal turned to Harry and said, "The big lad might be worth signing," and Harry, a brilliant scout who had brought so many good young local players to City, said, "He's already on the books, Mal."

'I was playing inside-forward at the time and scoring quite a lot of goals, but the coach said, "He could be a very good signing but not an inside-forward. That's not his best position. He's a central defender if I ever saw one." I had never even thought of myself as a defender, despite my height, but Mal converted me immediately and, of course, the rest is history. That was pure Malcolm. He saw things so quickly.

'I took over from George Heslop, who had done so well since coming from Everton and playing such a big part in the title win. I played a few games beside George but then Mal put me in the team to stay.'

Booth made his debut in a League Cup tie at Huddersfield, and as City achieved a clean sheet he could hardly have looked more at home. Immaculate on the ground, confident in the air, his introduction was especially notable in that Huddersfield's extremely talented free spirit, Frank Worthington, was the man to be subdued.

'It was around this time that Malcolm made his infamous "we're going to terrify Europe" speech, and I went to Istanbul as one of the subs. I was absolutely gutted when we went out in the first round of the European Cup, but in the wake of that defeat George and the goal-keeper Ken Mulhearn were dropped and they brought Harry Dowd and me into the team. We immediately went on a good run that finished with us winning the FA Cup. It was funny, really. I was so disappointed we lost in Istanbul but if we had won that game Mal might not have changed the team and you might never have heard of me.

'We went on to the Double of the League Cup and the Cup-Winners' Cup the following year, and for the next four or five years we could fancy ourselves against anyone. It makes it all the more painful now to recall that we missed out on two great chances to win the title. Of course we should have done it on both occasions, and the truth is that it became a time of us always going to do this and that and then failing.'

The disappointment of that still bites home and, he says, is only redoubled when he considers the scale of the miscalculation which brought it about. His diagnostic report on the misadventure is hardly original, but each version you hear only intensifies that haunting sense of lost horizons.

'When I first got into the team in 1968,' he says, 'I was lucky enough to be in a side that anyone could see was going places. There were great players around and the atmosphere was incredibly positive. City had just won the league and were going on to the win the FA Cup, the League Cup and the Cup-Winners' Cup. We had marched out from under the shadow of Manchester United and there really didn't seem any limits on what we might achieve. It all seemed inevitable, one step leading to another. We couldn't fail to achieve all our ambitions, but then we did, and when I look back I have to put a lot of blame on the directors.

'The big mistake, the fatal one, was that Malcolm would get bigger all-round responsibility, basically the freedom to do it all, and at the same time play down the role of Joe Mercer. That was the worst decision that could have been made. Together they were absolute magic. Set apart, they just couldn't make it work, and that became so obvious as the months went by. Mal was all over the place, an incredible box of tricks, full of ideas and inspiration. He was just brilliant at getting the team moving, convincing us of the value of new ideas, a new kind of thinking about the game, and of knowing that we would always be fitter than our opponents.

'Joe was a real leader. It was in his bearing and he would say, "Yes, Mal we can try that," but also say, from time to time, "No, that might be stretching it a bit." He was always watching Mal closely – and protecting him from the worst of his own nature, saying things like, "Hold back a little bit on that, you might just be going over the top on this one." The plan of the board was for Joe to move upstairs, but he couldn't take that, he felt sidetracked, humiliated, and so he went off to Coventry City.

'It was a very sad day when he left. The moment we heard he was going we knew how much we would miss him and how, sooner or later, Mal would feel his absence. But then again I cannot emphasise too much how terrific Malcolm was before the break-up. He was, surely, one of the all-time great trainers and coaches. He came out with so many things that were just stunning. You could get right away the point of what he was trying to do, and so of course you embraced it.

'Something people may not understand quite so well about professional footballers is how insecure they are. They have these terrible moods of vulnerability and take all kinds of doubts about themselves from the training field and matches, and what Mal had above everything else was the ability to make you feel better about yourself. It was as if he could shine a light on what you were trying to do, and when he did that you felt a great surge of new confidence. You felt taller.

'Joe was always the old head, giving Malcolm plenty of scope to operate but also pointing out where things might go wrong. He was like a great old craggy jockey, setting the right pace but always ready to weigh up the value of a big move.'

It could be any one of them talking now – Lee, Summerbee, Pardoe or Bell or Book on the subject of a flickering candle. It is the recurring lament for a bout of human folly, a signal failure to understand that sometimes in life it is essential to understand that you have arrived at a place near perfect for all of your needs – and all of your strengths and weaknesses.

Booth gives the now familiar shake of the head and roll of the eyes and goes on, 'When the directors changed the balance of the relationship between the manager and the coach, Mal became increasingly involved in things he wasn't good at. For example, we all knew Malcolm wasn't good at money. It slipped through his fingers. It was there to spend. So when a player went in to see him about his pay, ask for a certain level of rise, Mal's instinct was to give him a bit more than he was asking for. That just didn't work in the football of those days. It wasn't the way to do it. Joe was the old fox trying to keep everyone happy but not letting things run out of control. Sometimes you would see him in a corridor and you would say, "All right, boss," and he would reply, "Yes, fine, Paul," – or "Harry" – but then on the other hand he was very astute, he always knew what was happening about the place. He was on the other side, the directors' side, when he felt he had to be, and he could look after all of that while Mal was out on the field coaching us – and that's how it should always have been. If it had stayed that way I'm convinced we would have won at least two more titles and people would have spoken of us down the years in the same way they did of Busby's United, Revie's Leeds and Shankly's Liverpool.

'For a few years we could outplay the strongest teams, but then we lost some of those certainties and, in 1972, we virtually gave the title to Brian Clough's Derby County. A lot of blame is attached to Rodney Marsh, who came in the spring of that season, but there again there was another ten of us. However, Rodney would admit he wasn't fit. He used to come to training in bare feet – and wearing beads. One morning when he came into the dressing room I asked him, "Have you left your shoes in the car?" and he replied, "Oh no, I don't wear shoes," and I thought, "Blinking heck, we've got a right one here."

'It was inevitable that there was a real mixture of feelings when we went to Southern Cemetery to say farewell to Malcolm. I saw all the lads together again and I was right back there in the old days, thinking about the things we used to get up to. By comparison, when you look at today's players you see they are living in a fishbowl.'

Apart from briefly playing alongside George Heslop and then so quickly assuming command of the centre of defence, the young Booth was given another assignment. It was to be Francis Lee's *de facto* butler. 'The first time I went on the road Mal said I would be Frannie's roommate. We were staying at the Waldorf in London, which struck me as a very posh place indeed. As soon as we checked in Frannie had me running errands, getting him newspapers, cups of tea. He said, "Look, you're just coming into the team and I'm a senior player. It's your duty to look after me." I said, "That's all very well, Frannie, but by the time of the game I'm going to be completely knackered."'

The truth, of course, was that it was a huge and thrilling adventure. 'I had the feeling,' he confirms, 'I had made it into the company of a very special group of players who had come to believe that winning was not their challenge but their right. To my young eyes I had been given membership of what seemed to be football's version of a perfect society. Colin Bell had a special place in it for his phenomenal gifts and ability, and I suppose this is why there is such sadness among the lads today that he and Frannie fell out so seriously in later life – and why the rest of us still hang on to the hope that one day they will be able to celebrate each other's company again as they did when between them they were destroying defences – Belly with his unstoppable running, Frannie with his eye for every weakness in the opposition.

'Alan Oakes was another extraordinary performer. There was only one reason why he didn't win an England cap. It was Bobby Moore. Oaksie's commitment and strength were fantastic, and it was all the more remarkable that before a game he would often be soaked in sweat. Then the game started and he was a giant. He just ploughed through a game, always reading it acutely. He made great tackles, great passes and scored some great goals.

'None of us worried about all the attention paid to Bell, Lee and Summerbee. We all knew we were playing our parts well enough, and no one could, for example, ever doubt that someone like Neil Young belonged in the highest class. In fact, we all roared one night at a fans' do when Mike Summerbee was speaking and someone in the audience referred to the team of "the Big Three" and Mike said, "Hey, wait a minute, there's also Neil Young." We took that as more of a tribute to a wonderful player than a put-down of the rest of us. It was something I recalled at the funeral of a teammate we all loved for both his ability and his unassuming nature. Youngy was an aristocrat of football but he never lorded it in the dressing room. He was, truly, one of the lads.'

There is a place for all of them in the memory of Tommy Booth. If some of them were more prone to trouble, and weakness – if they could not, as in the case of Tony Coleman, totally embrace the team ethos – there was always at least a touch of redemption.

'The last we heard of TC,' says Booth, 'was that he was in Thailand after deciding that, with his marriage over and his children grown up, he was tired of living in Australia. He lived modestly in Australia on a pension, sold his medals and admitted, "It's a bit difficult, you know." He was a terrific player and thoroughly justified Mal's belief that, despite a bad disciplinary record, he could make a real contribution to the team – and this was despite the fact that off the field we were never quite sure of what he was going to do next.

'One night when we checked into the Waldorf before a game in London we heard they were staging the Miss World contest there. Joe Mercer groaned when he heard this, saying, "That's all we bloody need." The place was swarming with photographers. The following morning we were all down at breakfast and TC was missing. Joe and Mal went round the breakfast room asking everyone if they had seen him or heard what he had been up to. But there was no sign of him. Then TC came marching down the marble stairs wrapped in the flag of Miss Nigeria.

'He was a funny, strange guy – and a hell of a player. He had to be to last three years at the top at City in view of all the baggage he brought with him. When he left for Sheffield Wednesday we knew that, on the field at least, we had lost one of our certainties – a powerful, quick and skilled presence along the left.'

Still, no one questioned the fact that the Big Three were so enshrined at the heart of everything City achieved and Booth, like every other member of what was often, and so carelessly, thought of as a chorus line, is quick to acknowledge the weight of their impact. 'Frannie was the hardest of pros,' he says. 'When you talk to him now he says, at the age of 70, "I think, with the protection forwards get now, I could still be playing. You know, they cannot kick you from behind any more." In that ruthless mould, we also had Mike Summerbee. Within the new limits, full-backs are expected to have a go at wingers. With Mike, it was the other way around. He used to love playing against Leeds. They were the toughest team around and they brought out all his warring instincts. Norman Hunter was reputed to be the hardest man around but I'll tell you something, he didn't enjoy playing against Mike – or Frannie.

'Tony Book always said to us, "When you get the ball give it to Mike." And when you did you always knew he was going to drive at the other team with a superb cutting edge. A team feeds off confidence like that, and it meant that we were not afraid of anyone.

'Belly was, no doubt, a freak of nature. The strangest thing for me, though, was that he was never as dominant for England as he was for City. Frannie always said that you needed a run of 10 or 12 straight games for England before you felt really at home. Though he played a lot of games for England, Belly didn't really get that kind of run. It was tragic that he got the bad injury that brought the end of his career – and, of course, he still has a limp today. When he played his first game in a comeback, which you always feared was never going to succeed, the cheers at Maine Road were – you knew the moment you heard them – something you were never going to forget.

'That was also true of the comment of the man he replaced for the second half of a game with Newcastle United. We were still in the bath, congratulating Belly on his return, and still stunned by the reception he had received and how it had helped us storm to a 3–0 win, when Paul Power joined us. He said, "I'll tell you what, lads, and I'm not being funny, I couldn't believe the ovation I got when I came off the field. To tell you the truth, I didn't think I was playing that well."'

Booth slaps his knee and roars as if the incident came yesterday and, yes, there in the absurdities and the passions of grown men inhabiting such a small space and heightened experience were some of the jewels of Tommy Booth's professional existence. They still glitter beyond any sense of disappointment, though he does tell you how much he would have given for an England cap: 'It was one thing I wished for very much when I was playing, along with that league title which beckoned so strongly. I felt I was good enough to play at that level and I would have loved to get the chance. I did get a call-up for the squad but, of course, I had some very tough opposition, especially in Dave Watson, who eventually joined me at City, and Roy McFarland. They were both truly great players.

'When I had my best chance of playing, with McFarland suffering from a knock, I picked up an injury myself. I remember lying in bed recovering and watching England play Yugoslavia, thinking, "I should be there, I should be playing for England." The lad who was taking "my" place was Jeff Blockley, who had just moved from Coventry to Arsenal for a fee of £200,000. He had been signed to replace the captain, Frank McLintock, but it didn't work out for him at Highbury – the Double-winning manager Bertie Mee said it was his biggest mistake in the transfer market. Blockley, though, was a steady player who eventually signed for his home club Leicester City after making 62 league appearances for Arsenal in three years. He was two months older than me when he won his only England cap, but it was one more than me.

'Still, a few years later I got some perspective on my failed international career. I got an injury which required three discs being removed from my back and I thought, "Never mind playing for England, never mind playing football, I'll be lucky to walk properly again." I had a tough battle to get back into the team, especially when Bookie, after he had taken over from Ron Saunders, signed Watson. In those days a back operation put a huge question mark against your name.

'As a young defender, the man I looked up to most was Bookie. He had learned his trade so brilliantly. The greatest accolade I can give him is just to refer to our great record against United. They were a team, at least from my perspective, you always wanted to beat, not just because they were the bitter local rivals who had been dominant for so long but also because they were such a superb attacking team. The fact is when we played them the great match-winner George Best rarely if ever saw a light. That was down to Bookie.

'I remember when he scored his first goal for City – he scored four in eight years – no one went up to congratulate him. He seemed a bit bemused, even though he probably had an idea we were winding him up. One of my early games for the first team was against Spurs, and I thought, "This is going to be a hell of a challenge against the G-men, Jimmy Greaves and Alan Gilzean." But we won 4–0, with Bookie absent. Afterwards Mal said to me, "Wait till Bookie's back, then we'll really start flying," – and we did, all the way to the Cup final win over Leicester.'

For Tommy Booth, as for all his teammates, it was as though he inhabited a world proofed, at least for a little while, against ignorance – and false or worn out football formulae. At Maine Road there was this affinity with the game's realities. Things were as they were, hard won and working always to potentially optimum levels. It was only outside of this zone of opportunity and self-improvement that doubts could accumulate so quickly.

Lilleshall, the FA's coaching citadel, was the classic example. 'When I was made manager of Preston,' Booth recalls, 'I went to get my coaching badges, even though in those days they were not as important as they are today. Nowadays, you cannot get a job without the badges, no matter what you have achieved on the field and however deep your instincts for the game.

'During one session a lad came over to me and said, "Look, Tommy, the next time the goalkeeper throws the ball out to you, miscontrol it." Now, as a centre-half, I had a good touch. I was never the kind of defender who would just hump the ball downfield. So, anyway, I followed instructions, let the ball bobble away from me, and this coach, who I believe was a schoolteacher, came up to me and said, "Tommy, that's not the way to do it, get out of the way." He then went on to tell me that my body shape was all wrong and, of course, all I could say was, "For fuck's sake, you told me to miscontrol it."

'Another day the subject was an upcoming international with Brazil and how the South Americans were so good at playing the ball from the back. "What I'm going to do now," said the coach, "is show you how we are going to combat this problem." He called up the back four and said, "Tommy, you go centre-back and I want the goalkeeper to roll the ball to you at least three yards out of the box." He then called up two forwards and told them, "What you have to do is close him down." So the goalie rolls the ball out to me and when I get it and turn there are these two forwards in my face. The coach seemed very happy, but I had to point out to him, "I don't really think a professional goalkeeper would actually give me the fucking ball while I had two forwards up my arse.'"

Despite attempts to persuade him to stay, Booth walked away from the course after three days. He was just too appalled by a culture utterly separated from the practicalities of the professional game. He saw it as some kind of bureaucratic pantomime. Men invested with authority ran around with clipboards rather like, he thought, headless chickens. He was certainly less surprised, on reflection, by the earlier announcement of the FA's head of coaching, the most didactic of schoolteachers, Charles Hughes, that the Brazilians, the most successful football nation on earth, had somehow managed to get almost everything wrong.

Hughes said the nation of Pelé and Gérson and Tostão had missed the point with their slow–quick build-up, their fine passing and sublimely subtle running. What everyone had to believe in was his pet theory, POMO – position of maximum opportunity – which was, as Booth puts it, 'another way of saying whack the ball upfield to a target man and hope to feed off the scraps'. The notorious philosophy reached a natural conclusion in the session when midfielders, the natural-born creators of the game, were given yellow bibs and defenders were ordered to 'miss out the canaries'.

One of those urging Booth to stay in Lilleshall was his old teammate at Maine Road and future manager of City, Joe Royle. He said Booth's future in the game would be best served if he followed the example of Nobby Stiles, the World Cup hero who had to grit his teeth and listen in exasperation as Hughes lectured him on where he had gone wrong in the historic World Cup final triumph over West Germany at Wembley.

'Joe said I really ought to tough it out,' says Booth. 'But I had to tell him I just couldn't be doing with it. I told Joe I knew real coaches like Malcolm, who not only taught you things which you otherwise would never even have dreamed but also deepened your love for the game. They opened doors to new knowledge, new certainties about what was right and what was wrong when you went out on a training pitch or into a big game.

'In a perfect world I would probably have loved to have been a successful manager, and I certainly wanted to do my best at Preston, but when I coupled my experience at Lilleshall with the frustrations I had trying to deal with club directors, it all seemed too much.

'When I tried to tell Ken Barnes, a great player and a fine coach who had played that huge part in the Revie plan, about my Lilleshall experience, he just walked away shaking his head. He couldn't bear to listen to an account of the mockery of coaching which was officially sanctioned by English football's ruling body.'

If you had a straw poll of old City players to decide which one of them best represented the level of the support they displayed for each other, the security and consistency of their nature, Booth would surely be involved in an extremely close-run finish, probably vying with Glyn Pardoe for a winning margin. Certainly this sense that he embodied so much of the spirit of the team was strongly expressed a decade after the departure of Tony Coleman was a first reminder that in football, as in life, you can never be quite sure what tomorrow will bring.

At 32, and after 14 years as a City pro, Tommy Booth received a withering blow. 'A week or so before the Cup final in 1981 the manager John Bond told me that I would be playing against Spurs – even though I had missed the semi-final against Ipswich through injury. He told me in front of some of my teammates, including Paul Power, Tommy Hutchison and Gerry Gow. I'd scored in the quarter-final against Everton, but when I was injured, Tommy Caton, who was a brilliant young player, got the nod for the semi. When Bond told me I would be back for the Wembley game I just nodded and said, "Nice."

'We went down to London on the Wednesday, and after our first training session the manager said, "Right, lads, I'm going to give you the team now so no one has to stew over who is in or out for a few nights." He read out the names. Tommy Caton was in and I was out.

'That night we had a sponsors' table booked at the Professional Football Writers' annual dinner. I had already pulled Bond and said, "You know you told me I was playing. You really are bang out of order." I went to another restaurant and was alone with some very bitter thoughts and the certain knowledge that after this it was all over for me with City. Then, all of a sudden, the empty chairs at the table were filled. By Joe Corrigan, Tommy Hutchison, Gerry Gow and Paul Power. They all said they were eating with me, but I said, "No, lads, don't get yourselves in trouble, go back to the big do." But they wouldn't budge. They said they wanted to be with their teammate because they knew this was the parting of the ways. It was true because I had already decided I couldn't play any more for this guy John Bond.

'After the final we were due off on an end-of-season tour, and I didn't want to go but the lads persuaded me, saying, "Why not? We'll have a few drinks and a few laughs." One night on the tour I found myself having a few drinks with some of the lads and Bond's number two, John Sainty. Suddenly, Sainty blurted out, "Tommy, it was me who persuaded Bondy to leave you out of the final. I just argued the theory that you shouldn't change a semi-final winning team.'

'I said, "OK, but why did he tell me I was playing?" Sainty just shook his head and repeated that Bond had to be talked out of playing me. I thought for a moment and then I turned round to face him and said, "Well, I tell you what – if he had played me we would probably have won the fucking Cup."'

It is, like so many old football wounds, something that still nags from time to time, like a shaft of cold in an eroded joint on a winter's morning. But then there is always the spring that comes each year to warm the bones of an old warrior and for Tommy Booth there is also that one in which he rushed to a glory that would never leave him. It was the spring-time of a career which for so many of the City heroes will never slip out of season.

Chapter 15

Starbucks on the edge of Middlewich, Cheshire, is hard by the M6. The morning clientele comes rushing in and out, mostly for takeaway coffee, the dawdlers perhaps glancing at a newspaper headline on the rack beside the counter. However, the two casually dressed men at the corner table are not going anywhere in a hurry. If they did their share of travelling – under pressure that most of the commuters who now scurry by without a glance are unlikely ever to know – they now clearly rejoice in their option to stay put on another day when the rest of the world is about its business. Glyn Pardoe and Alan Oakes, local boys, cousins, are as comfortable in their memories as they are in their own skins and their own company and, most of all, in their own part of the world.

They ventured out to become big-city heroes as integral members of a coruscating football team, but when the glory was done they came back here as inevitably as the swallows return to Capistrano.

They are as philosophically and emotionally entwined in their own minds as they are in all those of their old teammates who, one after another, have seemed, even while extolling all their individual qualities, incapable of giving them an entirely separate identity. They are forever the cousins, the Cheshire boys, the alpha and the omega of lifelong consistency.

If there is one difference now it is that Pardoe is a little more tolerant of today's game, its excesses and its frequent failures to deliver evidence that its achievements, beyond such individual miracles as Lionel Messi and Cristiano Ronaldo, will ever be quite able to fully match and justify the available rewards.

We are talking in the wake of England's abject retreat from the Brazilian World Cup and 'Oaksie' is quite withering in his assessment of so much of modern football. It is expressed at times in a quite brutal detachment. 'I'll be honest with you,' he says, 'I have not watched through a single game of this World Cup. The truth is that when I try these days I go to sleep. But from all I can gather from what I've heard, and the snippets I've seen, England must have been an absolute disgrace – and how Roy Hodgson has kept his job I'll never know. As I say, I don't have the patience to watch a whole game. And then we played Costa Rica and got a draw, and were apparently quite happy to come home with that. Costa Rica!'

Pardoe nods in the direction of his cousin and says, 'I remember the last time he came to a game at City. It was a few years ago and we were playing United. Rooney scored a goal and Alan shouted out, "It's a disgrace. Does anyone pick up a player any more?" It's just as well he didn't see Brazil giving up seven goals against Germany.

'But then it's as I say to Our Kid here: what were we really entitled to expect? How many league games did Ross Barkley play before he went off to the World Cup as an England player? Fifty-odd. In the old days he would have been seen as someone still learning the basics of his trade.'

Oakes has a passing thought: 'To be fair to Steven Gerrard he's been brilliant for Liverpool but, let's be honest, he's gone a little. Unfortunately, time has caught up with him, as it does to all of us. To me the best manager for England is probably still Terry Venables, though he is getting on a bit now. The players would play for him because he is full of ideas.'

One of their regular debates is now swelling into vigorous life. Pardoe's riposte: 'Then again, it really doesn't matter what system you play, you need the players. I don't care what anyone says, you need the players who have the temperament and the background to go out and do it when it matters. I did think some of the teams looked good in the group games – teams like Chile and Colombia were tremendous the way they played when they had the ball. They attacked when they had it and when they didn't they got behind the ball, and of course that is so important. It's not a masterplan, it's a basic game.'

'There's another thing. You cannot teach someone to put the right weight on the ball when a teammate is running past someone. It's a natural instinct, like seeking out the right position to receive the ball.'

Oakes bridles again. He says, 'You don't need a bunch of coaching badges to figure this out. If you get a bit of space I'll give you the ball and then I'll move on and work to find another angle. No, let's face it, it's quite shocking the way England's international football has gone.'

Of all that they have in common perhaps the most extraordinary aspect is that neither played for England at the highest level. For their teammates it is, at the very best, a quirk of circumstances, and at the worst still another example of the neglect of some of football's most crucial values down the years. Oakes played once for a Football League XI; Pardoe had four under-23 caps.

Pardoe says, 'Just before I got my big injury I was being tipped for the England squad. But that finished me. Of course you can cry about something like that. But I've got no regrets. Alan and I had great careers.'

Prodigious, indeed, and marked by a stunning application and facility from an early age. Both hold City records, Pardoe as the youngest ever player when he made his debut against Birmingham City in 1962. He was two months shy of his sixteenth birthday. Oakes was not quite so precocious. He had to wait until he was 17 before making the first team against Chelsea but, when he left, 17 years later, he had played a record 680 games and was described by Liverpool manager Bill Shankly as 'exactly the kind of player youngsters should use as a model'.

Like all their comrades in the great City resurgence that erupted between 1965 and 1970, Oakes and Pardoe come most alive when they remember the impact the Mercer–Allison regime had on their careers and their lives. Their speech quickens, their eyes shine more brightly. Oakes, more vividly than most, conjures that time when everything seemed so perfectly pitched, so filled with reasonable expectation. He recalls, 'The team spirit was just unbelievable. Those were amazing days for a bunch of English lads, and they seem even more so when you think how things are now, the rewards available, the lifestyles of all the players and how they come from all over the world – and that when we won the league title and a bunch of other trophies we didn't even have a player from Wales or Scotland or Ireland.

'All right, Summerbee, Bell and Lee were special players, but to us they were never superstars. They were ordinary lads. Malcolm, of course, was in front of everyone, but unfortunately in the end he got in front of himself. There is much talk about the need for fitness today but I don't think the current players could have done what we did. I don't think they could have done our training. I think it would have just been too hard.

'The most exciting thing was that with every piece of work, every gut-wrenching session in Wythenshawe Park, we knew we were start-ing our real football education. We knew we were growing up. Malcolm had us believing there was nothing we couldn't do, and it was only later that we had the sadness of seeing everything break up. Then it was as though our world had come to an end for a little while. We didn't know much about the politics upstairs, the pressure on the relation-ship between Mal and Joe, and then when it came out into the open all we could think about were the chances of putting all the pieces back together again. When we could see they were just about nil it was a kind of death.'

As Oakes revives an old but still fervent regret, as he mourns that time of sudden and profound desperation, he takes me back to another football club and another set of players outraged by the stripping down of certainties.

It was Derby County in the autumn of 1973 and the day after the messianic Brian Clough had parted from the club he had revitalised no less profoundly than Mercer and Allison had City. I walked through the main door of the Baseball Ground and into a corridor filled with angry players. They were led by the goalkeeper Colin Boulton. Interestingly, he was carrying an axe. Naturally I asked its purpose and he said, 'Can't you guess, it's to hack down the door of the directors' room if they keep it locked and do not come up with any satisfactory explanation for allowing the departure of the most brilliant manager in the game.'

They didn't quite manage that but, understandably enough in the circumstances, there were quite a number of airy promises and a few platitudes. It was the old directorial routine, and though the club did appoint Dave Mackay who, with that significant help from Francis Lee, landed another title, that didn't mean quite so much when Clough, after unrewarding diversions at Brighton and Leeds, moved back to the Midlands and delivered two European Cup wins for Nottingham Forest.

There were, however, some major differences in style between Old Big Head Clough and the original Special One, Allison. As Oakes and Pardoe are so quick to say, they were never in doubt about the effect of their coach and the reasons behind it. For all his flamboyance, Allison never forgot that his essential role was to teach or, as so many of his players put it, 'to see around corners'. He could be a pedagogue, of course, but by comparison Clough was more inclined to outright tyranny. One of his finest players, the combative and creative little Scot,

Archie Gemmill, once told me, 'Sometimes why we play so hard for him can be a bit of a mystery. There are days when he can treat us like dogs, but, play for him we do – and I know we always will.'

Pardoe underlines the extraordinarily uncomplicated willingness of all the City players to submit to Allison's promptings: 'He presented so many challenges and we never ducked one of them. At first we might have said, "What's it all about?" but we saw the point soon enough. Also, though, I have to agree with Alan when he says that it was something that happened in another world.

'We used to go down to Wythenshawe Park on a Monday morning in the middle of winter to run off the weekend, and there would be so much water on the gravel. We had to run through it. Now, are you going to tell me that someone like Yaya Touré, who gets £200,000 a week and was so upset when the club didn't make a fuss over his thirty-first birthday, would be prepared to do that? No, not in a million years.

'The problem as it developed with Mal was that he thought he had done his bit as a coach and it was time for him to move on, in total command and at another level, which he believed he had attained. You've probably heard this a few times, but the truth was that he was a great coach but no manager, and if we needed evidence of this it came with the signing of Rodney Marsh. That was the critical example of what went wrong. Rodney's football could be brilliant, but it just wasn't our football – and the great irony, of course, was that our football was Malcolm's creation. Players like Belly, Summerbee and Lee were just perfect for the football he brought to us. It was sad to hear Belly complaining about running blind into the box, never knowing whether Rodney was going to deliver the ball. That sapped everyone's belief in what we were doing. I would make a lot of runs down the left hoping for the pass that never came, and in the end you ask yourself, "What's the point?" And that was the first serious doubt coming into what we had been doing so successfully.

'Before that you knew precisely what you were doing and what your teammates were doing, and there suddenly was this new guy in our midst making us look like idiots. Before that you could make a run in the certainty that you were going to get the ball. That was us, that was how we played, and the moment you lose that kind of certainty, well, you are finished.'

Alan Oakes was deeply impressed by Allison on their first encounter. 'He was manager of Plymouth Argyle at the time and you had to be taken by the way he had got his team together; there was a lot of cleverness in what they did and you could see that a lot of thought had gone into their game. They won a penalty and one of their players passed to a teammate from the spot and they scored. I'd never seen that before and I remembered it very well when many years later I saw Robert Pires and Thierry Henry making a mess of trying to do the same thing for Arsenal.'

Yet if both Oakes and Pardoe are still thrilled by the innovation and the stimulation provided by their old coach, they agree that their greatest debt to him came with the spirit and the unity that rose among them, a little stronger with each new challenge. 'As Alan always says,' Pardoe declares, 'it was as though we were more like a family than a football team. If there was a five-a-side game the Big Three were invariably on the same side, but we usually won. They couldn't say much about that because we tended to be better at that form of the game. So they just took their punishment.'

Of course the family broke up; whatever the strength of its roots and its ambience it always does in football, and it became depleted by the loss of such favourite sons as Neil Young and Mike Doyle and the richly admired George Heslop. But then Pardoe and Oakes are here to say that the maintenance of that spirit, right up to this sunny morning, remains the wonder of their lives. They agree it has always paid the freight of their ensuing existence, always been something that has enabled them to lift their shoulders in appreciation of the good luck they once had.

Pardoe is particularly affecting when he describes his reactions to the broken leg which effectively ruined his brilliant career – he was 24 and widely regarded as an England full-back in waiting – and a more recent heart attack.

'It kills you if you get bitter when things go wrong, and I might have done that after the Best tackle that really wrecked my career. You've just got to let it go. You have to make adjustments, balance up the good and the bad, as you go through. Yes, it was a terrible blow but, no, it hasn't gnawed at me down the years. If I had let it, where would that have left me? It was one of the things that happened to me. It shouldn't have happened, Georgie Best's tackle was a bad one, but there it was. Other bad things have happened to me. I've been disappointed by some people – and how some things have turned out – but my policy has been to just get on with it, to live my life however it came. I suppose it helps that I'm not a naturally bitter person.

'I've always tried to keep my reactions even because no one has ever needed to tell me that one minute you can be up and the next you can be right down there. I was up in 1970 when the injury came. I was playing out of my skin and I believed my best years were still to come. People were talking about me playing for England, and I had so much to look forward to. Then, suddenly, I was fighting for my life and my leg. That just showed me how quickly your life can change. So of course you cannot take anything for granted. Hopefully, it has made me a better person.

'About seven years ago I had a heart attack, a serious one. I was gone, apparently, and then the doctors brought me back, and since then my wife Patricia has worried about me. I go to town and if I'm not back in 20 minutes she's on the bloody phone. It has changed our life to a degree, and it is because of her concern for me. Before the heart attack I'd go golfing with Alan, and we would have some of the lads, like Tommy Booth, down from Manchester and then we would go for a drink afterwards and I could get in at 2 a.m. without hearing a peep from Patricia.

'I just get on with my life because the heart attack, like Georgie's tackle, is something that has happened and something I have to adapt to, and the reason I don't play golf any more is because I don't want Patricia worrying about me every minute of the day.'

His cousin and comrade interjects, sending out perhaps a waft of optimism that some of the old habits can be resumed. He says, 'But you're well over it now, aren't you?'

'Yes, maybe,' says Pardoe, 'but she would still be traumatised if I played golf. I couldn't really enjoy it now because of that – and I certainly couldn't linger over a drink. Anyway, that's how I look at it. I was very close to losing my leg. I have my health back and I have a good family I'm very proud of. As I see it, there is really no choice, you get on with it.

'I'd been at City 31 years when I got the call from the manager Peter Reid that said that I was finished. I'd been working as a coach for the youth team and the reserves and the manager said he wanted to bring in his own man. He had been at the club about three years by then. I was gutted, of course. Thirty-one years is a long time. I took 12 months off and then started working on reception at Barclays Bank in Winsford. To be honest, the football job was altering. You couldn't really say anything to the kids, they were getting most of their ideas from the TV. So I didn't try too hard to get back in.

'Nowadays the kids never play against over-aged players. At 15 or 16 we were playing against full internationals fighting to stay in the game. You were also playing every week, keeping your touch and your fitness and match sharpness. You were dealing with old pros going the other way but still full of tricks and knowledge of how the game went. Players are coming into action now without playing for eight or 10 weeks. I don't care who the hell you are, however talented you are, you just can't do that. You've got to be doing it all the time.'

Yet if Pardoe often looks askance at the new values of the game that was his home for so long, he does recognise there are some enduring qualities which still can make the difference between success and failure. It is a belief he holds with some optimism on behalf of his remarkable grandson Tommy, who spoke so impressively at the funeral of Mike Doyle, his other grandfather.

'Tommy is 13 now and he definitely has a chance,' says Pardoe. 'Like everyone else who comes into the game he will need some luck, but City obviously rate him. They have placed him in the academy and his education – with a teacher–pupil ration of one to 10 – is guaranteed until he is 16. He has lessons in the morning and trains in the afternoon. No doubt he has got a lot of ability, but then you never know. There are no guarantees but if he doesn't make it the problem will not be a lack of confidence. He made a brilliant speech at Mike's funeral, when he was barely eight.'

Pardoe was deep into the readjustments demanded by another life when his cousin left the battleground they had shared with such exhilaration. 'Oaksie' was pleased to go out as he had started 17 years earlier, albeit a rather more weathered and knowing version of the eager but sometimes apprehensive kid. He was 34 when Chester, who were just an easy drive from his home, finally persuaded him to say farewell to the highest level of football. That, he has always missed, but the third division club came bearing extravagant gifts: 'I left City in 1976 and I was happy enough at the timing because I didn't feel my first division career had trailed away like so many do. We beat Newcastle for the League Cup under Bookie, and I was delighted about that. I was also pleased that I had played 38 league games, which wasn't bad for someone hitting his mid-thirties. Chester had been tapping me up for a long, long time and at the end of the day I just couldn't turn them down. What they were offering me was ridiculous when you compared it with my money at City. They were paying me £400 a week, nearly double my City wages, and a signing-on fee that set me up for life. I could hardly believe it. On top of that they were paying £5,000 into my pension fund, and there were very good rates back then. So I had just fallen on my feet financially. I went just as a player but the manager, Ken Roberts, said, "You can have the manager's job shortly, I'm going upstairs."

'My big signing as a manager was Ian Rush, and soon enough he went to Liverpool. Rushy didn't want to leave. He went to Anfield, had his talks, received his offer and came back to Chester to tell me, "No, I don't want to go there." He was a quiet lad, a smashing lad, from down the road in Flint. I told Ken Roberts, "You know the lad is very happy here, he's going to take some shifting." The Liverpool chairman John Smith did all the signings and he called me to say, "The lad is adamant he wants to stay with you." Chester were building a new stand and they were desperate for the Rush money. A few months later the chairman of Chester, Reg Rowlands, came to me and said, "Look, we need £300,000 for the new stand, you've got to move Rush on." When we reopened negotiations with Liverpool I said to Rowlands, "You would be better taking a bit less on the fee and getting a sell-on clause," but he decided to go for the ready money. Eventually Rush moved to Juventus at the then British record transfer fee of £3.2 million.

'I used to give Rushie my old suits and lots of other gear. He had nothing but he was a great lad. He was a superb goalscorer, arguably the best I've ever seen. He was certain about everything he did around the goal.

'It ended for me at Chester with an argument with the chairman. When you argue with the chairman, it is goodbye, isn't it? I'd done six years and, to be honest, I was ready to get out. I'd enjoyed almost all my days there but it was time to go, and the important thing for me and my family was that we had become financially secure. I did a bit of coaching, at Port Vale and then back at Chester for a little while, but mostly I played golf. I just got on with trying to enjoy life and my family. I've certainly done that.

'My son Mike played in goal for Wolves and Aston Villa, and now he does a couple of days a week as goalkeeping coach at Wrexham. He's my younger son; my eldest isn't a footballer but he's a great lad – and he could probably drink you under the table.'

Like Pardoe, and for all his irritation at some of the manifestations – or as he might put it at his most irritable, infestations – of today's game, Oakes's debt to football was long acknowledged before the onset of that degree of financial comfort. 'The truth is,' he says, 'you never really thought about the money, it was always the game, week in and week out, and it was about relating to everyone at the club, including the supporters. Nowadays I think the big problem is that everything is so fragmented and dependent on any one club's situation. Take the FA Cup, for example: before, it used be a staple of football, now it's a matter of convenience – maybe you're interested in winning it, maybe not if you have bigger fish to fry.

'I was thinking the other day, if you told everyone there was a place in the Champions League for a team winning the Cup you wouldn't see reserves performing in games which, a few years ago, would have been huge. Everyone would play their best teams because the incentive would be huge. Yes, I do get very disenchanted with a lot of what I see today.

'What I really can't stand is all the diving and play-acting, tugging shirts and rolling over. In the old days when someone hurt you, you would be on the other side of the field before you said, 'Bastard.' You wouldn't want anyone to know you were hurt – and least of all the person who had done it.

'But then you hope it is just another phase, and that somewhere out there someone will discover, or remember, there is another way of playing football; something that Malcolm Allison brought to us at City, something that was so positive and very beautiful.'

It is where we started, and quite inevitably, it is where we finish. 'The hardest thing in seeing Mal slide down the years, moving from place to place, so often far below where he should have been,' says Pardoe, 'was that you could never forget all his shining gifts. When it all blew up at City, Joe wasn't so well and maybe the directors fed that into the equation. In the end it was just detail. We had had our time. What we would never have again was that sure sense of someone in charge who could make things work against the heaviest odds. Mal loved those situations when he would need to juggle the team, put David Connor on Alan Ball, say, and then see how things could fall so neatly into place.

'It was so strange in one way. Mal could analyse a football game so easily, know all the problems and the answers, yet couldn't take control of his life. I remember him at a party at Ralph Brand's house. Mal was dancing and, not unusually, completely pissed, and suddenly he fell back into a glass cabinet, completely smashing it. He struggled to his feet, put his hand in his pocket and pulled out 200 quid, handed it over to Ralph and said, "Here you are, I'll pay for it."

'Alan and me were lucky in one sense. We used to come away from games and training back here into deepest Cheshire, play a lot of golf and not get involved in too much of the nonsense. We felt we had the best of two worlds, and even in the team situation we had our group, Belly, Doyle, Alan and me. They called us the Big Four off the field (as opposed to Lee, Summerbee and Bell, the Big Three on it), but then in the dressing room there was no doubt we were all together. Even today when we meet up we are once again back in the dressing room.'

Oakes says, 'It's true that sometimes you got a bit exasperated with Malcolm. You thought, "Who needs champagne all the time?" But then he was committed to his idea of living life to the full, and maybe it was partly to do with the illness which cut short his playing career and threatened his life. I heard the story of when he was playing for West Ham and he got kicked in the chest and was lying on the field gasping for breath. Apparently he said later that his biggest concern was that he had £200 in his jacket in the dressing room and that it might go unspent.

'However, whatever made bubbly and big cigars and all his carrying on such necessities for him, they never interfered with the fact that we all owed him so much. He gave us the great days we will take to our graves. They were such fantastic days and now I don't have to make a conscious effort to think about them – and nor do I dream about them. It is more that they are part of me every time I get up in the morning.

'So many good footballers never get to Wembley – or win the league. In that last matter I really felt for Steven Gerrard when Liverpool just missed winning the Premier League last season. He is the perfect example of what I'm talking about. What a player he has been for Liverpool, and even as a City man I couldn't help feeling it would have been nice if he had got there after all the years of trying. Maybe he will never get there now. To be perfectly frank, he hasn't had the coach who could have helped him to make it happen.

'Not, certainly, as we did when we believed we could beat anyone in any situation. Malcolm, with Joe looking after his back, made us believe we could do anything if we just got down to it. We lost Youngy, Doyley and Heslop before their time, and we think of this when we meet up again and have our celebrations of the past because, as I always say, in our minds and spirit we became a lot more than a football team, and this means that all of us, those who have gone and those who are still here, will always be together.'

Pardoe nods a last affirmation. 'Some things you know you will have, whatever comes to you, and no one has ever needed to tell this to Our Kid or me. Everyone says how close we are, and it's true, but we also know we share something that goes wider than how we feel about each other, how easy we are in each other's company.'

It is, one is obliged to believe again, the rare gift that comes to only a small number of most fortunate people. Manchester City, circa 1967–70, may not have been the greatest, happiest football team ever assembled. But for that short and thrilling time they had a few reasons to believe it might just be so.

Chapter 16

Between them Wyn Davies and Freddie Hill played less than a hundred games for Manchester City, at a time in the early seventies when the trophy-hoarding team, while still capable of producing the most arresting football, had that first sense they may have seen the last of the best of their days. Though both had been admired down the years by Malcolm Allison – Davies for his ferocious and brilliant work in the air; Hill for his lovely creative touch – they came late to a tumultuous party.

The timing of their arrival will always be a source of regret to two fine footballers, both capped by their countries, both held in the highest regard by former teammates at a battery of clubs, but when I meet them again at the Olympus Fish and Chip Restaurant in Bolton they remind me in a fleeting way of an American gridiron coach I once knew, an ex-US Marine who, looking back on his service on the Nationalist Chinese island of Quemoy, used a phrase that lingered in the mind. Describing how it was being bombarded from the mainland, he said, 'I didn't go to war, but I sure felt the rush.'

Although Davies and Hill were never able to secure, after hand-to-hand fighting, fresh trophies for the team they admired so much, they did get a compelling sense of how it might have been. They felt, certainly, they had gained an unforgettable sense of being involved in sharply raised action.

I last saw them at Allison's funeral, where they said that they had come not only out of respect for the best football coach they had ever known but also to meet up again with old teammates with whom they had shared some of the last of their glory. And now again they are at pains to point out that it was better to have lived the last fragments of a great adventure than none at all. Certainly, they insisted, they too had felt a 'rush'.

Hill gives a haunting account of his halting, roundabout journey to City after 12 distinguished but ultimately frustrating years at Bolton Wanderers, four of which were in the company of Davies: 'Whenever I met Mal and Frannie Lee socially they said City were coming for me, but for so long nothing came of it,' he says. 'Mal would say things like, "I'm coming for you, Fred. I like the way you play, I like your skill." But after a while I took these remarks with a pinch of salt. It gets you down a bit when people keep saying they are going to do something but nothing happens. Anyway, I was at the party of a business partner of Frannie's, and Mal came up to me and said, "Freddie, we are definitely coming for you – on Monday." And, maybe naturally, I thought, "Well, I'll believe that when I see it."

'But then Monday came, and while I was training at Halifax Town the manager, Alan Ball Senior, came out on to the field where we were playing five-a-side and shouted, "Freddie, I need you in the office." I thought, "Bloody hell, is this it?" I was 30, I'd had some good years at Bolton, picked up a couple of England caps, but after arriving at Halifax I had begun to tell myself I could kiss goodbye to any chance of playing in the kind of great team City had become. That would have been an almost unbelievable experience after all those years as a pro at Bolton, and then heading over the Pennines to life in the third division.

'But here I was in Bally's office and he was saying the magic words, "Mal's been on and he says he wants you to go to City. It's up to you, and I would guess you want to go there, but as it happens I'm taking the job at Preston and I would like you to come with me. I would certainly do all I could to get you the best possible terms." I thanked him but said he was right, I did want to go to City and play with an already great team that looked certain to get more honours. It would be brilliant to finish up with such a team, one which put such a high value on skill and let their players get on with it. That had to be the dream of a player who had some skill and, yes, I wanted to be part of a story of success that would run for some time.

'Bally, who had done so much to develop the career of his son Alan, nodded his understanding and said, "You are right, Fred, a player like you would naturally want to play for a team like City. Yes, they are a great team – a beautiful team. We'll try to fix things up as soon as possible." So there was this great gift which had come to me on a Yorkshire morning. It was not to be a signing that would light up the football world and it wasn't the kind of key move that Mal and Joe had heralded when they signed the great trio of Lee, Bell and Summerbee, but I was being given the chance to end my career with a club that had already proved its great quality. Unlike Summerbee and Bell, Frannie and Tony Book, I wouldn't be in at the ground floor, I wouldn't be part of making a great team but, who knew, I might just be able to play a part in maintaining the standards that had been set so quickly, so brilliantly.

'One thing was reassuring. It wouldn't be the first time I would be keeping the company of great footballers. Apart from having Frannie as a teammate at Bolton, I had been around for the last playing years of Nat Lofthouse, the Lion of Vienna, and I had admired too the tremendous goalkeeping of Eddie Hopkinson. I also knew the character of blood-curdling full-backs like Tommy Banks and Roy Hartle.

'It was Banks who said at a meeting when the players were talking about strike action to raise the minimum wage, and someone said they should remember they didn't have to go down the pit every day, "Yes, but come Saturday afternoon those lads don't have to mark Stanley Matthews or Tom Finney."

'The atmosphere at City was terrific – all I had imagined. I felt the buzz the first time I reported to Maine Road for training. It was full of life and, ideally for me, a ball was never far away once fitness levels had been established. Malcolm was such a brilliant coach because he was so very sure about the kind of players he wanted to work with. He wanted players who could play, who could think for themselves and had the strongest creative instincts. He wanted those players and he always made it clear he would let them play. He wouldn't distract them from that main purpose, which would take away their effectiveness. He would say to the lads in defence, "Give the ball to those who you know can do something with it, give it to them and let them get on with it." Joe always backed up Mal in the team talks, saying, "Look, we've got the best players, and never forget that at any stage of the game."

'Mal loved skill, he revered it, and I was lucky enough to have a bit of it. Sometimes I'm afraid I have to conclude it is not the same today. The other night City should have won the big game at Liverpool, and maybe they would have done if Suárez had got the second yellow card he deserved for an act of shameless diving. That made me sick, really disgusted, because he is such a wonderfully talented player – it bewilders me when players of that quality try to cheat as much as exploit their tremendous gifts. But despite the Suárez issue, the fact is City got back into the game after going 2–0 down, and whatever the qualities the manager Manuel Pellegrini has, and they are obviously very considerable – on top of the fact that he seems an extremely nice fella – he didn't have his team, his hugely talented team, playing with the kind of authority Malcolm could inspire so superbly.'

Davies has followed his friend's account with intense concentration and now he shakes his head with a mournful regret worthy of an old Welsh bard intoning his gloom at the National Eisteddfod.

'When I went from Bolton to Newcastle in 1966 I did so without realising that another club had come in for me at the last minute – and that it was City,' he says. 'Had I known that I would almost certainly have gone to them, even though nobody realised quite then what a stir they were about to make. Going to City would have meant I could have kept living in Bolton, where I had a serious girlfriend, and I could have commuted to Maine Road.

'I did have good years in the North East, however. They were probably the best of my career. I felt I had truly arrived at the top of the game and was pleased to carry the nickname "Wyn the Leap". But then when Malcolm "Supermac" Macdonald arrived I had a sense that my time there was over. That was certainly my feeling when I stood in the tunnel at St James' Park when they were out on the field taking the official team pictures for the 1971–72 season. I'd hung back, and when the manager Joe Harvey saw me he shouted, "Wyn, get yourself in the bloody picture." I did it but not with a great deal of conviction. The word was that my style and Supermac's would not blend particularly well, and that his designated partner was John Tudor, who had made a big name for himself at Sheffield United and was a very good player. The plan worked out very well for Newcastle.

'Mal told me that he still thought I had a big future at Maine Road and, when he said that, I remembered driving back down the motorway from Newcastle after City had won the title at our place a few years earlier. It was a terrific game, one of the most exciting I had ever played in, and I was amazed by all the City fans going home like a triumphant army with all their flags and banners.

'Looking back, the great sadness for me was that I never played in a final. I'd played for Wales at Wembley, but I missed City's two appearances there, and then in the five years that followed my departure Newcastle made two appearances in the old stadium, when Liverpool beat them in the FA Cup final and then, three years later when City, ironically enough, beat them in the League Cup final thanks to an overhead kick by Dennis Tueart. Bloody hell!

'In my first season at City Mal made his ill-fated move for Rodney Marsh just as we seemed to be on our way to the title. On the first

Saturday after he arrived Rodney was in the dugout at Goodison Park when we beat Everton 2–1 and Fred scored, and the following week, with Rodney in the team, we beat Chelsea 1–0 at Maine Road in probably one of the worst games ever seen. Ten minutes from the end Ron "Chopper" Harris caught Marshy on the shin and Mal pulled him off. A lot of people, not aware of the knock inflicted by Chopper, were asking why Rodney was brought off and Mal said it was because the pace of the game had got to him after the second division and a lay-off with injury at QPR.

'We finished up missing the title by a point, and there's no doubt in my mind we would have won it if Mal had left things as they were. We'd had a lead of five points, in those days when you got only two points for a win.'

Hill played a high price for his goal at Everton. He got an injury that kept him out of the Chelsea game. 'That was the breaking point of my hope that I would play a part in a first title win,' he says. 'Rodney was brought in and stayed in but for a game at Old Trafford, when he was left out initially but came on and scored in a 3–1 win in which he showed quite a number of his skills. But then we all knew about those assets. The big question was whether he could stand up to a race to the finish line, and unfortunately the answer was clear soon enough.

'It was negative. We drew at Newcastle, lost at home to Stoke and Southampton, had a home win against West Ham, beat United, drew at Coventry, lost at Ipswich, and then, in the last match, when the race was already over, we beat the champions Derby County. Naturally, and frustratingly, Rodney showed a lot of his skill that afternoon.

'He was an exceptionally gifted player, but the fact was he just wasn't right for us at that time. He came from a different place and played a different game. I remember one day, when I was sitting on the bench during a game, Alan Oakes came racing up to the dugout shouting, "Get him [Marshy] off and Fred on."

'Derby had come back from a trip abroad very surprised to have won the title in their absence. It was a real shame, we had been playing so well before that slump, we looked like a team and, more importantly, we felt like one.'

The head that was once the most feared in football is being shaken again with much vigour as Davies says, 'Yeah, it was tragic all right. They had won those trophies between 1968 and 70 in a great burst of brilliance, and here was another that had gone begging. This was a good enough team to have won another title, at least one more. When I played my first game with City, I said to myself, "Wyn, boy, this is a really good team. It has everything you need to win titles." We had a bloody good defence, a midfield that knew precisely what it was doing, and a forward line, well, what more could you have wanted when you looked at those forwards?

'No, we didn't want for anything. At the very least we had all the qualities necessary to win a Cup, and so my consolation came when I told myself, "For sure you're going to Wembley now."'

Hill wants to clear up an old and, in his opinion, utterly erroneous tactical assessment of the team who gave Derby their default title. He says, 'Some people said we were great going forward but that defensively we were not so good, and I said, "No, you've got it all wrong." What was happening was that it was a defence dedicated to letting their forwards play. The forwards were never expected to mark back and cover for defenders. They were allowed to attack flat out, they gave us the ball and said, in effect, "Get on with it." I remember going back in one game when we seemed to be under a bit of pressure, and Tommy Booth saying to me, "Fred, what are you doing back here? Fuck off out of the way." He realised I was not much good at heading the ball so he was making it quite clear that in that part of the field he regarded me as neither use nor ornament.'

Davies again echoes Hill: 'The most important point was that Mal made us all, attackers and defenders, better players. It was a bit like when I went to Wrexham as a kid and Ken Barnes arrived as player-manager. I remembered him from his role in the great City Cup teams of the mid-fifties, when he was such a key element in the Revie Plan as an attacking midfielder. I remember seeing the City–Newcastle final of 1955 on black and white telly and I've never forgotten the excitement of that.

'When you're a kid people ask you what you are going to do when you're grown up, and even if you have dreams of being a footballer you say things like, "Oh, I'll probably be a plumber or something like that." I certainly didn't imagine I would be a professional footballer that day I watched two of my future clubs on that little telly screen in the parlour of my house in Caernarvon.'

The morning stretches into lunchtime at the Olympus, and as lady shoppers park their bags and sit down to most excellent fish and chips and bread and butter and copious amounts of tea some of the older ones call out cheerily to the heroes and, in one or two cases at least, maybe the heart-throbs, of their youth. I feel bound to ask the objects of this respectful familiarity if they do not envy, hard, the riches and the wider celebrity of contemporary superstars.

Hill says, 'It is unreal, isn't it? The truth is that people like Wyn and me and all the lads of our time really can't afford to think about it. It would probably make us ill if we did it too much. It's gone now, that part of our lives, and we've got more important things to think about, like how we find a little happiness and satisfaction in the rest of our lives. And, of course, if we are lucky, that has a lot to do with our families.

'Still, I have to be honest, when I saw Wayne Rooney walking off the field the other night after being knocked out of the Champions League by Bayern Munich I had to think, "Now what's going through his mind right now? Is he thinking, 'Oh well, it's all right because I'm another few hundred thousand pounds richer this week. It's not the end of the world.'?" Really, the whole situation is unbelievable.'

Davies burrows beneath our table into a shoulder bag packed with old photographs and cuttings and then brandishes, with a puckish smile, an article based on an interview he had done a few years earlier. 'Here,' he says, 'look at this – it is the only time I ever told a lie.'

The yellowing page is dominated by a Davies quote: 'I had my time in football and I enjoyed every minute of it. No, I don't begrudge today's players all their big money – not for a second.' He says now, 'When Freddie was talking my mind was going back to when I was a kid at Wrexham and people asked me, "Hey, what happens if you don't make it in the game? And even if you do you're only going to play until you're 30 – if you're lucky. Then you will still have to get on with your life and make a living."'

When Freddie Hill left the game he did so with the certainty that he was doing the right thing according to his nature. 'When I knew my playing days were over I never wanted to be a manager,' he tells me. 'From my perspective the best of football had come and gone. I didn't want to be dealing with businessmen directors who knew nothing about the game. I didn't want to be picking out young lads and then dropping them and telling them they had no future in the game they had set their hearts on, all that sort of thing. It just didn't rest easily with my nature. I couldn't tell a kid something that ruined his life and not bother about it. I wouldn't be able to drive home and shake it off by the time I got there.

'So I was very happy to go working for Frannie in his paper factory.'

He was most happy that he had, with that extension of his time among great players at City – and then 75 games with Peterborough United which helped win the club promotion to the third division and gain him a place in the Fenland's football hall of fame – played until he was 35, and with the satisfaction that he had never compromised his cradle gift of natural talent.

Davies is inspired again to rummage in his repository of memories beneath the table and this time he comes up with an old tape of an interview Hill gave at a Bolton Christmas party. 'He says about me,'

Davies reports, 'that when I first arrived in Bolton I was painfully shy and my English wasn't too good. And it is true enough. I spoke Welsh back in Caernarvon and I didn't get at all comfortable with English until I spent some time in Wrexham.

'When two big clubs, Bolton and Sheffield Wednesday, came in for me, the first thing I did was look at a map. I retraced the journeys back from both places to Caernarvon and saw that it was about an hour longer coming from Sheffield. So that was a no-brainer decision. When I came to City after five years at Newcastle I headed straight back to the familiar ground here in Bolton. Fred and I used to go to Frannie's house and join him on the drive to City.

'Those were lively days in Newcastle – on and off the field. One night, at the big club La Dolce Vita, I was introduced to two extraordinary women. Someone took a picture of us. The ladies were Diana Dors and Jayne Mansfield – and that, I thought, wasn't bad for a lad from Caernarvon. They had been up on the stage on high stools answering questions from the audience, and it all seemed very glamorous to me. I also met my countryman, Tom Jones, a great guy who was so natural and unpretentious.

'Everyone who got a number one record in those days seemed to show up at La Dolce Vita, and I remember well Del Shannon and the girl from Cardiff's Tiger Bay, Shirley Bassey. For a while it was one of the most famous nightclubs in the country, though some of the pilgrims would not have won the approval of my Mum, and these included the Kray Twins, Ronnie and Reginald. One night they showed up with a big party, and the word was that they were taking a break from talks with the local "firm". That night the American singer Billy Daniels provided the on-stage cabaret. It was sad to see the place go down over the years. In the end, just before it closed you could get a pint there for 29p – one of the cheapest prices in town.

'After training we used to go to a coffee bar favoured by local musicians, and one night I got talking to a lad from County Durham who was known as "Peanut". It was Peter Langford of the Barron Knights. It was not unusual to be poured into a taxi at 2 a.m. and then sweat it out at training in the morning.'

It is almost as though Davies is reaching out, not altogether successfully and maybe least of all in his own mind, to varnish over some of the harsher realities – and consequences – that came with the pattern of his career and his life.

Certainly his mood becomes more sombre when his friend Freddie Hill takes his leave. As he retraces the final stages of his football life, and then returns to his roots and the start of his working days in a North Wales quarry, he might be walking a high wire between exhilaration and regret and, well, a degree of bitterness.

When the disappointment of City's title drive hit home, when it was clear the fissure separating Allison and Mercer had gone beyond repair, he found himself once again in another of football's cycles of hope and despair. 'In the middle of the City crisis I heard that Frank O'Farrell wanted me to sign me for Manchester United and play me alongside people like Charlton, Law and Best,' he says. 'I could hardly believe it but I went to see the manager, who was having such a tough time trying to get a great club, and some great players, back on track. He was very pleasant, said how highly he rated my ability, and the deal went through very quickly.

'I was happy enough because United is United, and I was living just up the road in Bolton and didn't have to change anything in my life. Unfortunately, O'Farrell was on his last legs at Old Trafford and Tommy Docherty was arriving in his place. When O'Farrell's sacking broke a reporter called me up and asked me how I felt about the coming of the Doc and what my assessment was of the managers I would experience in Manchester – Malcolm, O'Farrell and now Docherty. He asked me if I was bothered about the fact that Docherty had such a liking for Scottish players – did I fear being edged out by somebody wearing a kilt? I said to the reporter, "Oh, give over." But in response to his other question, I said simply, "Malcolm was an absolutely brilliant football man, Frank was a gentleman and I don't know much about the Doc." I hadn't met him yet.

'Docherty arrived with his sidekick, Tommy Cavanagh, and I have to say I wasn't encouraged. After a few days Docherty had me in his office to tell me that the West Bromwich manager Don Howe had been on. I was non-committal and went back to training. About a week later Docherty told me that Howe had been back on and that I might as well go down to West Brom because I was only going to "die" at Old Trafford.

'I was stung by that and said to him, "What have you ever done in football except leave clubs in debt?" Of course, that made him very angry and he asked, "What's all this about me only going for players wearing kilts?" I said that the interview had happened weeks ago, the line about kilts was a reporter's invention, and I just wanted to do my job. I might have saved my breath. The West Brom move didn't happen but soon enough I was at Blackpool and running out the string of my career.

'One positive thing I do remember from the Blackpool days, in which I scored just five goals in 36 league appearances, was a very fine goal scored by my teammate Mickey Walsh. We were playing Sunderland at home and Mickey smashed it into the top of the net. It was voted the goal of the season [in 1975]. Some things stick with you always and the memory of Mickey doing so brilliantly that day is one of them.

'I was always a genuine player in as much as I gave it everything I had. I had scars and injuries and all that, but it did take me to a point where I think you apply a phrase I have always loved, the one that says, "What you see is what you get."'

There is no longer any need for the reinforcement of Davies's travelling bag of memory-spurs. Now he is back in the hills that surround his historic home town. 'I left school when I was 15 and went working with my dad in the quarry. My dad had TB and he died when he was 39.

He was a hard man and then he was gone, and my mother had to bring up three of us on a widow's pension. I don't know how the hell she did it. I earned £4 from the quarry and gave most of it to my Mum. When I was still 15 I went to United for a trial, and the game was at Everton. Nobby Lawton was playing for United – and I played well. The United scout lived just outside Caernarvon and he was very pleased with my performance.

'When I got out of the team bus at Old Trafford I was told I would be staying the night at the home of the United coach John Aston before returning to Wales the following day. I was honoured to be staying with a famous old footballer, someone who had played with United in some of their greatest days and had also won 17 caps for England. Over supper Johnny asked me what I did when I wasn't playing football, and I explained in my halting English how you cut the slate in the quarry.

'I had another trial, in the youth team of Aston Villa, and played well again, scoring two goals in a 3–0 win and, later at Villa Park, an official said he wanted to introduce me to someone. It was Joe Mercer, who was then the Villa manager.

'I didn't get an offer from either United or Villa but looking back on how it all worked out I cannot say I regretted that. If those clubs seemed very glamorous to a kid from North Wales I realised soon enough that it was very easy to make a big fall when you are so very young and inexperienced in both football and life.

'When I went to Wrexham I got the chance to work my way up. I got the opportunity to move to Bolton when I was 20. I reckoned I'd got to the first division with a lot of hard work, something I had been used to at such a tender age at the quarry.

'I didn't have an agent when I left Wrexham – not many lower division players did – and I tried to do a bit of negotiating. I was very anxious for Mum to get a thousand pounds, which I thought was only fair in that Wrexham were getting £25,000 for me and I'd given some pretty good service for quite modest wages. I told manager Ken Barnes this and he said, "Right, leave it to me."

'Back home in Caernarvon they were saying, "Oh, Lily Davies must be rich now because Wrexham have sold her boy for a fortune." After six weeks I drove down to Wrexham from Bolton and finally got to see Ken Barnes when he was leaving his house with his wife and son Peter, who would go on to make his name as a top pro with Manchester City and West Brom.

'Ken said, "Oh, Wyn, what a nice surprise, come into the house." He was less pleased to see me, though, when I raised the subject of the payment that had never happened. He said to me, "I don't know anything about that, Wyn, you better see the chairman."

'That was how it was in those days, and it can make you feel very bitter. I didn't lose my respect for Ken, who had been such a brilliant player and was a very good coach, and I met again a few times before he died. But that business comes back to me sometimes when I read about all the rewards received by some, let's face it, mediocre players. I was a naïve lad when I went to Bolton – I even mistakenly handed over some insurance payments to the club which were due to me, and it never got a lot better throughout my career. When I went to Bolton, Newcastle, City and United I never received more than my basic contract and some quite small win and crowd bonuses.'

That first bout of angst came 50 years ago in the house of a football man he hugely respected. Now there are days when it seems like a small rankle indeed. He has depression and recently he has been fretting about his health.

We are alone in the big and now empty restaurant, but for a waiter clearing away dishes. Davies tells me, 'I'm quite worried about my memory, it is not so good now. I put things away safely and then quite soon I'm wondering, "Where the hell did I put that?" Before coming here this morning I went to the hospital for a scan – today it was on my heart because, I was surprised to hear, your heart dictates everything in your body, including your brain. I'm also going to have a brain scan. One reason that I'm worried is that I've been reading about the campaign launched by Jeff Astle's family following his death at the age of 59 – and the conclusion of a coroner that the degenerative disease suffered by him could be linked to the number of times he headed a heavy leather football.

'The Astle family have accused the FA of telling lies – and reneging on promises to seriously investigate the theory. I want to do what I can to help the campaign, and maybe my situation now could be very helpful to the medical people who are looking into it. God knows, I headed enough footballs, and some winter days they were so heavy you felt like you were putting your head in the way of a cannonball.

'Depression is not very nice, so sometimes I have to keep myself going a bit more than usual. I do get emotional at times, especially when I think of my Mum, Lily.'

He makes one last visit into his bag and produces a strip of white cardboard on which is printed out, in block capitals, 'YOU CAN ONLY HAVE ONE MOTHER, PATIENT KIND AND TRUE, AND NO OTHER FRIEND IN ALL THE WORLD WILL BE AS TRUE TO YOU.'

'At the moment,' he says, 'I have the sad feeling that people are dying all around me. When I leave here I'm going off see the widow of a friend of mine who had a stall on the market in Bolton and used to take me to the races at Aintree and Haydock Park. I go to see Joyce regularly, and take another friend, Edna, but when I called her today she said she was very down and didn't want to see anybody, but we're going anyway and we'll try to buck her up.

'I sometimes wonder what triggers depression? I never married, never had kids. For a while I went out with Joe Mercer's daughter – she used to come running with me in Chorlton, but I don't really know why something didn't happen. I suppose, deep down, I've always been a bit scared to commit. Sometimes people say to me, "Oh, Wyn, get a couple of pints down you," but it isn't always so easy.

'When I first came to Bolton I didn't suffer too badly from home-sickness. I went into digs with two other players, and I got myself a girlfriend quite quickly. I should have got married then, and I don't really know why I didn't. Then I went to Newcastle and she used to visit me, and when I could I came down here. Her cousin ran a pub next to the railway station.

'I had two brothers – David, who died; and Norman, who lives in Caernarvon still. I go to Caernarvon every year to visit Mum's grave on her anniversary. I also go to Anglesey to stand at my brother's grave.

'Tomorrow I'll be up at about half-past five. At half-past six, after having my porridge, I go to the gym to do some stretching and work on the bike, have a nice shower and then go home to change. I also pre-record any racing on television and pop into the bookies to make a few bets. I come to this restaurant not later than 1.25. I then go to the park with my dog, give it a walk and then tie him up before I play some bowls. I enjoy it in the park. You bump into a lot of people, and that takes you out of yourself, doesn't it?'

So does meeting up with old comrades like Freddie Hill and going to the events like the one he is looking forward to now, a ceremony at Newcastle to install a plaque for his old manager Joe Harvey, whose success in the Fairs Cup and the FA Cup, Davies points out, were the last honours won by a proud club. 'I'm going with my old teammates Jim Iley and Pat Howard, and we will have to set off at 6 a.m. because the ceremony is scheduled for eleven o'clock. But I know it will be a nice occasion.'

Certainly it will be a little time when he will not be required to watch, or even to recognise, the clock that some days now seems such a tyrant. He will be Wyn the Leap again, ferocious, indestructible and aware once more that wherever he went, including to the passingly brilliant Manchester City, no one was ever mistaken in what they saw.

Chapter 17

When Mansour bin Zayed Al Nahyan decided to buy Manchester City in 2008 he made, in a stroke, a much loved but historically problematic football club one of the richest and most powerful in the world. It was the signal for a rush of trophies and ambition unprecedented but for Malcolm Allison's promise to fly City to the moon. The Sheikh also resolved a question that for the best part of 50 years had bewildered arguably the club's most revered player.

'I wondered all that time,' says Colin Bell, 'why it was that people with big money had never gone into City – and thought how odd it was that it hadn't happened. I had always believed that investment flowed naturally into a business that clearly had the backing of people coming through the door. In the 50 years since I joined them the action at the City turnstiles has been fantastic. To have something so close to a full house so often, over a time when they had mostly not been claiming trophies, proved to me beyond any doubt they had great supporters. So hence the question I kept asking myself: "Why have City not had their own version of Roman Abramovich?"

'Now it has happened in the most spectacular way, and there is every reason to believe the Abu Dhabi owners are here to stay. They want to build on strong foundations, and now anyone can see the possibilities are immense. If that sounds optimistic, if you think I might be over-looking the fact that nothing is guaranteed in football, not even by billions of pounds, the fact is I've been emotionally attached to City so long I probably have blue blood. This is a lot to do with the fact that over the years I have come to believe that City have the best supporters in the world. They are honest supporters. They take the pain.'

They certainly displayed that kind of resilience in the early days of the Mercer–Allison renaissance, when after claiming the second division title City had a season of tricky readjustment in the top flight. It was voiced in a plaintive chant on the occasion their team, fighting to stay buoyant on a torrid afternoon at Goodison Park against Everton's surging midfield of Ball, Kendall and Harvey, conceded an early goal. 'Two, four, six, eight, ten, fuckin' hell we're gettin' beat again,' they cried in masochistic union.

By this time, though, one of their most committed number no longer watched shoulder to shoulder with the people whose cause had long been his passion. Ian Niven had a season ticket now, sat in the stand and was no longer content to express his opinions in the supporters' club meetings he attended so zealously. He was well on his way to becoming a director, despite relatively modest wealth, and down the years would come to share with Tony Book, a man he admired so much, the honorary presidency of Manchester City.

At 90 he is, I'm reminded when I see him in his top-floor flat in a smart Didsbury building, a most remarkable example of how football can become so central to the happiness of even the most serious-minded, hard-working and erudite men. For him the arrival of Malcolm Allison at Maine Road was, soon enough, less an encouragement than a reason to stage a one-man Palm Sunday. He adored the big man and it was an affection which survived sturdily through the worst of the years that came after the coach's first, utterly transforming impact. This was never more evident than on those haunting occasions Niven and I collected him from his care home and took him to lunches that invariably re-identified, in a spark or two, the man we had known and always loved.

Two great motifs of his life are prominently displayed in Ian Niven's lounge. One is a badge commemorating his wartime service with the Chindit troops in the jungles of Burma. It is pinned on the wall next to a picture of Joe Mercer and Malcolm Allison drinking champagne in his old pub in Denton, which he made a bastion of City support – a place where the great players and their bosses regularly came to relax, comfortably, among their most ardent admirers. 'That was one of those nights I will always treasure,' he reports while pointing to the big, framed photograph. 'We had just beaten United 3–1 in the championship season.'

He tells me his life story in sharp and vivid detail and points out, almost as a warning, this is necessary for any proper understanding of what a football club can mean to both an individual and a whole community. 'I came back from the army in 1947,' he says. 'We had been flown into northern Burma by the United States Air Commando. President Roosevelt approved the mission in consultations with Winston Churchill. "Vinegar Joe" Stilwell was the commanding general. We thought he was a bastard. He hated the British. Our mission was to meet up with him in the north. He was coming down with a force known as Merrill's Marauders – or Unit Galahad. It was partly modelled on our outfit, Orde Wingate's Chindits. The whole show came about because at the Tehran conference the Soviet leader Stalin complained to Roosevelt and Churchill that America and Britain were not doing enough in the Far East. We were flown in a hundred miles or so behind Japanese lines in gliders to a point Wingate had picked out after a series of recce sorties. It was a fantastic mission and it came just a month or so before the Normandy landings. No one was really concerned with the Far East, and we were just to get on with it after Stalin had made his point that almost all the action was being concentrated on the Western Front. Apparently, Roosevelt had said to Churchill, "We had better see what we can do. Joe isn't happy." We didn't understand the geopolitics – only that we had to shoot any bugger we had to shoot.

'I had volunteered for the Royal Scots, the regiment of my father, who was a regular soldier. The first five years of my life were spent while he was in the army. He joined up at 18 and served in the last year of the First World War. One motivation was to get away from his father, who was very strict, as was my father in his turn. So he buzzed off from Dunfermline across the Forth Bridge to Edinburgh and served a seven-year stint with the Royal Scots. When he came out he was every inch the army man, spick and span, and my mother had to scrub and clean.

'We had moved to Manchester by the time I volunteered for the Royal Scots at the outbreak of the Second World War, and I had to go to the Cameron Barracks in Inverness. It was a two-day journey, like going abroad. When the gliders landed in Burma we had to march, walk and crawl for 200 miles, and we had to harass the Japanese on the way, especially in the matter of blowing up the bloody railway to Rangoon. We had sappers with us. I had trained as a signaller. At the Cameron Barracks we had been given something like an eleven-plus exam so they could get an idea of our aptitudes. It was quite sensible, really. Twelve of us became signallers. You were still an infantryman, rifleman, route marcher, but you had lessons in codes and ciphers while the lads were square bashing, which saved us a lot of monotony. A few months later I was on my way to India on a troopship that was part of the first convoy passing through the Suez Canal. Inverness was the furthest I'd been before, apart from a trip with the Boy Scouts to Paris.'

But if Ian Niven had set himself on a vast and unfamiliar sea, he did have in his kitbag two items of enduring reassurance. He had packed his football boots.

'My reflections on some of the greatest days of Manchester City are very happy now,' he says. 'When I look back on my involvement with the team, and the support I was able to give as a director to a brilliant man like Malcolm Allison, I regard myself as a very lucky fellow. When you are a little chap at school you are generally kicked and bullied, but it didn't happen to me because I could play football. Football saved my life, gave me a lot of confidence that was put under threat by my military father. That pressure made me a quite subdued kid despite that not really being my nature or my personality. The three kids had to follow a strict code: you sat down at the table and you didn't speak unless you were spoken to, you did everything at the double. School was very strict in those days and when you got home it started all over again. My mother was quite the opposite of my father, she was a lovely, gentle Catholic woman. My father was a Scottish Presbyterian, puritan to the last ounce. He was a City supporter because his father played professionally for Dunfermline and was friendly with Peter Hodge, who worked very well with young players at that club and then after stints at Raith Rovers and Stoke City, became an extremely impressive manager of Manchester City between 1926 and 1932, winning the second division title and signing a certain Matt Busby as a trainee professional.

'When my grandfather finished playing for Dunfermline he moved the family to England, living in Chapel-en-le-Frith and later, when my family moved to Chorlton-on-Medlock on the fringes of Moss Side, I remember my dad walking all the way to Derbyshire to see his father. Where we lived in Manchester was full of Catholics who went to the Holy Name church – and I went too because I wanted to play football with them. When my father caught me playing on a Sunday he gave me a beating because Scottish Presbyterians do not do that on the Sabbath. On the other hand, he supported me in every other way in football, buying me good kit and even my own football (that was locked away every Sunday).

'When I came back from the army I was still very much a City man. My father used to take me to the games. The first one was away to Liverpool, and the big attraction was that our former hero Busby would be playing for Liverpool. Matt Busby was my father's idol, even though he had played such a big part in Catholic affairs when he was playing for City. But in this instance, at least, football values took over.

'My father was the chief cashier of a credit company and he told me that I was going to Anfield, along with 20 of his agents, on a bus that he had arranged. I didn't have any choice. "You're on the bus," he said. In those days it was a great trip – today it would be a bit like going to a big show in Vegas.

'Matt Busby had just been transferred to Liverpool and they made him captain for the day. Nearly 80 years later, I have it in my mind now, me sitting on a wall and Matt Busby coming out at the head of the Liverpool team with the ball in his hand. Now, here's the twist. We won 5–0. That's how good we were. We could sell the great Busby and still do that. And what did we do with the money we got for him? We bought Peter Doherty, one of the greatest footballers of all time, who carried us to the title with his beautiful talent. I was 12 then, quite a promising little footballer and by the time I was 14 I was captain of my school team, Ducie Avenue, which was a very good team indeed.

'My father was a scholar, a good writer, because he was educated well in Scotland, but I knew I wouldn't be able to follow him in this. I had no chance of making it to a top grammar school. Ducie was a technical school with a commercial section and I knew I could handle that if I had the right results in the eleven-plus exam. The main attraction, though, was the number of Ducie pupils who regularly graduated to the Manchester Boys team. One of them was the only Irish Catholic we ever had playing for City in those days, Billy Walsh. United were blazing. They assumed he would automatically roll up at Old Trafford.

'I got to Ducie and I finished up playing for Manchester Boys. The other day I went past the old Chorlton High School pitch where we used to play, and it all came back to me, the glory of taking that jersey and putting it on. My football career carried on when I got to Deolali in India and played for the camp in a team of international players. A Scottish corporal, a very knowledgeable football man, saw me kicking a ball about and said, "Come along, you'll get a game." I got kicked near to death but I enjoyed every minute of it. When I said I had turned out for the City youth team, the old sweats said, "What a load of rubbish." And then I asked them if they had ever heard of Peter Doherty.

'That reaction was just par for the course. When I was about six years old I asked my father when I became a City fan and he bellowed, "When you were conceived." It was a bit like being christened a City supporter. He might have well as said, "You will support City and you will also believe in God."'

For a little while, Niven admits unashamedly, the big, swaggering coach and saviour of City Allison was a more than passable substitute deity. When he achieved his ambition of becoming a director, he never disguised his status as an out-and-out Allison partisan. 'I feel very sad about the way it went for Malcolm,' he says. 'There was a genius. He is still with me, there he is on the wall, and he's also in my heart. He always will be. When he came along I was sat in Block H, Row H, right behind the directors' box. By then I had "achieved" a season ticket. I say achieved because back then getting a season ticket – and I had to get four, for my wife Olive, my son Ian, my daughter Olivia and me – was like buying a car when you didn't know you could afford it. But I knew I was going to do it. The main reason I stumped up the money was that when I went to an FA Cup semi-final between Everton and Liverpool and stood in the Kippax stand somebody peed down the back of my coat and trousers, and I said to myself, "Whatever the cost you're never going to let that happen to you again." This was two years before that terrible day when a crowd of just eight thousand came for the 3–1 defeat by Swindon, when stones were thrown at the stadium windows, and then it was so painful to remember how it was back in the thirties when a crowd of 81,000 showed up. I remember my son saying, "Where are all the people?" and I said, "Something has to be done about this football club." When I said that I thought about City's great tradition and how much it meant to so many ordinary people.

'At the time I was making some progress in my job as a buyer [at a local engineering firm], which was something I didn't know anything about when I went into it. When I eventually handed in my notice a director of the firm said, "One hundred and 22 people applied for your job and I whittled it down to two, tossed a coin before giving it to you and now you're leaving." I had got on a bit after doing some other jobs and before that I had joined the City supporters' club, which at the time was so old-fashioned it wasn't true. But it did help me get to put names to the faces of directors.

'The board didn't want to accept the supporters' club until the secretary Mrs Whelan, a magnificent woman, forced her way into recognition in the fifties. She said the people in the boardroom had to understand that the supporters were the lifeblood of the club and should be treated as something other than a nuisance.

'I formed a supporters' club in the Lord Lyon pub in the heart of Moss Side. Bobby Johnstone and Ken Barnes used to go there, along with quite a few of the other City players. I was a very young man then, and a long way from owning my own pub. In the end I only got one because I was thrown out of a United pub, but I didn't just wander into the business. I went to a course at Manchester University organised by the Forte company and, bloody hell, I finished top of the class – Joe Egg this was, someone who had never passed anything but a bus stop, most of his life.

'Eventually I built up a pub a mile away from the man who threw me out (because he was United and I was City). His pub was the White House in Audenshaw, run by Bill and Sadie, and it was the only one I'd ever known which had a Jewish landlady. She was a lovely woman, a businesswoman apart from anything else, and I admired her very much. Her partner was Bill. He stood about 6 feet 3 inches, bigger than the goalkeepers, and when he stood behind the bar he did it from a very commanding position. Behind the bar there is a floor raised about three or four inches, and it is known in the trade as "the Olympian Height". I still have the picture, this giant staring down a little fellow like me. I felt as though I was looking up at the Eiffel Tower. He had told my friend, and fellow City fan, another Bill, to piss off when he responded to the bell sounding the last call. We had been sitting next to a fine old grand piano at which Sadie was tinkling the ivories very well. She really was a superb woman. When my pal Bill came back from the bar without the drinks and told me what had happened, I said, "What!" and he said, "Leave it, Ian," because he knew I could be a bit feisty and he wasn't one inclined to look for trouble. As I went to the bar the landlord Bill gave me a very elaborate two-fingered salute and said, "This is for you." I just told him to give me my tankard – I must have been drinking shorts that night – and walked out with Bill over the cobbles and into my E-type Jaguar. Just as we were about to drive off, Sadie came waddling out of the pub crying, "Ian, he didn't say it, he didn't say it," and I replied, "What didn't he say, Sadie?" There wasn't really much else to say but I did add, "Sadie, I love you but I will never see you again."

'Going home we passed the Fletchers Arms pub on the left of the main road going out of Denton. We both lived just behind the pub, which was a big place with a bowling green, but it clearly wasn't doing any decent business. It took me about a year to get it.'

He managed it through the crash training course and the cultivation of the failing landlord he planned to succeed. Initially, the brewery turned him down because of his lack of experience, but with the help of his prized certificate and Saturday mornings learning, unpaid, the mysteries of the cellar, he got his pub – and made an institution essentially dedicated to the glory of Manchester City. Niven had worked at Richard Johnson and Nephew Engineering, which employed 2,000 on a site which is now part of the great new City complex in east Manchester. This may be the story of just one, albeit extraordinarily committed, football supporter, but the more this sprightly, sharp-witted nonagenarian speaks the less he seems to be recounting a life as explaining an obsession. On his lips the old Manchester comes alive. Not the one that sprouted trendy discos and boutiques in the new world inhabited by celebrities like George Best and Mike Summerbee and Malcolm Allison, but one in which it was still possible to look up at the night sky and see the red glow of the city that had marched into the heart of the Industrial Revolution. This is Niven on his former workplace, which today looks like the fulfilment of an old futuristic fantasy: 'Steel rolling plants stretched all the way up the lane and you never failed to see the furnaces burning. You felt the intense power of so many men at work.'

As the years passed he also developed still more fiercely that yearning to see his and a large section of that workforce's favourite football team achieve some kind of parity with the developing Red juggernaut at Old Trafford. 'I think it is only by retracing my life like this,' he says, 'that I can explain where I came from and my feelings for Manchester City; how I am Ian Niven the fan who had his nose at the window looking at United's stream of big imports settling in . . . huge players like Tommy Taylor from Barnsley, Duncan Edwards from Worcestershire, with the biggest brown envelope in the history of English football up to that point, and his mum being given a fantastic washing machine; and then the emergence of Bobby Charlton, and Pat Crerand coming from Celtic, and our own briefly owned Denis Law arriving via Torino. And this was before the eruption of George Best.

'I said to myself, "One day we'll have all that being enjoyed by United now, one day it will happen – and of course it did – and long before all that money came pouring in from the Middle East. But then I possibly wouldn't have seen it all at such close hand had a United publican not provoked me into getting my own rival City pub. I wouldn't have come to meet Malcolm Allison and be his friend. I would never have become a City director. I had never envisioned being a director but I did have the ambition to be part of the organisation and do something for the club I loved so much. Yes, I would get into City. Their public relations was hopeless, and I thought, "Well, that's something I can improve."

'As a publican I did three things which are supposed to be taboo. I told everyone my religion, the fact that I was an out and out

Conservative, and a Manchester City supporter – the three things you are not supposed to discuss with your customers. I went the other way. I said, "Here we are, Manchester City, in the second division, so I'm not someone trying to jump on a magic roundabout. I was proud to put up those second division posters.

'People might have said, "Oh, there's a nutter come to Denton, have you seen him in his pub?" I didn't mind people coming to see the nutcase. I said, "Have a go if you like – then come again." I was working very hard then – scrubbing the walls, sorting out the cellar, putting in fluorescent tube lighting with the help of Hughie McGahn, who I'd worked with at the engineering firm when he was head of the works department. He was a brilliant lad, a Catholic and a United fan, but when I got on the City board I gave him the job of maintaining the ground. He did the work superbly, was full of innovations which transformed Maine Road, making it so much more comfortable for the fans – and providing much better sight lines.

'I told him that he would be in charge of everything to do with the ground and he would be working with another of his mates, the new secretary Bernard Halford. If you asked Bernard who was the best signing with connections to Ian Niven he wouldn't say Bobby Johnstone but Hughie McGahn. Bernard replaced Walter Griffiths, who was very hostile to Malcolm, and just happened to bar me from City's European Cup-Winners' Cup final in the old Prater stadium. That provoked the comment that the two things you shouldn't do to Ian Niven is tell him to piss off – and stop him going to Vienna. This was, I suppose, because the man who threw me out of his pub was not in his job in another 12 months, and nor was the man who prevented me from going to Vienna.

'The big problem was that Walter Griffiths was so jealous of Malcolm it hardly seemed possible. Walter was a petty officer in the Navy and I felt he came to City with a petty attitude. But for a while he ran City. The chairman, little Albert Alexander, had to knock on his bloody door. Albert didn't seem to have a bad bone in his body, he was always agreeable and well-mannered, and when I joined the board he seemed to understand my situation as an outright supporter of Malcolm.

'I took Joe Smith to Albert's house after he had bought the shares of the vice-chairman Frank Johnson. Joe had made a lot of money in the double-glazing business from his base in Oldham and wanted to spread his wings a bit. He had kept his dealings with Johnson secret and he didn't really know what his next move was. Joe had called me and said, "What do I do now?" Albert invited us to his house and we told him the story of Joe's move for control of the club. Joe could lose most people in business but he was very new to football and consequently rather naïve. But by then I knew enough about the workings of the football corridors to keep him in the mix. At the first meeting Joe told Albert what had been happening, what shares had been bought and who was involved. It wasn't a takeover, we told Albert, we were just coming in to join the board and have some input on what we thought were City's best interests. Some fairly heavy politics developed as the affair unfolded but at the end of that first meeting Albert said, "You gentlemen can join our board." I suppose he just thought, "The shares have been bought and now it's a fait accompli."'

It wasn't quite so straightforward, as I learned as a young reporter working on the story after a tip-off from Allison, the man who had lured Joe Smith into this new and exotic country. The coach was now attempting to orchestrate the club as a power broker as well as the inspirational coach. But there was fierce resistance among some directors who lined up behind the threatened Joe Mercer and saw the new men as dangerous intruders into their previously unchallenged empire.

As a deadline approached I was told I should call Joe Smith's mansion at the end of a crucial meeting he was having with his supporters. I was also given a code to establish my identity, which was, 'The sun is rising over Maine Road.' This was all very well until the subsequent conversation was all but drowned by the roars of laughter in the *Daily Express* sports room.

There was certainly a degree of ruthlessness when Smith and Niven took their place in the boardroom and Joe Mercer, once the chaperone of Allison's erratic brilliance, so quickly saw his leadership base collapse. Niven is quite candid. When he arrived in the boardroom beside Joe Smith it was as someone who believed it was the coach who had laid the most important foundations of success, and his priority was to protect Allison. He explains, 'If you saw a picture of the City of those days, Walter Griffiths would be stuck on the end of a row of players and you would look in vain for Malcolm. You were excused thinking the big men were not Joe and Mal but Joe and Walter.

'Malcolm arrived at my pub a little after most of the players, and in the days before I met him I reflected that though the team was an assorted group of characters they were unanimous in their opinion of the new coach. In the first days they came in complaining how hard he was working them, but they were in raptures when they talked about his know-how and his flair. At first they would say on a Monday night, "That bastard made me sick today – physically sick," but when they formed a wider view it was an entirely different story. Quickly, I had a picture of what was happening at the club. The thing I found appalling was that it was clear to me that Walter wanted to get Malcolm out despite the dramatic progress being made on the field. I believed that with so much already achieved, and Joe Mercer being so much better than when he arrived, and feeling much more able to handle the pressure, Walter saw the future with a new, young hustling guy in Malcolm's place and everything else staying the same. This seemed the overriding intention of a board shaped by Walter's thinking. I said to myself, "And these are educated men." Could they not see what was happening before their eyes? They thought they could get a strong guy, maybe someone like Dave Ewing, but of course they could never get another Malcolm.

'In the early days he wore a Cossack hat – the fedora came later at Crystal Palace – and sitting in the stand I thought, as some of us do about José Mourinho these days, "This fella is a bloody maniac." He was on the touchline, jumping up and down, waving his arms, screaming at the players and the officials, and I could only say, "Dear, dear me, I'm not sure about this guy."

'But then you noted the results, you watched the way the team were playing, how filled with confidence and invention they were, and then you were thinking, "No, I've got this fella wrong, he's not a maniac, he's a bloody genius."

'You also heard some of the tittle-tattle from the anti-Allison movement within the club. When I spoke to Malcolm I said, "What about the secretary?" And he said, "Oh I have a lot of trouble with Walter Griffiths. I send bills upstairs and he doesn't pay them."

'To a degree, I could understand Walter's perspective. He had been a strict petty officer and he was running the club like a ship, and everyone in the boardroom held him in the highest respect. It was all, "Yes, Mr Griffiths, no, Mr Griffiths." And then when I went on the board I could see how cleverly he treated the directors. I could see how the Griffiths scenario had developed. He was fastidious in his care of the directors and his reward was a freedom to run the club. I had to ask myself, "Who is it we want here: Walter Griffiths or Malcolm Allison?" My answer was that no one else could do Malcolm's job nearly so well as him. So I became . . . not a fanatic for kicking out Walter, then Joe Mercer, as some people still say, but [for] wanting to keep Malcolm there. I also knew that, basically, Joe Mercer wanted the same thing.

'There was another side to it, but I was no different to most people at Maine Road: I loved Joe. He was a sort of Uncle Joe to everyone, and Uncle Joe went to sleep a lot. When you went around to his house his wife Norah, a very intelligent, lively, lady was buzzing around and Joe would often be sleeping in an armchair. On a Friday, building towards the weekend climax, it was not unusual to find him in his office asleep with a newspaper over his face.

'My reaction was, "Good luck to him, I don't care just as long as we keep winning." The chemistry was there. Everyone knew Joe's medical history. He had health issues at Sheffield United and then struggled quite badly after a couple of seasons at Aston Villa. The pressure of the job had worn him down and, really, Norah wasn't happy that he was still working. She knew the score. She didn't want her husband to die early, and Malcolm, when everything got going and we started winning, was helping him get better. He got a lot stronger and in those circumstances – most people would have done so. One problem, I believe, was that Joe was lulled into the belief that he might do it without Mal.

'It was true he was getting better but he couldn't have taken on all that Malcolm was doing to make the team. How could he do it physically? He would have to get someone who Walter Griffiths could keep in tow. So that was the situation. Malcolm was utterly exceptional, and if there was anyone out there with anything like his quality he was unlikely to let himself be dominated by a Walter Griffiths – or do his work in the shadows.

'Even now, as I head into my nineties, those days are still with me, crowding my mind. I think of them all the time, and it was the greatest sadness to me when Malcolm came back to the club in 1978 and just wasn't the same man. There is another kind of sadness when I think of an incident that came many years later, when Malcolm was living up in the North East with his lovely partner Lynn, and his football career was really over.

'He used to come down to visit me quite regularly. He would arrive on a Saturday morning, and the following day I would drive him to the station and put him on a train. He had been banned from driving.

'One Saturday night after dinner we were talking about the old days over a brandy. In the middle of this rather quiet session – certainly neither of us was drunk – he suddenly stood up and started screaming and shouting and raising his arms. He shouted at me, "You were one of the best directors at City, so why did things go wrong?" It was a cry of rage. I was rather stunned as the words poured out of him. They were not in place or in any way coherent, and I sat there thinking, "I'll let this go – it will subside." It did, but it was only recently that I thought it was probably around the start of his dementia.'

Niven tells you in exhaustive detail of the nuances of boardroom life, the shifting alliances that, in his case, saw him variously as an ally and opponent of the controversial new chairman Peter Swales in the years after the Mercer–Allison regime. He speaks of his regret that, in the end, there was nothing left with which to defend his friend and hero Malcolm Allison but an old trail of glory. Yet, he says, there was a surviving commitment to the football club he knew would colour all his days.

'I got in many battles after that day I took Joe Smith to Albert Alexander, but I like to think that I always tried to act in the best interests of the club,' he says. 'My love for City took me in many directions, and perhaps they weren't always the right ones, but in the end I was never in doubt about the time that most lifted my heart. It was those years at the end of the sixties when my team played the most wonderful football and, for a little while, kept winning trophies. It is something I will cherish until the day I die.'

Chapter 18

Without exception those most affected by the legacy of the Manchester City team that flew so high, and the impact of the man most responsible for getting it to take wing, often find themselves walking back along the same haunting line. On one side is superb achievement, the life-enhancing sense that each new day is an adventure; on the other is the abyss which comes when such a time has gone – and can never be recovered. To a man and, also a number of women, there is a remarkable unanimity when they cross either side of this demarcation etched so clearly in their memories.

Then they encounter joy or sorrow. Also true, I discovered one sunny summer morning, is that no one re-explores this still vivid terrain more poignantly, or more tenderly, than Malcolm Allison's last partner, Lynn Salton.

Happily and securely married now to a retired surveyor, she still lives in the attractive house she once shared with Allison in a small, well-ordered estate on the fringes of the prosperous North-East village of Yarm. Her husband, Graham Longstaff, offers an amiable welcome and then goes off for his daily run when his wife returns from her duties as a much respected local schoolmistress.

Before this meeting, and the christening of Gina (the daughter she had with the coach), there was a conversation at Allison's funeral, but the last time I saw her was in Portugal in the late eighties, when Allison was enjoying a brief but exhilarating burst of success in Lisbon with Sporting, and then a little way down the coast in the fishing port of Setúbal.

Allison, it seemed, had stripped down much of the angst that had accompanied the meandering of his career at Manchester City and at Crystal Palace, in Istanbul, where he had suffered his first great setback, and then Middlesbrough, where he wooed Lynn.

He was a celebrity again, a winner, and she remembers it as the happiest, least complicated period of their time together. This was clear enough to any visitor anxious to know if he had managed to create a degree of equilibrium in his life. There were drives along the coast, a long, jovial but also reflective dinner in his favourite restaurant on a cliff overlooking the Atlantic near the beautiful village of Cascais. On the terrace of another restaurant on the seafront at Setúbal the chef brought for the coach's inspection the best of the day's catch. He was hailed warmly in the street.

'The success he had in Manchester first time around was something he liked to talk about,' says Lynn, 'and at times it became very clear to me that he thought he had made a mistake going back there. The signing of Rodney Marsh was a crucial mistake, he also admitted. He said it was probably true that you should never go back over old ground because it can never be the same. But then he never dwelt on this too long, he much preferred to talk about the times when things went so well, when he could take so much pride in the performances of the team he had done so much to make.

'One of the things that attracted me to Malcolm was that he would tell me so many stories. Often I would say to him, "Tell me some stories, Malcolm," – and then I would spend many happy hours listening to him.

'Something that sticks in my memory is the way so many people told me that while he was a great coach he was not a good manager, and that he couldn't deal with the directors, the elders, of a football club. He said he found it difficult to respect most of the directors because of their lack of knowledge of, and feeling for, the game. There was, he said, a huge gap between the professionals and the people who were supposed to be running the club.'

Quickly, she returns to the bleak place that, down the last years of their fracturing relationship, so dismayingly supplanted the brief idyll they shared in Portugal and the gratitude she felt for Allison's huge support when she confronted the onset of what they feared was a life-threatening illness.

'Towards the end we had a very difficult time with Malcolm, and the worst of it was that our daughter Gina became embarrassed by him. She no longer wanted to be associated with him, which was so heartbreaking because they were so close when she was growing up. One problem was that he found it so hard to deal with the fact that he was no longer in the limelight. I kept telling him that he shouldn't feel like that. A lot of people he liked and respected were never slow to say how much he had contributed to football and to their lives.

'When we went to Malcolm's funeral the thing that was most special to me was for Gina to hear all those people talking about her father, saying how great a football coach he was. She heard men like Mike Summerbee and Tony Book saying how he had made them the men they were. That moved me a lot – and especially when I realised how much it was registering with Gina.

'She is proud of her father now. He had taken to going around to the school and picking her up after he had had a drink, and it was just awful, that, and her coming home here not knowing how he was going to be. I used to take her around to my mum's and that too was hard.

'But I can see now how going to the funeral made such a difference with her hearing all those people speaking so highly of him, and also the great number who were there and how clear they made it that he had touched them so strongly, become so important to them.

'Another thing about Malcolm was that he learned so much from the fact that when he was a young player at Charlton Athletic his manager, Jimmy Seed, never spoke to him, and how he once broke that habit during training and it caused so much anger in Malcolm because he believed it was only done to impress some visitors to the ground. He never forgot that, and it informed a lot of the way he was around the football club, with everybody: people in the office, groundstaff, the ladies who made the tea.

'I'll always remember going to the games with him when he was coach of Vitória de Setúbal. I loved to go to the games and feel some of the affection the fans felt for him when he was doing well, but as much as I enjoyed it when we won I was very upset when we lost. I knew he was hurting a lot when it happened but he never showed it, not on the outside. The next morning he would go to the club with such a cheerful front, full of enthusiasm for the training ahead.

'It went very well at first, the club won promotion and when we went to dinner he would be fêted and, of course, he loved that as he sat back sipping a glass of wine and lighting up one of his big cigars. It was wonderful when things were going so well and he had confidence in the future, but then soon it was also typical Malcolm that he fell out with the club president.

'Malcolm told me it was a matter of quite fundamental principle. The president wanted him to play one of his personal favourites, an old hero of Sporting Lisbon, but Malcolm said the player was past it and refused to play him by command of the president. His job was to make the team and run it, and if he had to take orders from someone who didn't really know the game, he was off. Of course, we were off, because if Malcolm didn't get the last word in any dispute over selection that was that.

'He only rarely saw eye to eye with the chairmen and the owners of the clubs. One notable exception, he always told me, was Robert Daniel at Plymouth Argyle. Malcolm said he respected him because he showed some understanding of the nuances of football.

'It always hurt me when people dismissed his ability as a manager, and I thought of the story about when he told everybody that Mike Summerbee was finished and it got back to Mike's mum and she confronted him about it, and told him, "My boy's going to show you who's fit and who isn't fit." And there was his vindication after fighting so hard to get Joe Mercer to sign Tony Book.

'No, there was never any doubt in my mind: Malcolm had brains to burn and he was so innovative in the way he employed the talents of people – Lennie Heppell with his dance movements and Roger Spry with his fitness regimes. He set these men to work on things which he believed needed to be done, without ever being threatened by the specialist knowledge he didn't have. The most remarkable thing about Malcolm was his tremendous belief in his own ability, and that isn't so common in life.'

The decline was at first quite gradual, and for a while Lynn thought she could check it, perhaps even put it into reverse, by a series of initiatives. 'In the beginning it wasn't too bad,' she reports. 'I encouraged him to go down to Fisher Athletic, a little club in London which had been taken over by some ambitious people. I thought it would be good for him down in London, getting him out of a rut he was slipping into up here. But you know what it's like in London. Everybody is so busy you don't get much time to see people and, of course, it didn't work out.

'Then he got a little job with Century Radio up here, and again I thought this would be something good for him because he would be travelling the country and meeting up with old friends in football. But the drinking was getting worse, he swore on the airwaves, was fired and then he was a bit lost.

'The drinking became dominant. He couldn't adjust to the changes in his professional status – or his finances – all the limits which had been placed on what he could do. In the end it seemed that the drinking was all that was important to him. I could never understand why he drank as much as he did. When he was at Bristol Rovers, when things had begun to fall apart, we had Gina and I just couldn't commit to going down there. And he found it increasingly hard to be on his own.'

Even in the contentment of a new and tested life with her second husband, and her pride in the brilliant university career of Gina and happiness at the prospect of her marriage to her fiancé Liam, Lynn still sometimes tastes the sediment – a guilt, no matter how many times she is told, as she is again this morning, how unfounded it is.

'I loved him dearly,' she says, 'and I have so many good memories, but I don't think too many people understand what it was like in the end. I've only confided this to a few close friends, but there were some terrible scenes. He would go away drinking, out of control, and then come back and break down the door. We had to separate. I had to force that for my sanity and, more importantly, Gina's.

'Recently we went to the sixtieth birthday party of Malcolm's elder son, David, in Manchester, and it was interesting that Gina most wanted to go. Soon after the funeral Gina and I went down to Manchester for a shopping trip and we met up with Alexis, Malcolm's daughter with Sally, and we had a lovely weekend. At David's party he was introducing Gina to everyone, making her feel part of the family, maybe for the first time, and at the end of the weekend he told her, "I'm your big brother, if you want something, or need to talk to someone, give me a call."

'I sometimes felt a little bit guilty when I was in the family's company because I wondered if they thought I had abandoned him, but as time went on they became more involved and I think they began to realise how difficult my life had become. Dawn, Malcolm's eldest daughter, was very kind at the funeral, lovely with Gina, and Malcolm's first wife, Beth, was there – 81 now but fine after recovering from a hip operation. All those who loved Malcolm have in some ways a similar story to tell. He had a very selfish streak, after all. You loved him and you admired him, but sometimes you just couldn't fail to be exasperated by the way he was. This was most sharp when you thought of the waste of all that talent. I do often hope the family understand now my situation because, in the end, I was dealing with someone who had a very serious illness.

'Oh, the stories I can tell. So many times I would try to stop him going out drinking too early of a night. But there was really nothing I could do or say to stop him. On one occasion I took away his shoes but that didn't work. A neighbour recalls how she looked out of her window and saw Malcolm getting into a taxi in his socks.

'He ran up so many bills in Yarm, partly because people were afraid to challenge him. Of course, he did have times of severe regret, when I think he had flashes of understanding that he had taken wrong turnings at very important stages of his life.'

Now, she can only wonder and be grateful for the repairing of her own. 'I met Graham on a blind date through mutual friends eight years ago, and we've been married four years now. Gina did biochemistry at York University and got a first-class degree with distinction. She's doing her Ph.D now. I just don't know where she gets her brains from. Was Malcolm scientific? I have to say that Malcolm did play a big part in her early progress at school. They were very close, which was very different to his situation with his first family because he was so involved in his work – and his own life – when they were young. Sometimes I think Dawn was a little bit envious of that time he had with Gina. Bobby Moore came to Gina's christening and made a very witty speech, which included that line about him being more worried about the behaviour of Malcolm than the baby.

'Gina was very pleased when I got together with Graham. I was on my own after separating from Malcolm. I was quite happy with my career as a teacher but as Gina was getting older, going seriously with Liam and working so hard at university, she was pleased to see I was getting something more from life.

'I met Malcolm at the Tontine restaurant [on the edge of the North York Moors], one of the best in the area. I was there with my mum and Malcolm was having lunch. I was 28 at the time, didn't have a boyfriend, and really had never met anybody who interested me. My mother once said, "I'm going to knit you a man," because she thought I was so fussy. And then there was Malcolm. As we left the restaurant he asked the barman, "Who was that young lady?" As we lived in such a small community, he was able to give him chapter and verse.

'I was in the Tontine a few nights later with some girlfriends and Malcolm was there again. Surprise, surprise, he sent across a bottle of champagne. At first I thought he was interested in one of my friends, but very soon he came across and invited me to dinner. To begin with I thought it was probably a bad idea, but I said, "Oh, yes." I don't normally drink, but on this occasion I had a glass of champagne. So I was quite responsive. I had always loved football. Maybe I was a bit tired of living in the same village for so long and thought it would be nice to get to know someone from a different background.

'We agreed to meet for lunch the following day, but when I woke up I had cold feet and was thinking, "No, I'm not going to get involved. Though he's separated from his second wife, Sally, it's probably not a good idea." So I didn't go to the restaurant and I didn't send my excuses. I just stood him up. However, he knew where I lived and he telephoned me that evening. My brother Richard answered the phone and asked who was calling. Malcolm said his name was Roger, but Richard shook his head and said, "I don't think so," when he handed me the phone.

'I tried to explain why I hadn't turned up, but he was persistent and in the end I agreed to see him for dinner the following night. It was 30 years ago but I remember all the details. My university friend Kate was having a birthday party for her baby and I went up to Sunderland. That left me running late for my date with Malcolm. I called the Tontine with a message that I would be a little late, and when I arrived Malcolm said that by then most of the staff had come whispering in his ear that I might be 15 minutes late.

'It all started from there. He was so charismatic, so different from anyone I had ever met. I liked to see his hands, he had lovely hands. I remember well the first time he met my parents. I told him, "Look, don't order champagne and don't smoke a cigar, show them you're not like your public image." Of course that had to go into the category of a nice try.

'When we were in Portugal and reporters came out from England almost all of them brought champagne and cigars as props for the photographs. It was as though they wanted him to play out endlessly the role in which, to be fair, he had cast himself, but now, it seemed to me, at the cost of being imprisoned by it. I would take away the champagne and the cigars and tell the reporters that they were part of the image he was stuck with whatever else he did or said.

'I was struck at the funeral not just by the affection shown for him by the players but by all the people who came out to line the streets, all the generations of them, and I noticed the older people talking to the children – it seemed to be they were explaining that this was somebody they should know about.

'As I said, I was very conscious of the impact on Gina right from the start of the service. In fact, I had been impressed by that even before we arrived. When David called to say Malcolm had died I immediately rang her at the university. I didn't want her to hear about it on the news. She had some pals around when I called and I was pleased about that. Her first reaction was that I didn't need to drive down to York to bring her home. She insisted she would be fine. But then she soon called back and said, "I think I would like to come home."

'I was a little surprised because after all that had gone on I didn't expect her to react like that. I didn't think it would touch her so deeply. I thought we had gone past that point. I had an idea that she had spoken about it all a lot more with Liam because she perhaps thought it would upset me if we went too deeply into things.

'Prior to the funeral, City had a match against Arsenal – the first one since Malcolm died – and Gina said, "Oh, do we have to sit through a whole football match?" while I was thinking to myself, "Well, it will probably be a great game." So we went – and it was special. We had lunch with the family. Alexis was there with her three beautiful daughters. Her mother had died of cancer and I got the impression that had left her feeling for a while that she was on her own. It was really moving when the family walked out onto the pitch with the great old players and we felt the warmth of the crowd when they cheered and clapped for Malcolm. There was a minute's applause and it was very strong.

'The last time I saw Malcolm was at another match at City. I went with Gina and Liam and we brought Malcolm from the home. It was very sad. I didn't think Malcolm registered much, and when you remembered how vital he had been it was very hard to see. It was the hardest part.

'Now, when I look at Gina I think of all the good memories I have of Malcolm from those lovely early days, and I have to say that at that point in my life he was the best thing that had happened to me.'

Their first crisis came when she developed a tumour, a sudden frightening shadow cast over the bright Portuguese sunlight. 'I was told it had to be removed. We were always aware of the huge age difference between us, but when I was quite ill, and I was told they didn't really know my situation until they operated, I would say to him, "You thought you had found yourself a young bit of stuff but it looks as if I could pop my clogs before you."

'We went home for the operation in Newcastle, and Malcolm was hopeless at driving anywhere. Whenever he went up to Newcastle from Yarm he would always come back a different way, usually via one of the pubs. But he did get me to the operation on time and afterwards the surgeon said the best way for us to see if it had been successful was for me to have a child. This was because the tumour had attached itself to my pituitary gland, which is responsible for all your hormones.

'Malcolm almost had to pick himself up from the floor, and I pointed out that Malcolm already had five children – at least that we knew of. I love children but I wasn't sure it was right for us to have one of our own. Malcolm had his children and there was the age gap, and the fact that I was 35, quite late to have a first child. But now, of course, I believe it was meant to be, my having that illness and the end result of Gina.

'She's such a lovely, bright girl and Malcolm had those wonderful early days with her. He would play games with her and tell her his stories. I would stick to the books, but he would veer off the well-beaten track. Everyone in Yarm knew Malcolm and Gina. They would walk down the main street and go to lunch while I was teaching at school.'

The image is touching enough, if you once knew any of the sensitivities that could so swiftly surface from beneath a brash façade, to remind you of Kris Kristofferson's song 'Jody And The Kid' and so many of the kind of days most of us wish we could have again.

'People say that he was arrogant,' says Lynn, 'but I know he cared about the people who went to the matches, and very deeply. I remember going to a Cup game between Middlesbrough and Bournemouth and I was surprised how concerned he was about the impact of a poor performance on the people in the stadium. You know how it can be in the Cup, when the team from a lower division raises its game, and there was a lot of tension in the ground and at one point he was almost tearful when he thought of the consequences of defeat. Middlesbrough did squeak through but he was unhappy about the way it had gone.

'It's strange, really, but even at the end when things had got so difficult, I still hated it when anyone said a derogatory word about Malcolm. It didn't matter how awful things were, or how destructive his behaviour, I just couldn't bear it when somebody put him down. I would think of the good days in Portugal, the best of the days, and when once he said to me, "I want to forget the bad days, I want to enjoy these good ones." When we left Setúbal the team's Hungarian goalkeeper came around – it had broken his heart that his coach was leaving.'

At Allison's funeral Wyn Davies stood at the back of the chapel with tears in his eyes and said that he had always felt cheated that he'd had just one season with 'the best coach in the world'. He shook his head and said, 'He made you feel you could do anything you wanted.'

Lynn nods and says, 'There were so many statements like that. When people say he couldn't handle success I think that is such a mean and simplified view. The main thing I carried away from that day was that Gina finally understood what her father meant to so many people. She stood among her brothers and sisters and together they mourned his memory, all the excitement of it, all the laughter, and, yes, of course, the pain.

'But more than anything I remember the pride.'

Chapter 19

There is a winter mist over the Cheshire fields as I drive to the last of my appointments with the men who, one by one, have not so much recreated their past as weighed the undying impact of one part of it. I'm seeing Mike Summerbee, which seems perfectly appropriate because no one is more emphatic about the daily relevance to his life of a long-gone time. It might be his football version of Hemingway's days in Paris – his time when he believed he had been empowered to meet any challenge set before him. It might be the gift the writer described as his Moveable Feast, a repast always simmering on the hob of his recall.

From that time of burgeoning and (for a few years) brilliantly burnished achievement, Summerbee, like all his teammates, is now separated by half a century – by all the hopes and pleasures and disappointments which come to shape all our lives; but however deep the autumn, they can still, each one of them, and with such little bidding, evoke the warmth and the buoyancy of their brightest spring mornings. In the case of Summerbee, who is a few weeks away from his seventy-second birthday, there is an additional leavening of memory.

It comes from the yeast in those who believe they may have survived the worst of their fears, who reach a point in their lives when they know that whatever else happens to them they have reasons to celebrate which have become robustly secure. They have a certain ballast to carry them through come what may.

He welcomes me in the driveway of his unostentatiously beautiful home. It is not the house of many of today's football glitterati. It is, rather like its owner, a place which rewards closer inspection.

We go to a small library/study, where he shows me proudly some of his first editions. His education in a West Country secondary modern was, he admits, almost nominal, unlike that of his wife Tina, who went to a Quaker boarding school. He mostly played football in school. Now, though, he reads voraciously, and is especially keen, like his old coach, on biography.

He also reflects strenuously on the good fortune that culminated a few years ago with his appointment as ambassador of Manchester City, which came at a time when he was winding down his bespoke shirt business and, worryingly, beginning to contemplate the possibility of a loss of focus, even purpose, in what was left of his life.

It was a question that occupied him, he says, long before his superb 10-year career at the top level at Manchester City quickly wound down in the moorland hollow of Burnley and was then wrapped up, after a three-game misadventure at Blackpool, with a two-year player-manager stint down the road at third division Stockport County. Indeed, it was something that was always part of him from his first days as a professional footballer. He knew, as well as anyone would ever do, how cruel the game could be. He saw it in his father George's face at that time when, after a journeyman playing career, he lost his last job in football as manager of Cheltenham Town, a devastation exceeded only by the swift advance of terminal illness.

Summerbee says, 'I think my father would have been proud of my success if he had lived long enough to see it. He had a real struggle in the game, and the only benefit for me was that it gave me a view of the bad side of football. I saw him as manager at Cheltenham and I saw him when he died, and there were so few people within the game who helped him.

'So I knew football as a boy, looking at Dad's struggles and frustrations and that despair which came to him in the end.

'I was very lucky to start my career under Bert Head at Swindon. He was a football man who always put faith in young players, and then it was Malcolm and Joe, so what more could I have asked for in the way of football education? They pointed me to the future, a very rewarding one indeed, but of course they couldn't wipe away the memory of what had happened to my father before he died.

'It meant that when my own career came towards its close I didn't have any illusions about happy endings. My father's career was cut short and he was very ill and that was it for him. He knew it was over and there was no going back. So because of my background I knew what to expect.

'My City teammate Frannie Lee seemed to know it all along – he had thought it out, and that's why he worked so hard at his business. He knew he had to live a life beyond football. He saw so many old players struggling along, nursing their regrets, trying to come to terms with the fact that their old horizons had disappeared. Every day of his life he worked to get where he is today.

'I had my shirt business. I knew it wasn't going to make me an extremely rich man but it was something I could do to provide a living for myself and my family. When my playing career was over I threw my boots out of the window and sold some shirts. I never forgot what happened to my father, that when the day comes they can just cut you off in a word or two.

'However successful you are on the field you have to understand it will not all be roses, that one day they are going to take away a piece of your heart, if not all of it. On a practical level, the money stops, you have to go out and do something.

'My father played in Preston, and when I was a young boy Tom Finney was always someone to look up to. He had such beautiful talent, he wanted to be a great footballer, and at one point the club prevented him from playing in Italy, where no doubt he would have been a sensation. But his father insisted that first he become a plumber. And that's what Sir Tom was. He was one of the greatest players the game has ever seen, but at an early age it was hammered into him that nothing lasts for ever, nothing in life is continuous. Football, however you get to the end of it, is ultimately humbling.'

But then if you are one of the very lucky ones you can come out of it whole, proud of what you have achieved – and what you have survived.

Summerbee tells me that he has perhaps never before felt so relaxed about his place in such company, not even before his marriage to Tina, when he and George Best were the tigers of Manchester nightlife and his success on the field with City had carried him into the England team. He feels he has outrun the shadows cast by the pain of a father who never lived to see his strong and open-hearted son fulfil so many of his old dreams, and whose grandson, Nicky, followed his father into the City side and played, as a sharply inventive midfielder, more than a hundred times.

The composure is with him, he says, in all the places he inhabits, as he potters in his scrupulously tended garden, presides over family occasions as a proud grandfather, retires among his first editions and, not least, when he travels the world as the diplomatic face of the club for whom, before it became steeped in wealth, he once waged such ferocious football warfare.

'Until a year or so ago I was leaving the house at 6 a.m. going to places like Scotland on business, but now I make time to do some of the things I want to do. I feel very fortunate to be still connected to the club, and at a time which promises to be the most successful in its history.

'I think I can go down there to City and make a contribution in an environment I love – and do it without people nudging each other and saying, "Oh, here he comes again." When the day comes that they pull the plug there is no doubt I will find it a little difficult. For the moment, though, I can say that I've never been more content.

'I enjoy meeting all my old teammates on a routine basis – and mixing again with so many players I once battled with so hard out on the field. I saw Bobby Moncur, the fine Newcastle player, the other day and I said, "Congratulations." He said, "For what?" and I said, "Well, you never got this close to me before."'

It is the amiable swagger of an old pro comfortable in his unlined skin, and most happy that a relationship with the club he served so brilliantly, and which was briefly fractured when he moved to Burnley at the age of 33, has been repaired.

'I was upset by what happened when I left for Burnley,' he says. 'Sometimes change can be good, it can put a couple of years on your career, and I had been at City for a long time. I was supposed to be on a free transfer when Burnley came in for me, but then suddenly the chairman Peter Swales slapped on a £25,000 fee and that really did me with him. They bought me for £35,000 and I had given them my best years. I came back to City in Burnley colours a few months later and received a presentation – from the fans, not the club.

'It hurt both me and Frannie that we were not as influential as we might have been as senior players who had put a lot into the club. Frannie is a very strong guy and, though success didn't come on the field with his chairmanship, there's no doubt in my mind he got the club's financial affairs in good order – and the deal he made with Howard Bernstein, the leader of Manchester council, for the Commonwealth Games stadium, was a huge stride forward. Sometimes it is also true that in life you have to take a few backward steps before going forward.

'When I went to Burnley to do the deal I was accompanied by the great cricketer Colin Milburn, who was a good friend of mine and still missed badly for his huge appetite for life.'

Chairman Bob Lord, Mr Burnley, was in the boardroom. This master butcher, notorious for his hard opinions and apparent iron rule at the old Turf Moor ground, made a formidable figure as he stood at a large table, on which some forms were laid. He was wearing a light grey suit and, as always, he reminded Summerbee somewhat of the Mekon, the evil genius in the Dan Dare space adventures in the *Eagle* comic.

'When I was introduced to him he pointed to the table and said, quite brusquely, "There's your contract." It made rather astonishing reading. At City my top wage was never more than £150 a week and now, with my best years done, I was being offered £240, on an inflation-linked contract. I read through it quickly and said, "That's fantastic, Mr Lord."

'He said, "You deserve it. You've been talking to our manager Jimmy Adamson for two weeks and he tells me you haven't mentioned money once. All you've said is what you might do for Burnley Football Club. That's an attitude we very much appreciate in this place."

'The sadness in this story is that Frannie went to Derby and won a title, and I got relegation. I still very much wish it had gone better. Mike King, the comedian, once introduced me at some dinner occasion by saying, "Burnley paid £25,000 for this man and regretted every bloody penny of it." Whatever the truth of that I know that the lack of success there was not for any want of effort. That didn't make it any easier, though, because Burnley is a great club, with a wonderful atmosphere in the ground. It was built up over the years on the communal pride that came with being able to compete so well, for so long, with the big guns in the English game, and in the process claim both the league title and the FA Cup.

'It was very late for me at Burnley, but still I wanted to feel again some of the exhilaration I had at City. I liked wearing their strip, I thought of great players like Jimmy McIlroy who had done that, and I enjoyed my days at an excellent training ground. I didn't think so much about the money. I tried to emulate Frannie, playing so well and working so hard at his business, and, to be honest, sometimes I wondered how he did it. When it was over I could at least tell myself that I was doing all right: I was working at a business, I had a good marriage, a good family, and, well, I told myself, "Life goes on."'

Unlike so many of his contemporaries – though not, it has to be said, almost all of his old City teammates – there is no angst in Summerbee, no pained conclusion that he was born at an unpropitious time in the football evolution. He doesn't yearn for a Rooney mansion. He says, 'For me there is no real difference between the players of my time and today. Of course, today's men are lucky to have such big financial rewards and, of course, the playing conditions are so much better – along with scientific advances in training and fitness and nutrition. But there are huge pressures on them that we didn't have. Players like Pablo Zabaleta at City just don't get a break. He was travelling to China with Argentina recently, then coming back for a Champions League game.

'I also believe that here the competition does run deeper. In Spain and Germany, Italy and France, there are two or three teams and then it falls away quite sharply. It's true that we can only be envious of a lot of the conditions today, and for this reason I think the old players would have done very well. But then if you sent today's players back in time I do think they would struggle. No disrespect to David Beckham, who had such fantastic talent, but he just wouldn't have got in the team of Best, Law and Charlton. There are things today which do annoy me deeply. For one thing, I never thought you could pass or cross the ball straight through human bodies, which quite a few of today's players seem to believe. Another thing which really pisses me off is the way so many place the ball at corners, apparently desperate to get every available inch, and then so often waste the kick.

'You have two main options taking a corner. The first is to drive it towards the near post with somebody coming in – and if the cross is missed, have someone behind the man at the post meeting it. Alternatively, you can send it long. But then for me there was the option I would call the Wyn Davies situation. This would have him about 25 yards out of the box, then running in with me attempting to play the ball into his path. The advantage in this was that he was 6 foot 2 inches tall and by the time he met the ball he would be around 9 foot 8 inches. (I once remember Wyn coming back from a corner and asking, "What colour is your car?" and when I told him he said, "I thought so, I'm sorry to tell you that somebody's trying to nick it in the Platt Lane car park.")'

If Summerbee is generous, sometimes to a fault, about the pressure on today's footballing plutocrats, it does not blur his critical faculty when it comes to judging supreme achievement.

One touchstone is Wayne Rooney. 'Recently in a derby match,' says Summerbee, 'he showed his ability when going past two or three defenders and coming close to scoring a remarkable goal. But, along with Beckham, you couldn't put him in the same class as Best, Law and Charlton. Tina once said that she could never imagine George being an old man.

'Messi is a truly wonderful player, but I don't think he occupies the same world that Bestie did, when you think of the conditions he had to deal with and what little protection he got from being kicked up in the air so often. When we played United I used to say to him, "Now don't start trying to take the piss out of me today, stay on your side of the pitch." He was just phenomenal, unplayable at times, though I have to say Bookie mostly made a good fist of marking him. Mind, you "Skip" was a hard bugger. I was 15 when I first played against him, for Swindon Town against Bath City, and he kicked lumps out of me. He was so quick, and he read the game in a way you could hardly believe.

'It was a bad tackle George made on Glyn Pardoe, a bit similar to the one that Noel Cantwell performed on Dave Mackay when he broke his leg, but I don't believe that kind of result was ever the intention. You know, it was a very, very hard game in those days. There's no doubt, though, that the injury to Glyn was a tragedy because otherwise he would have been England's left-back for many years. As a kid he could score goals for fun, and then when Malcolm moved him to left-back he looked as if he was born to play the position. He had such an inner confidence, and I always found it so strange that you so often saw this in lads who off the field were very shy and unassuming. Then you saw them go out there and suddenly the self-belief was coming out of their ears. Oaksie was also a quiet man off the field who just grew before your eyes when he went on it.

'Belly was different to Oaksie, and Pardoe and Bobby Charlton, in that though he too was shy he tended to build walls around himself. Still does. Yet his son Jon is quite different. He is a surgeon and a very easy communicator.

'It was a big mixture we had in the City dressing room. There was the stability provided by Oaksie, Doyley and Glyn, who had been there since kids, cared passionately about the club and were desperate to bring success. They had such a hunger for it – and when people like Frannie, Belly, Bookie and me came along it spread into us. Like them, our blood had changed to blue.'

You notice again how seamlessly Mike Summerbee lets in the past, or at least that part of it which most moves him. It is not a fading memoir but a living force, a point of reference for all his theories on what is best, and most damaging, in the game that has filled so much of his life.

'People talked all the time about Bell, Lee and Summerbee and how we brought the edge, the creativity and the ability to score goals, but it became a bit of an embarrassment because it seemed that the engine room was being blocked out to a certain extent. Those boys who had been there from the start were the history of the club, they told you where you were, told you about the meaning of the place, because they had always been at the heart of it. And then we had the greatest coach the country had ever seen, so forward thinking it was unbelievable. There's no doubt the latecomers did bring a necessary edge after we got out of the second division, while losing just two games, but no one could ever doubt that the will and the unharnessed effort had been there all the time.

'Jimmy Murray and Ralph Brand came in after Joe and Mal arrived but though they were talented players they were not what Mal had in mind, and then the rest of it just knitted together.

'I don't believe I would have played for England if I hadn't come under Malcolm's influence, which was so great it is almost impossible to overstate. Joe was like a father to me, he knew my father when he was a professional player, and then a manager, but this didn't get me any preferential treatment. It didn't spare me some tremendous bollock-ings, and in this Joe was very much like Malcolm. They wanted to get to the heart of someone.

'I played my first game for England at Hampden Park in 1967, so soon after the World Cup win, and I still shiver with pride when I think about it. I wished my father had been there, because I could have told him, "This is for both of us." It was the time I had done so well when Malcolm switched me to centre-forward in the drive to win the league title.

'But then things got a bit harder, opposing defenders were on to me, and for a comparison today I would cite the kid at Aston Villa, Christian Benteke, who in the 2013–14 season was looking nothing like the player who had made his first big impact. You have to adjust to the situation your success brings, you have to keep looking for another edge in your game, a little more commitment and willingness to explore new ways of developing the talent you have. This season there are signs that Benteke had made it through that difficult time, he has won back a bit of that first arrogance, and the assumption that everything he tries has a very good chance of coming off.

'It was also true that I had got a bit carried away with myself. I found myself struggling, because you have to be careful not to become overconfident. It was arrogance rooted in our success, but a turning point came in the Charity Shield game against Leeds United in 1969 after we won the FA Cup. I had just got married to Tina, and that was a very big development in my life, but I didn't feel that anything had been taken from my game when I went to Elland Road to face the fine full-back Terry Cooper. At half-time Malcolm said, "You might be finished here. If you carry on as you're going I'm going to pull you off in the second half and you will not be playing against Sheffield Wednesday next Saturday." After the game Malcolm told me I would be working with the kids in the B team the following week. Nothing more was said on a very bleak drive home over the Pennines. He made his point very heavily. I wasn't even training with the "stiffs" the reserves. It was as if the blinds had been drawn on my life – right up to after training on the Thursday, when Malcolm called me into his office and said, "Right, the boss and I have had a talk and we're going to give you one last chance."

'Well, I really motored against Wednesday. We won 4–1, I made three and scored one and Malcolm said, "That was OK, that was more like it." He had simply smashed down the barrier I'd built around myself with the idea that I had become a superstar. He brought me out of the clouds and right down to the ground. It was a pivotal moment in our relationship, and I know such things were happening between him and other players all the time. It was how he maintained that incredible momentum we found so quickly; and, if along the way he did outrageous things, the truth was you could forgive him anything. One day my wife said to me, "I think you love him more than you love me."

'Sometimes it is hard to explain the camaraderie that grows around people who share a challenge, but for myself I can see it even in something like *Strictly Come Dancing*. When someone is voted out of the competition you can sense the impact on the other contestants is very strong. You might think this is stretching it a bit, but I do see elements of my own experience as a footballer in the feeling you develop for the people who, like you are, are striving to do something well under quite a bit of pressure.

'In football you can see a very powerful example of this when you consider the Munich air tragedy. You could see how close those Manchester United lads became before the tragedy, and how devastated survivors like Bobby Charlton, Bill Foulkes and Harry Gregg were. When you play football you are not going to war but you travel together constantly, you share each other's hopes and fears, and so you get to know the guys you sit beside and share rooms with very well indeed. You leave your families and enter a separate world. I imagine it is a bit like soldiers going out on patrol. I've come across quite a few lads coming home from active service and they've all told of how important it was to understand every aspect of their comrades' nature. In their cases, of course, we are not talking about winning a football match but matters of life and death.

'For another example, you could look at the breakdown of the all-conquering England Ashes teams in Australia. They were slaughtered so soon after beating the Aussies in England and it was so clear that they were not bonding together, that something had gone very badly wrong. It seemed that there were just too many egos. Malcolm would never have tolerated that, he would have waged war against such attitudes.

'He was a day-to-day man, but he always insisted on being in control. I remember going to Highbury for one match and Joe Mercer was fêted as one of the great players of Arsenal's past, a distinguished club captain, and they didn't bother with Mal. He didn't react in any way except by delivering a particularly brilliant team talk.

'After Malcolm's funeral we all went our different ways because we all had our different and very strong emotions. I hated to see him in the care home after he developed dementia. I went a couple of times but I could hardly bear it. And it was the same when George Best neared his end in the clinic in west London. Denis Law and Bobby Charlton went down but there was no way I could do that.

'A big difference between players and coaches of today and back then is that we used to live so much of our lives together, we were in each other's houses. We were so much more intimate then. Losing Malcolm was like losing a member of your family, and it was the same when Neil Young and Mike Doyle went.'

As inevitably as each of his old comrades, he is drawn back to some of the details and all of the emotions of those days which flew through the late sixties and then crash-landed into a new decade. 'I will always say,' he insists again, 'that there's only one great football coach this country ever had, and it was Malcolm when he was clear-headed and knew exactly what he wanted to do, what he was out to create. The momentum was so strong. We were so fit and so believed in ourselves. We travelled all over the place together, and the most amazing thing, considering we were young men and liked to have a good time, was that we couldn't wait to train. Some of the best mornings were at the little Cheadle training ground. We changed in a small hut and also sheltered there when the weather got very bad, and I suppose it was because we were so happy there, so sure about what we were doing, that one stark incident was as bewildering as it was tragic.

'One morning we retreated to the hut to find a kettle boiling on a Primus stove. Eventually we went looking for the groundsman and found him face down in the bath in the dressing room. The coroner's verdict was that he had drowned himself, and with typical morbid humour one of the lads said he must have finally despaired of ever making a decent cup of tea. Maybe at that time we just couldn't comprehend the plight of someone who may have decided that life was too hard, too lacking in hope or purpose.

'Malcolm only really started to go off at the end of our time together. He couldn't get his head around the fact that his gift was to be a coach of men, and that as a manager he would have responsibilities that he could never take on successfully. We knew that he was frequently flying down to London to see his girlfriend, Serena Williams, at the Playboy Club in Park Lane and other Mayfair watering holes, and we accepted that to some degree he would always be a free bird.

'But then as affairs at City became more complicated, as the old sweet simplicity of his relationship with Joe began to break down, we could see he would never deal easily with the directors, and all those issues which build up beyond the touchline. All his players knew that as long as he was coach we would live happily. But then it was clear enough it could not last. When he was manager he just couldn't go on waltzing into town with a new girl on his arm.

'And then, of course, it was as we most feared. We had lost our guiding hand.'

Summerbee nods when I recall the time the coach filled in a thin day for his ghosted column in the *Express* by telling me that it was time for football to ban the back pass to the goalkeeper. It was killing the game, enabling poorly equipped defenders to take up the easiest of options; bad coaches, bad players, were hiding behind the killing formula of the back pass and the long ball from the goalkeeper's hands.

His proposal was derided by almost all the football cognoscenti – only to be acted upon 20 years later after the dismayingly negative

World Cup of Italy in 1990. Fifa realised then that they had to renovate a product that had to be sold on the last frontier of the game, in the World Cup in America in four years' time.

'We used to train never passing the ball to the goalkeeper,' says Summerbee. 'The forwards had to pick up the ball and go. We worked from the halfway line, usually on the big field at Maine Road. Mal would stand at the edge of the playing arc and the defenders were told to push up so they were practically up our backsides. For me to get the ball I couldn't step into the other half. So I had to take the defender away, run him, check out and get the ball to my feet, and then when I got it I couldn't pass to anyone. I had to take the ball past the defender and have an end product. The man who was marking me had to stop me scoring. I had to beat the defender and put the ball past Joe Corrigan.

'When the ball went to Joe he had to knock it straight back to Mal for the process to start again. If the ball didn't go to Mal Joe had to come out of goal and collect it. Everything had to be done accurately, and you had to do it going forward all the time. Going forward was written across our hearts in the end. We always went forward, and we always had the players and the tactics to do it. Mike Doyle knew his limitations but he played brilliantly within the group. In fact we all had our limitations, but we got over them because we worked so closely together. Doyley was a major force. He was a good talker and a genuine fighter, which gave everything he said added weight.

'Neil Young was a player who was on his way out when Mal arrived at Maine Road. He was one of the boys who had been there for years, and some people had come to believe he couldn't play. Certainly he seemed to have lost all confidence in himself, but Malcolm gave it back to him. Not only could Youngy play he could do it in a way that marked a great player.

'Doyley was a typical wing-half who battled. Alan Oakes was the same but he could ping a 50-yard ball to your feet from one wing to the other. He would be going down the left and I would be really wide on the right. Malcolm always said to me, "Stay wide, don't go in," and Oaksie would find me perfectly.

'In the end every member of the team involved in the great years, from big Joe out, had to say that if Malcolm hadn't arrived we wouldn't have reached the pinnacles of the game.'

If there is a degree of sadness in Mike Summerbee it lies beyond the story of his own life in and out of football. It concerns not only the profoundness of the changes that come to all our lives but his belief that the world has shifted beyond the possibility that another group of young English footballers will ever know the particular thrill that came to him and the rest of the boys.

'I can't tell you the reason, at least not precisely, why there are so few outstanding home-grown players today, how it would be impossible for a Premier League manager or coach to do what Joe and Mal did, which was to race to the title so brilliantly with eleven Englishmen.

'What I sense is a lack of hunger, a lack of love of sport for its own sake. In my day kids had to work for everything they got. People talk about obesity in kids today but there was little of it when I was in school. The girls played netball and rounders and we played football and cricket all the time. There was no organised Sunday football for kids – the only Sunday football was up at the Rec, and all the lads were involved.

'Today there is nothing like that, and it's the reason why so few kids are coming through. Parents are spending more time working at the weekend, and when games are organised I don't think it is with the same love. The kids have wonderful gear, the same as the top players, but I do sometimes worry about what they have in their hearts.'

Outside, a wintery sun has cleared away the mist, and maybe he will go into the garden and do a chore or two, clear away a few late fallen leaves. His garden, like his memories, is better ordered than he could ever have imagined in some of the wilder days he shared with the coach and the players on the brief journey that made their lives.

'The greatest gift given to me,' he says as we part, 'was the understanding that if you wanted something you could get it, but there were no short cuts. You had to put in the time, the sweat and the hurt, and then you just might have something to keep for ever.'

Epilogue

Maybe it is true that it is dangerous to go back. Perhaps it is better to carry the past lightly, remembering the best of it and discarding the rest. This way you keep the baggage manageable enough to pass easy inspection at the customs posts of experience.

There are other benefits. The dwindling days are not weighted with old burdens. If you do not look so hard then better the chance that some certainties stay in place, uninvaded by disillusion and regret over false turnings – or the suspicion that for so long you may have been too comfortable in who you once were and what you became.

Yet, rightly or wrongly, none of this was cause for concern when I drove away from the home of Mike Summerbee, the last stage of my year-long odyssey into the collective mind and surviving emotion of the team that I once loved so dearly. This was because I could say that I loved them still. I loved not only the generosity of their spirit but the sturdiness of their gratitude for the best that had come to them so many years ago.

I loved the enduring compassion felt for the fallen Young and Doyle and Heslop and, just a few months ago, Dowd – and their willingness to acknowledge, through the clearest of lenses, that because something goes terribly wrong, as in the fracturing of the relationship between

Malcolm Allison and Joe Mercer, it doesn't mean there is no redemption to be found in the wreckage.

I loved their overriding instinct to celebrate so much that had gone so thrillingly right rather than dwell too heavily on that which had made it unravel. I loved their fierce pride in what had been achieved and their devotion to maintaining the links which it had first created.

If I found a point common to all their memories it was the overwhelming belief that there was something else apart from the trophies, which came in such a rush of acclaim – a sense of wonder at the most luminous of the performances. And maybe it was this that ran deepest. It was the sense of a team that had held together for 50 years.

Yes, Bell and Lee have their issues, but all of them are transcended by their concession that the other's contribution to the great sporting legacy of their lives was immense.

Such bonds are recognised virtually on a daily basis – and not least when Mike Summerbee calls at the home of his old captain Tony Book and they drink tea and seek to drive away the bleaker moods that sometimes descend on the older man. Together they also spend time in the extraordinary environment of today's Manchester City, the team of unbridled wealth and high ambition.

Whatever the new, fabulously geared City achieve though, the veterans can only hope that they will know the kind of kinship that lasts to the end of their days. But in the new world of football it is impossible to imagine that such as Sergio Agüero, Yaya Touré and David Silva will grow old so comfortably in each other's company because it is indeed a phenomenon that could only have been born and nourished in another age.

This is not a judgement but a statement of reality, and it certainly does not preclude a septuagenarian Agüero, maybe reflecting on the terrace of his hacienda back home in Argentina, remembering how it was performing alongside some of the most talented footballers the world had ever seen, and before some of the most passionate and steadfast supporters of the game.

We are, after all, creatures of our time, and maybe the best we can do is celebrate the greatest of our luck and wish for some of it to pass on to those inhabiting a different world and different challenges.

That certainly is the message of the team that helped colour my youth.

It is five years now since we buried their coach, but it doesn't seem so long, no more than that time when they reached for the sky and for a little while, give or take a misadventure or two, resided there.

This, perhaps, is another way of saying that for me, at least, spending one more year in their company had the effect of a reviving heartbeat.

James Lawton,
Padua, Italy,
January 2015

Acknowledgements

No doubt many debts accumulate in the writing of any book and those accrued in this one are surely self-evident. It could not have happened without the generous support of those who did so much to make the story. Mike Summerbee was especially unstinting.

Colin Bell, Tony Book, Tommy Booth, Joe Corrigan, Roy Cheetham, Wyn Davies, Steve Fleet, Freddie Hill, Francis Lee, Ken Mulhearn, Alan Oakes and Glyn Pardoe took me back to the old dressing room. David Allison, elder son of the great coach Malcolm Allison, and Lynn Salton gave haunting but still loving accounts of the turbulence of life in his shadow. Fred Eyre – businessman, writer and once a young footballer who shared the ambition and dreams of his close friends Neil Young and Mike Doyle – relived the days they once shared. Ian Niven, the veteran City director and partisan, was inexhaustible on the subject of his beloved obsession, Manchester City Football Club. Also most valuable was David Tossell's excellent biography *Big Mal*. I thank them all.

I am also most grateful to Charlotte Atyeo of Bloomsbury for her guidance and encouragement, the skill of copyeditor Ian Preece and, not least, the inspiration provided by my agent David Luxton. My wife Linda's patience was, by me, a source of largely unrecognised wonder.

Index

INDEX

INDEX